GENESIS
For the Space

CH00925949

The Inner Earth and the Extra Terrestrials

by John B. Leith (1920 – 1998)

via Robyn C. Andrews, owner

GENESIS For the Space Race
The Inner Earth and the Extra Terrestrials

Library of Congress Control Number: 2015909831
CreateSpace Independent Publishing Platform, North Charleston, SC

TIMESTREAM PICTURES & BOOKS
4412 Wild Horse Court
Ooltewah, Tennessee 37363 USA

ISBN 978-0692449660

Genesis for the Space Race

Cover Design
TR-3B © RHI 2015
Operation High Jump © RHI 2015
Randy Haragan, Sr. Illustrator

Genesis for the Space Race

Preamble
by Donald M. Ware

John B. Leith was born in 1920, possessing a photographic memory. In 1937, after high school, he went to Lhasa, Tibet for spiritual training. While spending 90 days meditating in a cave "to get to know himself," he learned that in a previous life he was the Roman centurion that pierced the "Spear of Destiny" into the heart of Jesus to make sure he was dead. That action was part of the procedure for crucifixion. Jesus had already left his body. Centurion executioners had to prove that before removing the body from the cross.

A thunderstorm was approaching, and they were anxious to get off that hilltop called Golgotha. After using the spear, Centurion Longinus laid the spear at the base of the cross. His partner used a small ladder to place a rope under the arms of the corpse and drop the ends over the crossbar. Longinus held the rope while his partner removed the nails. As Longinus lowered the body and laid it on the ground beside the spear, he looked up and saw about 300 people who wanted to desecrate it, to cut Jesus' head off. The body was in his custody. Longinus covered the head and shoulders with his shield and put his foot on the shield. With his sword in one hand and his knife in the other, Centurion Longinus kept the charging Jews and their allies away long enough for his partner, 10 other centurions, and a lightning bolt to drive them off Golgotha. That allowed the 30 followers of Jesus to bring a stretcher up for his body.

In this lifetime, Leith was used to lead a six-man special-forces team to keep the Christian relics of Europe out of the hands of the Russians. That story, Leith documented well in his first book, The Man with the Golden Sword. It was published in November 2014 by Robert

Miles, available at www.timestreampictures.com.

I found both of Leith's original typed manuscripts in May 2013 in the home of Robyn Andrews in Chamblee, GA, an Atlanta suburb. Leith's son found a copy of both manuscripts when John died. Greg Gavin, Onelight.com, edited this Genesis . . . book and published it in 2009, not knowing who owned the original copyright. Only a few people had read the first manuscript that tells who the author of this book is. I first became aware of this Genesis . . . book through my fellow MUFON researcher friend in Tampa, Florida, Mike Forte.

The CIA chose John Leith in 1975 for this official disclosure because both Leith and his research partner, Leland Frank Hudson (known as Frank) were agents of the Office of Strategic Services (OSS) during WW II. Leith won the top award for valor from seven nations while leading a special-forces team on 62 missions behind German lines. In 1945 both were restricted from acknowledging they had any wartime service until after both were dead.

Unfortunately, a lady borrowed the manuscript of this book to read, illegally made a copy, and self-published it in Birmingham, Alabama under the title Secret Development of the Roundwing Plane in the United States. Researcher Frank Hudson was furious. He wanted to sue her, but that was not possible. The CIA would not allow him to acknowledge his wartime service. They sent an agent to take the map of the inner Earth that was provided by the Atlantean cartographer Haammooud from Shambala. That agent also retrieved photos of ranking German officers and of construction in New Berlin. I suspect the CIA also stopped the circulation of the illegal 1996 book. Frank Hudson did not die until 1997, and Leith not until November 1998. Carol Hammond, a talented researcher, recently looked for that book on line, without success.

To help you sort out the disinformation from the revelation in this important disclosure, I will describe my best assessment of the reasons for the disinformation. Since the 1950s I have studied covert education, as documented in my 1994 paper, The Long-term Government Covert Education Program on Alien Visitors in Vol.1, #1 of the Journal of Exopolitics, www.exopoliticsinstitute.org, also archived at www.

freewebs.com/donware. Over many decades, especially as a Director of the International UFO Congress for 18 years, I have developed a sense of how the process works and why it is necessary.

Humans are eternal spiritual beings. This planet has been a 3rd-grade classroom for the soul since the first humans were seeded here over 900,000 years ago. The 3rd-grade curriculum is to use free will to make choices that polarize our souls toward service-to-others or service-to-self. Now billions of humans are ready for the 4th-grade in the evolution of the soul where the main curriculum is to learn to express unconditional love of others. It is a joint ET/human/angelic project to transform Earth to a 4th-grade classroom.

Throughout the past 30,000 years, ETs have preserved those humans with the greatest capacity for intellectual growth and spiritual aware-ness when large numbers were threatened by natural disasters, plague, or war. They were taken to the inner Earth to continue their spiritual evolution. Naturally, they evolved more rapidly than those in the warring nations on the surface of this planet. When inner Earthlings have proven that they have put war behind them, they are allowed to leave this planet to explore and interact with our space brothers and sisters. At this point, it is quite helpful to acquire an upgrade in our biological computer. Humans on the surface and below are getting a bigger hard drive, a faster chip, and improved telepathic ability. The genetic engineers assisting us are Zeta Reticulans, highly respected, almond-eyed, and gray-skinned "doctors". They use shorter bio-logical robots to shuttle selected subjects to the doctor's office. They choose 4th-grade humans to raise their Indigo, Crystal, and Rainbow children. Other children, with heads too large for natural birth, are taken at about 3 1/2 months and raised in the inner Earth or on our off-planet bases. Of course, Leith was not authorized to mention the hybridization program. He finished his input for this book in 1980, and his research on the results of his WW II missions described in The Man with the Golden Sword in 1985.

The CIA and the Atlantean, J. B. Aacceerson, who provided the map of the inner Earth did not want the wealthy and selfish people on the outer surface to spend their money to try to enter the more advanced society beneath our feet. Hence, the 125-mile-diameter holes at the poles are disinformation, to discredit the map and the supporting text written by Leith.

Three neutral nations assisted in the relocation of many thousands of Germans after their military forces were defeated on the eastern front in March 1943. President Juan Peron sold 10,000 Argentine passports to Martin Borman, Hitler's close assistant. General Francisco Franco allowed giant 500-seat submarines to depart through cities on the north coast of Spain where night trains carried Germany's finest young blue-eyed soldiers and women.

Third, the Vatican, under Pope Pius XII, had an amnesty program for anyone willing to dedicate the rest for his life to the work of God converting people in hidden places to Christianity. When Hitler was trained for priesthood, he did not choose the name of a saint or keep his own name, as customary. He chose the name of an Italian playboy who was in trouble with the law and chose the name of a Saint. Hitler took the Italian's name, Father Krespi, sometimes spelt Crespi. He also chose Ecuador, a country where the state had no claim on the property of the church or those who worked for the church when they died. He actually left Germany in late 1944, on a submarine with Martin Borman, for a beach 30 miles south of Guayaquil, Ecuador. To provide a cover story for the Catholic Church, this book says that Hitler went to New Berlin below the Antarctic. Neither he nor Borman would have been allowed to enter New Berlin.

Another cover story in this book is that Hitler II (Hitler's son born to Eva Braun in 1940) came to Zaragoza, Spain for his Father's funeral in 1974. He actually came to Cuenca, Ecuador for the funeral in 1978.

Finally, I want to encourage all who read this book to read the "Fifth Epochal Revelation" free at www.urantiabook.org (or in a paper copy). Urantia is ETs name for Earth, and the "Fourth Epochal Revelation" is the life of Jesus as described in the Bible.

Contents

CONTENTS

PART II - THE INNER WORLD OF EXTRA TERRESTRIALS

Genesis for the Space Race

DEDICATED
TO AN UNSUNG HERO,
JONATHAN E. CALDWELL,
INVENTOR OF THIS
CIVILIZATION'S FIRST
SPACECRAFT

Genesis for the Space Race

Introduction

Some of the most closely guarded secrets of this century -- and perhaps since time began will be discovered within the pages of this book. At the heart of the long kept secrets is the phenomenon, euphemistically known as unidentified flying objects, which certain nations of this world have developed with the aid of outer terrestrials from other planets.

The manuscript is entirely original, from primary sources, most of which must remain anonymous. Over 100 interviews were conducted. Research for the project took three years of two men's time, plus thousands of hours contributed freely by others, some of whom placed their careers in jeopardy to do so. Material was gathered mostly in the U.S.A., but also visited was the USSR, Mexico, Germany, Canada, France, England, Spain, Brazil and the Vatican.

Washington was where the real struggle was fought to pry the truth from bureaucratic vaults. During the task of researching projects related to the UFOs, a few allies who wanted the entire story explained were gradually located in all walks of the Capitol's life. Some of those who came to our aid were Senators, Congressmen, top military men in all the services, and high-ranking civil servants, as well as agents and retired agents of the Central Intelligence Agency and the Federal Bureau of Investigation. Through the efforts of all those sympathetic people the book was completed. Its contents simply attempt to open up, without apology, the post-war history of the so-called UFO for examination.

The U.S.A., Canada, as well as Britain and Germany are the main custodians of the secret UFO knowledge revealed herein. But only in such a freedom-loving nation as the U.S.A. could there have surfaced bold men willing to defy tradition and disclose the buried facts about the new age of visiting space ships, and inner and outer terrestrials.

The manuscript did not begin on a theme of development of the so-called UFO. It was started more as a doubtful question about the phenomena in general, and as ensuing facts were enlarged the story of an international competition was recognized which had begun in the 1930's and which the author's labeled "The Space Race." Quite soon, in the uncovering of additional information, it became apparent that Earth was no longer a singular planet on which men looked and listened for the reality of similar life elsewhere in the universe. Instead it was evident that Earth itself was that sphere in this solar system which sister planets had been monitoring closely for years. We were not alone was the discovery which we the authors and countless others had made. But who would believe that report if we were to tell? This was the mind-boggling dilemma.

Right from the start it was anticipated that much of the new information sought on the space age could not be freed from security wraps for national defense reasons, which indeed proved to be so. Sympathetic to this corollary, the authors did not inquire at all into military secrets. But a recurring irritation was the unavailability of certain material of related UFO importance which will not be released for 50 years from its happening. That keeps many relevant events hidden till the 1990's or later. In this latter case perhaps only history, or time, or unknown witnesses will come forward to expose the truth. But aside from the military considerations, this explosive knowledge had also been suppressed simply because of its phenomenal and disquieting aspects and the effect they would have in the public mind and spirit.

Nevertheless, if the story of man's sudden immersion into the interplanetary world of extra terrestrials isn't unfolded in part, at least, the telling may come too late. For the inhabited solar system in which we dwell and the equally inhabited space beyond is far more complex than the average intelligent person would realize. It is in fact a universe of principalities and powers that have traditionally been visiting and perhaps seeding planet Earth for a thousand millennia and which probably will continue whether or not we accept their incredible reality. It is this knowledge that will confound most religionists and many scientists and educators in the next span of years more than any other current revelation about outer space. An eminent physicist of Stanford University has stated that "committed Christians of all faiths will likely be the most unbelieving -- as in Galileo's time."

It may be that the greatest danger to the thoughtful reader will be his despondent reflection that God does not exist or at least has become remote and impersonal. On the other hand, the revised rationale of the agnostic may be to elevate man into God's abode, raising man's ego-image still higher. What to rightly believe will become self-evident to thoughtful people when they know for certain that the horizons of the heavens are endless and that there is a Force unlimited by time and space which must be omnipotent and omnipresent to fashion and turn the endless wheels of the cosmos, wherein Earthman may be only an insignificant figure.

For those who will think this material is science fiction in disguise, they are asked to delay judgment until the conclusion of the book. Meanwhile, a few of the problems encountered are shared with the reader.

One foreign government complained to the U.S. State Department that the authors were badgering their embassy staff. In another country the stay of the researcher was cut short when he was asked to leave. The Vatican registered a strong diplomatic protest with the President of the U.S.A. that one of its top emissaries was interrogated and forcibly searched while bringing material into the U.S.A. for the authors. A special hearing of congressional and senate committees met in Washington to act on the refusal by a government agency to release unclassified information as required under the Freedom of Information Act. In another case, the researcher was taken into custody for attempting to photograph non-classified National Archives exhibits, and an executive order was secured to release him from detention. And just as offensive was a forceful reminder that the collecting of information and pictures from our former German enemies was treasonable under a still existing wartime statute.

The drama of subterfuge on both sides went on and on and in itself would comprise a book of skirmishes with the military and science worlds that would be both laughable and yet lamentable. But as the story of the round-wing plane unfolds, it will be realized how the authorities became committed to a bond of silence going back 30 years. Nevertheless, the gathering of information for this book was not simply a game of the pen versus the sword. It was a rivalry of serious intent by the authors and those who came to their aid to persuade the government sources to reveal long overdue facts on the UFO enigma. And for those opposing forces who had been made keepers of the secret by the previous generation, it was a concerted attempt to dissuade the authors to go home and forget about UFO's and the nation's possible involvement.

But curiously the whole series of episodes has produced a grudging respect for the thrust of science in the free world and the hidden might of its military. Only in a democracy could the forces of constraint and openness meet in confrontation, and the lesser of the two protagonists be allowed to survive and tell of the struggle.

As this century ends, a reluctant United States has been shoved onto the world's stage at the most critical time of our civilization. Whether America likes this role or not, she and her friends are the star players who must take major parts in shaping this planet's destiny here and beyond. For far from being weaklings, the U.S.A. and her allies are the noble giants who hold aloft over our planet the shield that would keep our world intact and still free.

Prologue

There are a dozen nations on planet Earth capable of making nuclear bombs. There is an estimated stockpile of at least 30,000 heavy, nuclear bombs among major countries, and three new ones are being added per day. If only a fraction of this destructive force were delivered, it could kill nearly all life on the face of the Earth, contaminating the planet and its survivors for decades. The atmospheric and geological upheavals would so change the Earth as it is presently composed, that the highly civilized areas would disappear in the dust of war or beneath rising oceans.

As man's technical ability has pyramided to overkill his fellow men, and to destroy their abodes, peace in the heart of mankind and nations has become only a hollow phrase, or at best, a fleeting hope.

Onto this mad planet has come a new phenomena, the unidentified flying objects -- and with them, the outer and Extra terrestrials.

Genesis for the Space Race

PART 1

Chapter I

Earth under Surveillance

The sun was two o'clock high on June 24, 1947 over Mount Rainier in Washington State, U.S.A. A commercial pilot flying northerly in a clear sky over the Cascade Mountains fixed his sight to the left where a flash had occurred at the ten thousand foot elevation of the towering mountain.

As experienced, 50-year-old Kenneth Arnold scanned the reflection, little did he think that his description of the objects seen near the burst of light would result in the coining of a new universal word.

Here is how Arnold expressed himself that afternoon as reported later in newspapers around the world: "The nine objects I saw flew like saucers, if you skipped them across the water." Although what Arnold saw was highly technical, he pictured it in a simple, idiomatic term that thereafter caught the imagination of kings and commoners across the globe.

Thus was born the age of flying saucers in the twentieth century. And no one, scientist or seer, could turn back the clock ticking toward the arrival of the new aerial age. Hundreds of thousands of similar sightings in the current years would leave the world divided about the controversy. Simply understood, the question raised would be: Are the flying saucers real pieces of hardware or are they figments of imagination?

Unknown to Arnold in the immediate post-war years, the unidentified flying objects he observed, had been constructed and had taken off from the geographical area beneath which he flew. In his reflections, he would not surmise that he had just witnessed the evidence of an aeronautical secret that had been kept under official wraps for over twenty years.

What the veteran pilot of fixed-wing aircraft had watched were his own countrymen piloting a revolutionary break-through in aerodynamics named "round-wing aircraft."

Today, the latest versions of those early round-wing planes which Kenneth Arnold glimpsed over the Cascade Mountains have escaped the bonds of earth's gravity, and thus weightless, patrol the outer skies of this planet and venture fearlessly into the realms of vast space.

At this juncture, before the wider explanation of the intriguing aerial phenomena is revealed, the average reader will recognize this unanswered riddle. Never has it been told to laymen the identities of the thousands of aerial sightings seen by professional airmen and ordinary spectators in the last half of this century.

To state the conundrum briefly, the so-called flying saucers seen by Arnold and countless others across the globe were called "unidentified flying objects" by the United States Air Force. The terminology became commonplace but deceptive. Hence, the shorter euphemism, UFOs was used to describe such aerial sightings the world over. This being so, the reader will first become acquainted with four identifiable aerial happenings which have been declassified. They are all researched and documented cases from the years 1947, 1948 and 1955, and are actual crash landings and subsequent encounters with beings from other worlds.

Following these reports the story will be revealed of the round-wing plane as it was developed on Planet Earth. And when the revelation is unfolded, quite imperceptibly, the following conclusion will dawn on most readers:

The genesis of a new age has already begun for Earthlings. And it is self-evident -- we are late in joining the interplanetary creatures that have ventured into the vastness of the universe in search of other intelligent beings.

Case Number One:

Riddle of the Crashed UFO's

One night in 1955, three manned space ships from beyond earth's own solar system crashed into the desert near Farmington, New Mexico. Their unscheduled landings shed a display of fireworks that was seen by hundreds of people for 20 miles.

Yet, few Americans more than 22 years later have heard of that hushed-up accident -- except those in classified military circles.

The three intergalactic space ships, with 28 beings aboard, brought to planet Earth its most revealing evidence that mankind was not alone in the universe and that Earth was under military surveillance by unfriendly invaders. This revelation also sobered Earth's scientific communities. Beyond a doubt, the alien craft were right out of a space odyssey of the future.

For reader understanding of the alien space craft crashes, known as the Farmington Incident, it began about 450 miles from the crash late on the evening of January 17th. At that time and place a team of communication specialists, code named "Bootstrap," were monitoring Army maneuvers with sophisticated long-range equipment.

As the monitor spun the dial he picked up traffic on a distant amateur band. What he heard was highly unusual "ham" talk. The ham's remarks were, in fact, an introduction to what was to become, in the next 48 hours, America's most dramatic attempt to apprehend live aliens from outer space.

The radio ham in a staccato voice had told his listener "a large, bright object had streaked down from above and crashed in the desert near Farmington." As it struck earth it had skidded and bounced, making a path over a mile long. Rumbling, grating and tumbling along over the desert it finally stopped. The ham then called it "a whopper of an aeroplane or meteor crash," but ended his message by saying, oddly enough, that there had been no explosion. Then he signed off advising he was heading for the site.

So were dozens of others who had witnessed the unusual night display.

Twelve hours later by direct order from Offutt Air Force Base, monitors from "Operation Bootstrap" had become a communications and rescue team arriving in the vicinity of that night's drama. Traveling at high speeds and with top priority they sped on, still monitoring police and amateur airwaves. Each band they tuned in convinced them the object of their all night thrust was a downed military aircraft, containing either classified equipment or high-ranking military or civilian passengers.

En-route as instructed, the team had acquired an extra communications truck, jeep and live ammunition.

Then the unexpected happened again. Another ham, corroborated by a State Trooper's radio, reported a second crash at 2:00 P.M. in the same vicinity. "Move it faster!" the commander urged his night convoy.

It was 8:30 A.M. on the morning of the 18th when the team arrived on site.

As Major Robert Farrel (not his real name) of St. Petersburg, Florida, endeavored to clear a path to the wrecks, another meteor-like blob zoomed out of the sky from directly above. There was silence as the thing slammed to earth.

The third object cut another desert swath of billowy sand and buried itself within a mile radius of the first two crash sites.

Approaching the last crash, the security team almost immediately confirmed they were not at the scene of an accidental crash of a conventional aircraft. The silhouette of the disabled object also indicated that it was no rough meteorite.

What they saw in the total scene were three strange, unidentified airships of similar design, somewhat saucer shaped.

As the "Bootstrap" crew mingled with the crowd to survey the scene, people began banging on the hulls with a variety of tools and rocks. One man was about to fire at the hull of one of the downed ships with a high-powered rifle when the ten-man rescue squad took positive action. Dissuaded by cocked rifles of the Bootstrap crew, the curious backed off.

But the Bootstrap Major instinctively felt uneasy -- he sensed there could be intelligent life inside. Powerful microphones were held against the skin but no internal sounds or voices were picked up.

Peering inside through a hole about seven inches in diameter, the Air Force Major glimpsed the craft's scorched interior and observed two badly burned bodies reclining on seats.

Eventually a five by four foot door (totally invisible from the outside) was located and opened. Venturing in, the Major could see the ship's occupants had perished in a flash fire. Had the alien ship struck a magnetic vortex high above the earth or was it the victim of a high altitude aerial encounter?

First the bodies were removed and placed in military bags. The charred bodies averaged 32 inches in size with one giant corpse of almost four feet. Weight was estimated by the medical autopsy records as 65 to 75 pounds, with the giant weighing close to 100. (See appendix). The hands of each corpse were still gloved, but they had not been wearing their glass-like helmets at impact.

Closer examination showed that a touch of a finger near the col-

lar automatically unzipped a one-piece suit to reveal bodies with a
skin pigment of golden tan. The hair on each was black; their eyes
had no irises, and were occidental in appearance. Their feet were
slender and unusually long, as were the toes. Hands and feet each
had five appendages with nails. The sexual organs were pocketed
in folds of skin when apparently not in use.

Major Farrel had gained entry to the first ship by a fluke as his
hand touched a door release while he felt around the inside of the
window hole.

Another fortunate blunder now took place. Totally on his own, one
of the rescue crew began yanking at the controls on the ship's console. The Major spotted him and rushed to prevent further damage.

The vandal accidentally fell against a hidden panel door that simply opened under the sudden impact from the man's weight. The
11" square door had been totally invisible as were all seams on the
outside and inside of the craft. Inside the hidden panel lay a crys-
talline, metallic ring about 18 inches in diameter and three inches
thick.

Overhead on the roof the Major recalled having noticed an impres-
sion, barely visible, about the same size as the ring. When the ring
was placed in the circular groove it clung magnetically.

The humans investigating the alien craft were hardly prepared for
what happened next. As the ring was twisted counter-clockwise,
about 40 degrees from the set point, the magnetic adhesion that had
held the ship intact was de-energized.

Bedlam broke loose, both inside and out, as the ship began falling
apart outwardly into nine petal-like sections. The inside rescu-
ers tumbled down among the separated sections as those outside
leaped away. None was hurt except for bruises as the sections
disjoined themselves and the interior console doors and all access
panels opened exposing their contents. Only the center housing, located in the bottom of the ship, remained intact. It was cylindrical,
three feet in diameter and three feet high. This piece was slightly
radioactive and was later ascertained to be the power source for the

ship's anti-gravitational force field power system.

The storage access areas contained extra flight gear, food wafers, spare parts, medical supplies and mapping tools unfamiliar to the rescue crew.

That the alien ship was from beyond Earth's own solar system, the U.S. Air Force later concluded, and maps within showed its home planet could be in a remote part of the Milky Way or even from a constellation in another galaxy. But stellar coordinates of the home planet could not be ascertained. Its mission and that of its mother ship were to map Earth and report this intelligence to their home base. The men found charts showing the Earth's conformity with rivers, mountains and cities plainly visible. Square map sheets of a metallic substance showed Earth's charted grid lines running along magnetic variations. The results were unlike existing Earth carto-graphic methods that show position by longitude and latitude.

This alien ship was measured at 27 feet in diameter and nine feet thick. The underside was slightly concave with three round caster type protrusions 120 degrees apart, which, when extended, became the ship's gear. Ship design was shaped somewhat like a Coleman lantern except that the bottom skirt was flared outward.

On the third day after arrival, rescue operations were moved to a second ship. This craft was saucer-like, 36 feet in diameter, and had the same three caster type landing gears as on the first ship entered. The crew sandbagged the outside, applied and twisted the tool ring to the center top. Again the craft parted in nine equal sections with the center pin power source remaining upright on the bottom.

Inside, four more burned bodies were found and the rescue crew again removed the bodies of human counterparts from another world. They placed the four dead aliens beside their two comrades from ship number one. Various medical, technical and scientific experts were now on hand. The smaller ships and their contents, along with the bodies, were loaded gingerly by cranes aboard lowboy trucks for eventual air delivery to Wright Patterson Air

Force Base, Hanger No. 18, in Dayton, Ohio. Air Research and Development Command, under the watchful eye of Air Technical Intelligence Command, would now take over their transportation and ultimate study.

At Offutt and Wright Patterson Air Force Bases the nation's experts from all across the U.S.A., in whatever field needed, were already being assembled -- and sworn to secrecy. These experts would attempt to comprehend the significance of these visitors from outer space and compare America's progress with that of an alien society's space technology.

By now the team of expert personnel had grown to approximately 150. The largest craft, approximately 100 feet in diameter, was now approached. Unable to find an opening after digging it out, the magnetic ring again was found to be the tool for opening the ship. It was sprung apart, as were the others. The center core of the anti-gravity propulsion device measured nine feet in height by nine feet in diameter.

Its radioactivity, higher than the others, was less than the emissions from a hospital X-ray machine. Lead shields were used to cover the core.

Inside 22 burned bodies were found. The ship was functionally the same as the smaller ones but measured 99.9 feet in diameter. It was armed with deadly laser ray guns and had probably been shot out of the sky by another spacecraft with superior firepower that had also dispatched the first two craft.

Additionally, galleys, sleeping quarters and baths were revealed. Utility panel buttons numbering 81 in blocks of 9 were laid out, with nine other functional discs, for use by pilots and navigators. These discs had slight indentations for fingertip control. Fingertips placed on various indenture combinations apparently gave swift commands to the different electrical systems. The earth experts wondered how the aliens' fingers were maneuverable enough to operate the system until their hands were examined. The fingers pivoted forwards and backwards in a 180-degree arc. The entire crew had this physical anomaly.

The scientists also confirmed that certain navigational equipment in the flight guidance system was tuned to register mind patterns or vice-versa.

Each alien had four lungs enabling him in a given time to slowly compress and comfortably breathe Earth's atmosphere. Their blood was a brownish color and thicker than ours. The autopsy showed they probably had been breathing within their life support system a mixture of air with less oxygen than Earth people breathed.

The brown, central part of the eye was solid in color. Beneath the outer layers the focus membranes were hidden. Apparently the beings were able to look into the sun without eye injury or see into the darkness of space.

The corpses were undressed and immersed in alcohol. The group was so nearly identical that they seemed to be genetically cloned. Unless they were seen walking our streets in a single group, their variances to humans would probably go undetected. Each appeared to be about 25 years of age as Earth time is measured.

Concentrated food wafers were discovered. Each of these was about 1 1/2 inches long, the size of a single stick of Dentyne gum. One wafer found near a body was dropped accidentally into a tub of water and dissolved immediately. Its aroma was like that of vanilla extract. It bubbled and frothed over the rim of the bucket, finally rising into deliciously tasting dough that would have filled a 30-gallon vat. The rescue team jokingly called the mixture "desert manna." Later it was proven that one small food wafer kept a person alert and without the need of sleep for at least three days.

Measurements of the big ship showed it to be 99.9 feet in diameter with its outer rim forming a perfect circle. It was 27 feet through the true center of the dome and 18 feet at the center risers' edge. Color was a metallic gray with no visible markings, windows or openings.

Within two weeks the operation was over. The remaining bodies were placed in glass cylinders, and along with them, their dismembered ship, covered with tarpaulins, was hauled out of the desert. County police assisted in directing traffic. By night, the ship and other remnants of the accident were shipped to Kirkland Air Force Base near Albuquerque, New Mexico. From there they were placed on board a huge six pusher type propeller aircraft known as a C99. Three trips were required to transport the material to Wright Air Force Base.

In January, a report was made to assembled Congressmen, Senators and military in the underground Command center of Offutt Air Force Base. Viewers were shown the bodies, films, samples and other supporting graphs and data.

Presentations on the findings were made by approximately 20 technical experts called in over a five-hour period. Sobered by the firsthand account of so many reliable witnesses, was Captain James Ruppolt who headed up the "Official" Project Blue Book on UFO sightings.

By agreement of those present, and with approval of President Eisenhower, the lid of secrecy was screwed airtight on the Farmington "incident." The official line on all encounters and sightings grew harder -- beings from outer space did not exist. Notwithstanding, secretive undertakings began thereafter to assess the outer space technology and scientific advances found on the ships and to compare them with U.S. Air Force accomplishments.

A nation's strength or weakness ultimately lies with its people. The official attitude of Air Intelligence was that the American people could not comprehend that beings from light years away were spying on Earth for purposes unknown.

As the official books were closed on the Farmington incident, Air Intelligence began rounding up film and tapes taken at the crash. Newspapers made brief mention of the story, talkative people were coerced and the Farmington affair was buried where it began -- in New Mexico.

Since 1955 the "secret" has seeped out into several related scientific, medical and technical areas through writings, speakers and references referring to the phenomena. Today it is estimated that at least 1000 persons have knowledge of the crashes of the three alien spacecraft.

But only a handful of people, mostly U.S. Air Force personnel, knew what really happened high above America that day when three alien ships spying on planet Earth tumbled out of the sky with dead crews near Farmington, New Mexico.

Case Number Two

The Robot Earth Watchers

Hundreds of sightings were analyzed over a three-year period in several countries, but there are no better cases than those contacts recorded in America between Homo sapiens and beings from beyond.

Many helpful intelligence authorities believe a national awareness of alien presence must be expanded. And quickly too, they say, in order to prevent any mass fear or hysteria. Certain of the aliens who have already arrived among us want their presence known, too. They may be the vanguard of intelligent beings scattered throughout the cosmos whose plans call for opening up total communication with earth before this century ends.

Therefore, only a brief mention of the next two cases is essential to portray the reality of yet another kind of alien "eyes" used to watch earth's military installations.

It was in 1958 near the town of Irrigon, near the Columbia River that the episode took place. The unknown occupants were "captured" and removed, their craft downed by a support-firing unit for protection of the air force bases at Fairchild and Tacoma. Later the ship was transported to the headquarters of SAC at Offutt.

Upon gaining entry, there was found not humans, or humanoids, but four robots at the controls. After failing to remove the heads using conventional methods, an attempt was made to carry one of the robots by lifting the feet and back of the "head." On raising the "head" upwards a corresponding movement occurred in one of the arms revealing an unseen release mechanism in the back of the "skull" which uncovered the robot's "brains."

Literally hundreds of light sensors composed the eyes of the robot -- with signals from these sensors sent by instantaneous replay tape to the robot's computer located in its chest cavity. As the computer accepted the impulses from the light meters (eyes), it sent the response orders to the arms, legs, feet and fingers or head telling each or all members to take what action was necessary to properly operate or adjust ship controls.

After the computer received the taped instructions, they were logged in a memory bank, the reel or tape continuing back to the light sensors and thence to the computer or brain for continuing instructions.

The robot's feet and hands had only three digits each.

The robot craft was navigated by these analogue units to map planet earth and do surveillance. Of the four units found at the Irrigon crash, only one was undamaged. Six months after the Irrigon recovery, the U.S. began making its first thermograph pictures.

Earth scientists are now convinced that the technology of one planet or solar system may differ vastly from that of another.

Thus, a mother ship situated high in the sky over Irrigon on the day of the "robot" crash was used to initiate the master surveillance plan of earth and record same from its drones located perhaps over various U.S. strategic military areas.

An engineer rushed to the Irrigon site for the record, concluded that the analogue ship had struck an uncharted magnetic vortex at 15,000 miles per hour, but not everyone agreed.

The crash landing of this alien ship from some unknown planet also was reported by the Air Force as a meteorite; although, when tracked by radar it was seen to have made a 90-degree turn when pursued by another object. Then the subject craft lost power and tumbled to the ground.

At least ten alien ships have crashed in America since the first one was found. And aside from robots, perhaps as many as 40 bodies much like ours have been recovered and autopsied. Today reports on them are filed in the large library of information on the premises of the CIA in Arlington, Virginia.

Case Number Three

The Mantell Incident and the Live Aliens

In UFO annals one of the most repeated stories is that of Captain Mantell who was shot down by a UFO over Godman Field, Kentucky on January 7, 1948. The official version stops there except to add that his remains were recovered followed by an appropriate military funeral that ended the episode.

But the story of the 25-year-old World War II ace was far from finished by the recovery of his remains. At that point the real story begins. Just seconds prior to Mantell being shot down by the UFO, he had landed a lucky burst of machine gun fire into a vital section of the alien craft.

Simultaneously with Mantell's P-51 fighter plummeting to its hillside crash site, the UFO also fluttered to earth within three miles of the military airfield over which it had been intercepted.

The tower at Godman Field had reported initially an object, which could not be identified, on their radar. Meanwhile, flying a routine flight over the field was a group of Kentucky Air National Guard of which Captain Thomas J. Mantell, as flight leader, was requested to investigate, and if possible, challenge.

On reaching the 8000-foot level, Captain Mantell radioed to the tower that a bright, circular object was hovering below him. He kept contact with the tower as the object moved fifty feet below his plane and began passing him. Next, the object hove silently along side Mantell's starboard wing. Inside the 30 foot craft Mantell saw three figures observing him through portholes.

The scrutinizing UFO then rose to 30,000 feet with Captain Mantell unable to close the distance in pursuit. After chasing the UFO in a futile attempt to overtake it, Mantell reported an about turn by the UFO as it turned down on him at a fantastic speed in what seemed a suicide course. At the last moment Mantell fired a burst at the object. It stopped abruptly in mid-air and a collision was barely avoided as the UFO fell toward earth. Hot in pursuit, Captain Mantell rolled and followed. The tower maintained radar contact and was able to observe the chase. As the UFO descended with the P-51 on its tail, those below saw a blinding flash, as though perhaps a burst of explosive light had struck the P-51. The aeroplane broke apart and crashed on the side of a mountain about five miles from Franklin, Kentucky.

The day was cloudy with a slight haze as trucks on the field rolled out after ground crews witnessed the flash of light that had struck the P-51. The P-51 fell earthward in pieces. An Air Force Captain and Sergeant photographer rushed through the gates towards the falling UFO. As they sped to the site, the photographer, using a zoom lens, also caught the tragic scene of the P-51 breaking apart within sight of the base.

Meanwhile, the unidentified flying object skipped and tumbled slowly to earth glowing like a ball of fire. It was this bright glow emitted by the UFO that enabled the emergency recovery crew and the photographer to spot exactly the alien crash landing site.

The foregoing is the story of the chase. Captain Mantell shot down the UFO. The UFO in turn, destroyed him. Before either craft had crashed, the air base had hurriedly dispatched two emergency crews. One rushed to the P-51 wreckage and the other vehicle raced to the site of the unidentified flying object. The photographing team had orders to head for the UFO, but en-route was able to photograph the disintegrating P-51.

Air Force intelligence reached Mantell's crash first. The plane had disintegrated into thousands of pieces. There was no fire and no odor of burnt flesh or fabric. They found Captain Mantell still in helmet, suit and boots. As they removed the clothing the emergency crew recovered a clean skeleton, intact from head to foot.

The remains were taken to an Air Force laboratory for identification and autopsy. The skeleton of the deceased Captain Mantell was later placed in a sealed container and taken to a nearby undertaker where it was put in a coffin and sealed.
The story at the UFO crash site had a different ending. As the photographer continued to shoot pictures of the crash, they saw the glow of the craft cease as they arrived. A door opened and slowly three beings emerged with hands in air. The color of their complexions was light tan; they were tall in stature with high and narrow foreheads. The airmen rushed towards the UFO, guns drawn, as one of the beings in perfect English, said calmly, "We mean you no harm. We have come in peace."

The photographer sergeant began snapping official pictures of the exterior and interior of the craft. (These pictures were to remain hidden in a Washington vault for almost 30 years.) The aliens were hustled back to the base as the confused gate guard was ordered to permit entry of the group without identification of the airmen or aliens.

Three days later, at the administration building, the aliens were still being interrogated by a battery of Air Force Intelligence Officers from the Pentagon.

Their alien story: They came from Venus, the capital planet of this solar empire. They said other alien craft in the air at the time had crews from Pluto, Saturn, Mars, etc. Earth military installations were being scrutinized carefully, they said, with no hostile intentions except to record earth progress for interplanetary travel and nuclear war, the earth stigma that had alerted our sister planets to keep up constant surveillance. They said that upon being disabled by the P51 they instituted no retaliatory action.

Rather, their craft was programmed to beam in by radar fix on any adversary who shot first. The human-like beings repeated that they were sorry and had not intended to take the life of an earthman.

The Air Force was undecided just what to do with their unexpected visitors, who, in fact, had entered American air space only to observe.

As base radar scanned the sky, it tracked additional space ships hovering high above. Therefore it was deduced that to try the aliens for murder would bring reprisals from above.

The three aliens were placed routinely in the guardhouse. It was while they were incarcerated the second night that the problem of earthly law and ethics was solved without earthly help. During the night, the military policeman in charge of detention left his guard duty and ran to the officer in charge. "They're gone," he shouted. "The prisoners are gone!" Quick examination by security revealed the cell door was locked; the barred windows still intact and no escape holes had been cut into the walls.

Less than an hour later the answer came. Without human action a message began to appear on the station's telex. Simultaneously in the tower and communications room the same message was audible. In effect it said:
"We are a companion craft of the one shot down. We regret having killed your airman. The act was not intentional. In future, please instruct your pilots not to fire on our ships to prevent further loss of human life. Our spacemen kept in your prison were just rescued by a means totally unknown to you. At another time, after friendship is established between us, we will tell you how the secret escape was made. We are in your space to observe. We mean you no harm. Again, please forgive us for the unavoidable killing of your pilot. We are truly sorry."

At the time of the alien disappearance several witnesses made some unusual and verified observations. Here is what is described as being seen. "A 100 foot unidentified craft dropped down from above, and hovered over the guardhouse. From the craft there emerged a beam of white light, with a greenish tinge. On, or within this beam of light, the three aliens ascended or were taken up through the ceiling by unknown means to the presiding ship above the guardhouse."

A non-earthling who has been seen in Washington for several years and has been a confidant of Presidents described the escape ray. He said it was a solid beam that disintegrated objects in its path by disassembling the atom structure while the ray shone and allowed reassembling of the atom particles when the ray was turned off. The Washington spaceman, whose name is Plateu, explained that the ray principle had been used in Venus long before the present earth civilization began (which he declared was 33,000 years ago). Plateu said the ray was also developed on earth's sunken continent of Atlantis, but that its principle was lost when the continent sank 12,000 years ago.

As ethereal as the beings appeared to be at the time of their escape, they bore unmistakable human characteristics. Body shape was human; features occidental; hair blond; fingers long and slender: height 5' 6" to 5 '10"; appearance youthful. Habits while in detention: they took water into which they dropped red or white pills at different times. They used the toilet facilities and the official reports say they passed nutrients and urinated as do human males. No wonder! They insisted they came from the ancestral planet of earth's white races.

So ends the Mantell incident, except for over 2,000 pieces of official correspondence between the base, the Pentagon, and other agencies at Maxwell Air Force Base and Wright Patterson Air Force Base where the Venusian's ship finally ended.

After the Mantell "incident" Air Force Intelligence privately wondered why, if the aliens were able to retrieve their people, why hadn't they retrieved their ship?

But, publicly, the Air Force gave out this version of the Mantell incident: (1) Mantell lost consciousness due to oxygen starvation. (2) The object that Mantell was chasing may have been a "Sky Hook" Navy balloon that had been released in the area.

Case Number Four

United States Receives Visit from Beyond Earth

Washington, February 18, 1975; time - 10 P.M.

A hovering squadron of high altitude lights had just placed America's capitol under a blanket of surveillance. Before departing, they would send shivers through the security surrounding U.S. President Gerald Ford, and their mission would also change the U.S.A. scientific thrust in outer space within 60 days.

On this winter's night in question, the sky over Washington was clear and visibility was excellent. High above at 50,000 feet, twelve unidentified and stationary lights had appeared. The lights were not celestial bodies, mirages or balloons, nor were they conventional aircraft. They were, in fact, UFO's, a name first applied in 1966 by the U.S. Air Force to describe growing numbers of unidentified flying objects sighted around the globe.

At the three major airports around Washington several monitor systems handle traffic and also act as an early warning vigilance for unidentified aircraft. There is the AACS, i.e., Aircraft and Airways Communication System, the sophisticated radar at Andrews Air Force Base and the GPR, Ground Position Radar, etc. Therefore, besides untrained street personnel who spotted the mysterious lights, there were also the competent operators of the AACS, Andrews Air Force Base Radar and GPR, who were continuously watching the activities of the unidentified flying objects.

At 10:16 one of the lights detached itself from the formation and, peeling off to the right, dropped toward the city. Its color changed from blue to white. In a park in Georgetown, the northwest section of the capitol, the light landed and as it went out, there appeared in its place a solid object. Standing where the light had been was a 30 foot, saucer-like object with dome, supported by tripod legs. Underneath the craft a door opened from which a stairs extended to the ground and an ordinary looking being with occidental features descended. The six foot tall man moved briskly away from the perimeter of the craft and evaporated before his viewers.

As he did so, curious onlookers who had seen the craft's landing in their neighborhood ran toward the machine. But ten feet away from the craft an invisible force field kept the sightseers away. The hatch closed, and the machine stood isolated and alone.

About 10:20, after the being had departed from the craft, there simultaneously appeared a stranger before the security guard at the street entrance to the White House. In perfect English he asked to see President Ford. The being's request was refused.

At approximately 10:21, a being in a flight suit was seen walking down the hallway to the Oval Room. A secret service man challenged the figure from behind. It continued on. A bullet from the gun of the President's guard apparently passed through the being without drawing blood.

At the next instant, the stranger disappeared from the view of the secret service pursuer and silently passed through the locked and closed door to the Oval Room. Thereupon it stopped in front of President Ford working alone at his desk. The startled President looked up at the figure of a tall, slim man with black hair, dressed in what appeared to be a trim flight suit of silver colored jacket and pants tucked into calf length boots.

The being spoke calmly: "President Ford -- I am sorry to intrude in such an unearthly way, but I have a message of great importance which must be told," He continued, "I am a scientist from Earth's sister planet Venus, which, regardless of Earth's scientific postulations, is inhabited by a people identical to those like yourself on Earth. But my mission in being here tonight concerns special knowledge which others in this solar system have elected to give the United States as our chosen custodian for planet Earth."

Much of the alien's conversation remains classified but some of the subject matter has been verified from executive sources. In general, the visitor spoke of the dawning of a new age for Earth in science, medicine, and other wonders -- but hinged his remarks with a single admonition: "Earth must first denounce nuclear war," The verdict of the outer-terrestrial stemmed from an inerrant moral law of the universe, which Earth nations had broken by splitting the atom to destroy their fellow men.

Almost an hour later the outer-terrestrial departed. Upon leaving, he placed on the President's desk a dull, silvery object of elliptical shape with rounded edges. The stranger called it a Venusian book – a gift from his planet to America.

Simultaneously, several miles away, the being re-entered the vehicle in which he came. It took off and joined the lights above, at which time the formation disappeared off the radar screens of the nation's capitol.

This meeting between an outer-terrestrial being and a world leader is only one of the hundreds recorded since Earth's first nuclear explosion took place in 1945. American Presidents alone have had a minimum of 60 visits.

Outsiders for at least 45 millennia, throughout the pre-Adamite civilizations, have watched Earth. According to their spokesmen they have witnessed this latest civilization's: advent of the railroad, the discovery of electricity, the aeroplane and auto, the rocket, the smashing of the atom and lately, the fearful number of nuclear test explosions. Finally, the uncontrolled aggressions of nations cause them to make their own atomic bombs -- with intentions to deploy them.

As the President picked up the object, and examined it that night of February 18, 1975, he called for secret service personnel. He also asked for the Secretary of State and scheduled a meeting of the General Staff to be held at the Pentagon as soon as possible to evaluate the disk.

During the Presidential dialogue with the extra terrestrial being, he had declared the U.S. Air Force should learn the formula encased in the disk. Mr. Ford had gingerly examined the object, but laid it down, perplexed as to why the alien should leave such an indecipherable thing as a parting gesture.

Was it really a goodwill gift of science from another world, or was it some diabolical, destructive force that might enslave onlookers or destroy a city?

Like his predecessors going back to Franklin D. Roosevelt, President Ford must have asked himself some startling questions about this peaceful outer-terrestrial invasion, whose spokesmen looked human and acted like friends, notwithstanding their arrivals were always without warning or prior signal.

And, in a broader sense, U.S. officialdom was also asking, "Why all the sudden attention which Earth was now receiving after years of comparative isolation?" Even more perplexing questions were being asked by the suspicious military and science worlds. If these outer-terrestrials were so advanced scientifically and metaphysically, what did they know about the future destiny of mankind that made them suddenly want to share their knowledge with a single nation, the U.S.A.?

Aside from these basic quandaries, other sobering judgments had already been established -- which authorities had long hesitated to pass on -- and for an understandable reason. Those claiming to come from our solar system and even beyond were often nearly identical to certain Earth races in appearance and in biological, functional and mental ways. Obviously, there existed a correlation between Earth beings and inhabitants from certain other planets.

As President Ford may have pondered these revelations that historic night, he was well aware that alien ships of countless origins were now bridging the time and distance barrier between various planets in the universe, the knowledge of which leading nations of the world had denied the public. Furthermore, appraisal of the combined worldwide UFO phenomena by military consultants was singularly conclusive.

They concluded that all of planet Earth was under systematic surveillance by three distinct classifications of alien intruders. Those were labeled: (1) friendly, (2) presumed hostile and (3) unknown.

Category (1) friendly were usually round-wing in shape, originating within our solar system, whose human occupants have openly made themselves known to certain earth governments and their leaders from time to time (such as the foregoing visit to President Ford).

The same outer-terrestrials had also occasionally appeared by accident, for example the Captain Mantell incident over Godman Field, Kentucky in 1948.

Category (2) presumed hostile. These aliens generally came in round-wing planes and were of human resemblance from diminutive sizes to over six feet in height. They had, on occasion, attempted to infiltrate Earth by establishing hidden bases in remote areas, and their spacecraft were also engaged in mapping Earth and other questionable activities. It is believed they originated from one planet or constellation. Example: the Farmington affair of 1955.

Category (3) unknowns (Chapter XIX, Strangers in Our Skies), who were patrolling Earth skies and watching our people and military installations increasingly in the late 1970's. They arrived in spacecraft of various dimensions and shapes up to 1,000 feet long. Occupants were observed to be of a variety of physiological descriptions, some of which, by Earth's standards, bordered on the ridiculous or grotesque according to their own admissions which are delivered telepathically to Air Force pilots and airport controllers, etc. Observations of their spacecraft by competent observers suggested that their space technology might be more advanced than that of this solar system.

One repetitive warning had been delivered by all the friendly outer-terrestrials with whom physical and voice contact had been made. According to informed Air Force sources, that constant warning stated a nuclear holocaust on Earth was possible within a generation unless immediate plans were made now to prevent it.

As President Ford may have reflected on the promise of sudden increased knowledge for this world in exchange for abandoning the international nuclear race, 2700 scientists, engineers, physicists, astronomers, geophysicists, mathematicians, geologists and radio engineers were occupied 24 hours a day at the Goddard Center in Maryland, keeping watch on a more disturbing phenomena.

A magnetically weak but inhabited alien planet, over twice the size of Earth, had wandered into our solar system and attached itself to the force field between the sun and Earth. By the year 2,000 this oncoming intruder could possibly regress the climate where a third of the world's people are located towards another ice age. Its effects were particularly being felt in the northern latitudes where teams of American, Canadian, Japanese and Russian meteorologists and weather men daily gathered the evidence of an abrupt change in world weather patterns.

Underlying these hidden discoveries and new knowledge of outer space, the real question being asked by the world's leaders was how to tell the public without creating panic?

Collective scientific minds working on the secret already were aware of these explosive truths and the problems they presented. But how much of the biased viewpoints of our history, religion, philosophy, and science would have to be discarded in order to make way for the new 20th century revelations? These revelations clearly indicate: Earthlings are not isolated, but in fact are part of an interplanetary league of intelligent creatures. Our counterparts from planets nearby and other destinations light years away are trying to give warring Earth nations a message. The aliens are telling us to stop the nuclear race and destroy our stockpiles before we destroy our planet and its civilizations. In return for heeding this advice, they would provide Earthmen with the advanced technological, scientific, and medical secrets of the Universe.

Chapter II

Early American Development of the Unconventional Aeroplane

The reader already must be asking questions. Why haven't I learned of these cosmic visitations before? Why doesn't the government explain? Why the suppression of UFO landings? The authors asked the same questions when they began to dig into the mystery three years ago. Today there are many thousands of persons around the world who are engaged in keeping the alien presence and their unidentified flying objects under censorship wraps.

This unchangeable posture of silence exists in both democratic and totalitarian countries. It began with typical military reasoning that the public should not be informed, if to do so, national sovereignty would be jeopardized. It proceeded with the assumption that the public was not prepared for such astounding revelations, and could not cope with them.

American governmental censorship of UFO information seems to be typical of that in other countries and extends back nearly 50 years. In the mid 1930's, military secrecy about an unusual American invention in the field of powered flight triggered the first blackout of public knowledge.

It all began in 1935 because of a young aeronautical engineer with a high school education and two years study in the School of Mechanical Engineering at Oregon State College, who later became a World War I flier. His name at that time was Jonathan E. Caldwell and he lived near Glen Burnie, Maryland. He invented and built a lighter than air machine which in addition to conventional nose propulsion, was driven by a nine cylinder, 45 horse power French engine with controlled speed blades, each three feet long by 12 inches wide, mounted on top mid-ship which enabled the plane to ascend or descend vertically and even hover. The blades were attached to the cardinal points of a 14-foot wooden disk that was free revolving, deriving its momentum from the power-driven nose prop blast.

The canvas-covered, tubular steel plane, christened the "Grey Goose", had been constructed in a tobacco warehouse and then tested on the Maryland farm of Caldwell's friend Lewis Pumpwrey on State Road Number 3, Anne Arundel County. The machine flew fairly well; it was actually the wingless forerunner of today's helicopter.

Not satisfied with his initial achievement, a few months later Caldwell completed a fundamentally different design named the "Rotoplane". The spectacular lifting capability of this had been tested successfully in Denver, Colorado in 1923. Notwithstanding its lifting power, this machine proved to be less maneuverable. Its energy source consisted of six large, pitched, rotor blades encased in a single 12-foot-diameter rim or flange, above and in the center of which the operator sat. A news story at the time referred to the contraption as a "flying joke".

But regardless of critics and lampooners, Caldwell was not deterred from his dream of a round-wing air machine. He began his final prototype that would indeed prove successful. The latest model was 28 feet in diameter and would disappear before the press or public was allowed to examine it closely, although it had been used openly to provide rides and give demonstrations to interested observers and investors.

The machine resembled a huge tub with a set of six blades projecting out from both the top and bottom of the "tub". In the center of the affair was a round tubular housing or cockpit containing seats for two persons, plus gauges, gears and levers and of course the motor. (The first motor was an eight-cylinder Ford V8 gasoline engine with the block cut in half. This motor was considered heavy and troublesome in operation and was later replaced by a newly cast four-cylinder lightweight aluminum block, along with aluminum gears which were later substituted with bronze.)

The operator sat in the top of the center tubing or hub with his head and shoulders above for the purposes of sight navigation. Hands and feet operated with ease the levers and pedals for speed and direction. The bottom set of six lift blades were wide, fixed at a slight angle, and they turned clockwise. They had a controlled speed operated by one of the gears.

The six, maneuverable-pitch blades located topside were for lateral direction, projecting from the housing; they turned counterclockwise. In essence, the structure and design of the craft, as well as its mechanical movements and controls, were of utmost simplicity.

The two sets of rotors, set six feet apart, revolved in opposite directions around the ship. They were power driven during ascent but turned freely in pure aerodynamic descent if the motor failed, thus allowing the craft to float down under direction from its chosen height at a slower speed than that of a parachutist.

Airborne directional control was attained by changing the angle of the upper set of rotors: that is, forward or reverse thrust was accomplished by a tilting mechanism attached to the top bank of rotors. Thus slippage took place toward the lower side with advancing blades riding downgrade and retreating blades gaining altitude. According to Caldwell's description it was the same principle which birds used in flight, substituting rotors for feathered wings and tail.

The bottom of the craft could be made water tight, enabling it to take off from land or water. To raise capital for his forthcoming enterprise and float costs, Caldwell attempted unsuccessfully and repeatedly to sell stock in his aviation marvel names "The Rotoplanes Inc.," even offering up to $5.00 for a trial ride in the machine. The stock certificates read in part: "That the stock is for an invention, which invention is used in the development of an aeroplane designed to fly on the bird principle of flight, and that the stock is worth $10.00 to $100.00 per share, depending on his (Caldwell's) success in developing the aeroplane.

Eventually, a curious Army-Air Corps Colonel, Peter B. Watkins, dressed in civies, appeared as a prospective buyer whom the delighted inventor took for a test flight. The Colonel was permitted to take the controls, and was astonished at the craft's advanced maneuverability over the bi-wing and mono-wing airplanes of the 30s.

The Colonel flew the machine 45 miles to Washington, D.C., where he made 100-mile-per-hour passes over Washington Monument, and the White House. The Colonel was elated when he actually stopped the forward motion of the machine and hovered for a few minutes directly over the 241-foot high Washington Monument. Upon return to the city he was granted an interview with President Franklin D. Roosevelt.

He told the President that Caldwell's mystery plane was so advanced in design that to avoid copy by foreign military, the United States should immediately obtain control of patents and production. Roosevelt agreed with the Colonel, asking him to reevaluate the project and report back in 30 days for Congres-sional approval.

Within 30 days, without apparent Congressional approval Roosevelt acted.Caldwell received a letter from the Attorney General of Maryland, advising him to cease and desist the sale of the stock in his new company. Previous solicitations to sell stock in New York (1934) and New Jersey (1932) had likewise been stopped by their State Attorneys General. Caldwell, in effect, was forced out of his new aviation venture before it got off the ground.

In the autumn of 1936 Caldwell disappeared and officially was never heard of again.

The question of who was Jonathon E. Caldwell and how he could have disappeared so completely from society was a mystery that baffled the author for almost three years. So little information could be unearthed, only scraps of newspaper accounts that had been quickly denied. And then in November of 1978 a break came in the case of the missing inventor, Jonathon E. Caldwell, who had been 37 years of age when last seen or heard publicly. He would be close to 80 years old today. Was he the one to whom we had established a vicarious attachment and to whom we had dedicated this book -- before we were certain he existed or was still alive?

The American who was to become the world's greatest genius in the field of aerodynamics, and who invented the world's first round-wing plane that millions of viewers have labeled UFO's, was born in St. Louis, Missouri, in 1899.

His name one day would become greater than the Wright brothers, and the city of St. Louis where he was born would gain an even greater fame in years to come than had been bestowed on the city by Charles Lindberg when he named his historic aeroplane that took him across the Atlantic, The Spirit of St. Louis.

But before Jonathon E. Caldwell was to become pre-occupied with a vision of how man could overcome his own absence of wings, World War I would break out. To Caldwell, the war would be a chance to fly aeroplanes, and 1917 would see him volunteering for the service of the United States Army where his training at Kelly Field, Texas in fixed winged bi-planes would be a forerunner for overseas duty in France. Caldwell came out of the service a lieutenant in 1918. He rejoined the Army/Air Corps Reservists in the summer of 1921 and again found himself stationed at Kelly Field with a small group of World War I fliers who had returned for retraining and to brush up on their flying ability.

One day of that 1921 summer at Kelly Field a few young officers including Caldwell took out some saucers and tin plates and began tossing them through the air at each other to be caught during a few minutes of relaxation and horseplay. It was during this period in young Caldwell's life that he became enthralled with the idea of developing a completely new design of aircraft. At first he was hardly aware of his own intentions.

From saucers, Caldwell tried paper plates. Whether the object he threw was a saucer, or a paper or tin plate, or even a military wide brim hat, Caldwell made some pertinent observations. Such round objects when thrown and spun into the air or wind, sailed smoothly, traveled faster, and climbed higher than any other form or shape.

Caldwell while in France had learned the hard way about a fixed wing plane. He knew that if the propeller turned at sufficient revolutions per minute and the prop pitch was properly set, the plane could ride along on the air flow induced by the propeller's own current. But if the motor were to fail and the prop ceased to turn, the unbalanced plane would nose dive or spin to earth out of control. Caldwell himself had crashed and though unwounded, knew of several young acquaint-ances to which such a tragedy had resulted in death. But young Caldwell realized that what made the fixed wing plane such a fearful conveyance was not primarily the problem of engine failure and resultant prop stoppage which prevented an air craft from planeing through the air. Fundamen-tally, the first requirement of an aeroplane was one of design and the basic design of the present aeroplane must be changed. He reasoned that the hurling of the plates and saucers with only one leading edge to cut the air was the primary requirement for perfect aerial transportation.

Another problem to be overcome was one of balance. He had seen airborne dandelion and milkweed seeds floating along majestically and had observed maple leaves spin to earth in a gyrating fashion as they landed gently on the ground. Added to earlier observations of nature's use of air currents to propel seeds, Caldwell never for-got an experience on the battlefield of Flanders, when lying injured on the ground beside his downed plane, he kept his mind occupied by studying an artillery wagon turned on its side, one of the wheels of which periodically kept turning in gusts of wind. Thus, keep-ing in mind nature's methods of aerial movement along with the Flander's wagon wheel, these observations were added to his own study of the kitchen saucers that he had tossed repeatedly.

That summer of '21 Caldwell decided to build himself a 12" round model of a new aerodynamic structure. He would use a delicate balsam wood frame and cover it with shellacked tissue paper. The continuous circular edge would be down lipped so that when it was released inverted into the wind, it would ride on its own cushion of air. Thus was born the idea for the first round-wing plane. A simplification of that first model of a new type of aerodynamic structure eventually became the plaything of children all over the world -- a Frisbee.

As Caldwell watched the Frisbee-like object skip and sail through the air, propelled by elastic bands and riding on its own cushion, he was fascinated by the same recurring thoughts. Some day he would try and build a model large enough to hold a man in the exact center point, and if he could install a motor in such an aerial conveyance to give a constant density to the cushion beneath the circular plane, and if that cushion of air could be manually directed, he would overcome all the disadvantages inherent in a fixed wing plane.

Caldwell kept his vision alive. He retained his balsam prototype and all the drawings and design ideas scribbled or traced on scraps of paper or the backs of envelopes.

The idea that he would build a circular plane never left Caldwell's creative brain. Some day he knew he would invent one that could hover, or develop forward thrust and turn and bank far better and faster than the vintage planes of the early 1920's.

As the Reservists packed and left Kelly Field in 1921 to return to their jobs, the young Caldwell was careful to keep his notes and drawings and to pack along with them his first balsam and tissue paper model. At that time he lived in Denver, Colorado. Sparked by the enthusiasm of fellow pilots at Kelly Field, the young inventor seriously began his first motor-operated model of the new round-wing plane design. With the aid of a welder/mechanic friend in the round house of the Rio Grande Southern Locomotive Works in Denver, in 1922, they turned out a 12" model powered by an erector set toy motor and a single cell dry battery used in telephone transmission.

Wires connected from the battery to the model, as well as a three-foot rope hitch, provided lift for purposes of studying the operational characteristics of the model. Battery contact was made and the round-wing model spun and rose in the air. The attentive trio watched as the rope became taut. As the amazed Caldwell observed the performance, he and his helpers saw the battery and 52 pound table on which it sat, rise slowly in the air as the model plane ascended vertically and lodged itself and its suspended contacts against the shop ceiling. Electric current was cut and the heavy table and plane fell to the floor with a bang. Caldwell swore his helpers to silence and took home his 12" model (which today is in the Washington, D.C. U.S. Patent Office).

After the Herculean lift by the 12" model, an elated Caldwell immediately began work on a 12-foot model, which truly was the forerunner of the round-wing plane of later years. He and his railroad friends completed the project in 1923 and tested their machine in the yards outside the Denver roundhouse. First, about 500 pounds, then a ton of weight, and finally 3000 pounds of rails were tied together and attached to the model plane. Those rails were lifted with apparent ease. Then the speed of the revolving blade was decreased and the rails lowered to the ground from their highest elevation of twelve feet. Next the twelve-foot model was attached to a mountain locomotive type of the Rio Grande Railroad. As all watched the experiment, they saw the round plane lift into the air as the front end of the big locomotive rose slowly at least three inches from the tracks like a reluctant steed. The yard mechanic called out, "Oh Lord, what power have we let loose?" But the plane's bottom frame broke and the engine fell down onto the tracks again.

Caldwell was unable to raise venture capital in Colorado for the new aerodynamic invention and several years later this failure would result in his going east, first to New York, then New Jersey and finally Maryland where a decade later he would attempt his venture again.

During the 20's, the U.S.A. found its renewed industrial strength. As people like Henry Ford mass-produced his Model T automobiles, the growing use of which would eventually link the country with a system of roads and change the American life style, Jonathon E. Caldwell thought of future highways in the sky.

In the years ahead he flew the early mails in fast, single engine planes and hauled bananas in cumbersome air freighters for the United Fruit Company. The same decade also saw the two and three motored planes make their debuts, and pioneer flier Caldwell could also be found at the controls of such aeroplanes flying geologists into the wilds of Venezuela or Central America, seeking locations for a source of new liquid gold called petroleum. When not on a scheduled flight he loved to rent a plane and barnstorm around the countryside and provide rides in the new aerial wonder that most people had never seen. He also became a test pilot for a large aeroplane manufacturer, now out of business, and worked on and tested Lindberg's Spirit of St. Louis with Lindberg, who later reciprocated by trying out an early prototype of Caldwell's Grey Goose helicopter machine.

Also in the '20's Caldwell worked with Robert Edward Lee Cone of St. Petersburg, Florida, head of the Army/Air Corps. Cone was Billy Mitchell's adjutant, and he became one of Caldwell's most important contacts. Several years later, Billy Mitchell would remember about the maverick flyer Caldwell who seriously toyed with a new circular design principle for air travel.

Mitchell would write a letter to the young Caldwell urging him to keep up his research and be careful not to let his project fall into the hands of a foreign government.

After twelve years of earning a living flying aeroplanes (and a stint as a licensed Colorado stock broker located in Denver from 1928 to 1930 during which time he was married), Caldwell decided he must attempt a full-scale project. In the year 1933, he had built his last twelve-foot model and believed he had taken all the bugs out of the latest design. That summer he returned to Kelly Field for the last time as a Reservist. With him he packed a twelve-inch miniature model to show friends. Many Airmen watched Caldwell's round-wing model plane perform in a series of maneuvers that got people talking.

Word soon reached high Army/Air Corps echelons.

Plans for what he named a Roto Plane were later drawn up and perfected in the early thirties, and in 1935 Caldwell incorporated "The Roto Planes Incorporated", listing his new address as Glen Burnie, Maryland and showing his wife, Olive, as secretary-treasurer and brother-in-law Carl H. Davis as vice president. The next year he began his last full size model intended to be used on a commercial basis.

Thus, before 1936, the industrious Caldwell had already built and discarded his Grey Goose plane, the forerunner of today's helicopter. From the Grey Goose idea he had improved the design in a revolutionary concept and by mid 1936 had built his final round-wing plane, in which Army/Air Corps Colonel Watkins had taken a ride and tested to his satisfaction.

Then on October 27, 1936, Caldwell received a letter from the Secretary of War. It went: "Pursuant to our recent conversations . . . we feel your invention is too important to fall into enemy hands. The U.S. government, therefore, is offering you $50,000 for patent rights on the Grey Goose and Roto Plane, and is also prepared to allow for future royalty payments. The Army/Air Corps is also prepared to enlist your services as a full time officer with higher rank than your present captaincy."

The next day Jonathon Caldwell boarded a train for Washington. He sat down in an Arlington, Virginia hotel and discussed his future with Chief of Staff, Army, several aeronautical experts, key Congressmen and members of the cabinet. The delegation reconvened at the White House where Caldwell met President Roosevelt and came away with the rank of Lieutenant Colonel and an annual salary of $10,000.

"For the good of the service," Jonathon E. Caldwell that day had to make his most difficult decision for himself and his wife. He would surrender his family name Caldwell, and never again be known as such. For all intents and purposes he would disappear from society -- till the day he would die.

In August 1949, long after Caldwell's disappearance, some children ventured through a broken window into a so-called haunted tobacco barn in Maryland (the location of which is now in the city limits of Baltimore) - and later told their parents they had seen a flying saucer. Old F.B.I. files and newspaper stories dated August 21, 1949 filed by United Press and Associated Press appearing in the Baltimore Sun, Washington Post, etc. told briefly what had been found. The Deputy Sheriff of Anne Arundel County, father of one of the boys, was asked to accompany the boys back to the scene. He confirmed their story, unknowingly having found Caldwell's original Grey Goose and first Rotoplane. On notifying the Air Force, the barn was placed off limits, and a new generation of Air Force investigators, unaware of Caldwell or his inventions, carted the strange craft off to Wright Patterson Air Force Base, in Dayton, Ohio.

Air Force officers at the Pentagon were red faced when they finally found the files that explained the mystery. For since the day Caldwell vacated his original workshop environment, his inventions had lain forgotten and neglected in the old tobacco barn.

On November 8, 1978, at Kensington, Maryland, an historic book on Caldwell was brought up from the vaults for the researcher to read for two hours. On the leather bound cover, hand printed in gold leaf, was the name Jonathon E. Caldwell, and on the flyleaf inside the 16" X 11" X 6" book, it was written that some of the most valuable records of mankind were preserved herein. The contents were perhaps as important to the U.S. as the Bill of Rights or the early life of President Abraham Lincoln, and to the rest of the world, the knowledge discovered by Caldwell as told by the memos and letters in the leather bound scrapbook would also be a treasure which they some day would share.

As permission was given to peruse the book before it was returned to its deep underground vault, the rules were explained. Guards would be present, the entire contents could be read and studied, but no notes or diagrams were to be made, no pictures taken. Just to see and read the book briefly had required the signatures of the

President of the United States, the Chairman of the Joint Chiefs of Staff, the Commanding General of the U.S. Air Force, the Director of the National Archives, and the Director of the Library of Congress. As the researcher looked at the cover and opened the book, he was filled with awe. For what he saw, was a pre-glance at history, the full contents of which would not be made available to the public till after the year 2000.

Chapter III

International Response to UFO Phenomena

President Roosevelt may have acted with justifiable reason in placing the nation's immediate rights above those of inventor Caldwell. In Roosevelt's mind, and that of certain Congressional and military men, they regarded Caldwell's round-wing plane as perhaps a crude facsimile of that outer space version, that is, as related to aerodynamic design. Earlier in 1936, on two occasions the President was made aware of the presence of strange unidentifiable objects in American skies when he received his first visit by an alien who said he came from another planet in our own solar system.

But even more terrifying than the 1936 visit to the U.S. President by an alien who was human in all aspects, was that of another suppressed landing the same year involving weird creatures stopping at three airports located throughout the northern part of the country.

According to intelligence sources, the creatures' resemblance could best be described as octopus-like, with multiple tentacles rather than human appendages of arms and legs. The beings slithered along on their tentacles and were able to communicate that they came from a planet beyond Earth's solar system and that their celestial wandering was exploratory but their intention peaceful. They showed a fear and nervousness of the curious looking at things called Earthmen, so the feeling between the visitors and the visited was of mutual intimidation. The Earthmen had seen creatures with eyes, ears and mouths who communicated from an intelligent center in their beings, and with exposed organs in animalistic bodies, whereas the pilgrims from outer space saw Earth creatures activated by fingers and hands and feet plus a variety of clothing which must have seemed obnoxious if not at least bizarre. As terrifying as the spacemen were, huge seven feet tall, hairy monsters accompanied the travelers as guards. Today these creatures, called Yeti, have been reported all over the globe indicating that they may have been planted as "information censors" by outer spacemen.

Nevertheless, aside from differences in anatomy, the shock to those Earthlings who witnessed the sighting of the outer terrestrials was terrifying.

Following the 1936 episode with the humanoids (subsequently with other intelligent beings), the Executive Branch clamped a censorship on the arrival of the spaceship and its grotesque looking (by human standards) interplanetary visitors. That experience of select Earthmen being wakened out of an insular lethargy that ordained that all God's creatures had to look like us is still hidden in classified records of the Library of Congress of the Roosevelt era.

Caldwell's genius and his Rotoplane became the beginning by which the U.S. would secretly attempt to duplicate the more advanced interplanetary UFO's. And even then, as today, the U.S. military recognized that a nation with mastery of the air could command others in times of war or peace. Caldwell's Rotoplane was typical of other similar inventions drawn to the attention of the Army/Air Force as it geared to help Caldwell develop an improved version of the round-wing plane.

An official attitude of suppression grew concerning the sharing of knowledge of this type of advanced aerodynamic structure. In 1936, the non-revealing name of A-2 Army Air Corps Intelligence concealed the Air Corps' first efforts to improve Caldwell's round-wing design and duplicate an interplanetary space vehicle. A military awareness was born with presidential blessing to develop a temporary, secret military air arm of technology and industry around the round-wing plane. But what was needed first was where to hide the project away from the prying eyes of increasing numbers of German espionage agents.

Meanwhile, as previously noted, President Roosevelt had been disturbed in 1936 by his first meeting with an outer space being, not to mention the terrifying visit of the octopus-like creatures. A hasty cabinet meeting was called. The President was adamant in his remarks at that meeting that the American people must be told. It was Postmaster General Jim Farley who first suggested an informative radio show to prepare the public. A sense of unbelievable doom was present, the feeling that an interplanetary invasion of earth, like that fictionalized on the Buck Rogers radio program, was a possibility. Worse still, cabinet members were inclined to believe that earth technology was incapable of any defense, and consequently, destruction or slavery of our people was not unthinkable.

Roosevelt invited several electronic media leaders to a private conference. The meeting developed around a radio dramatization of H.G. Wells' book, War of the Worlds. Present that day were Lowell Thomas, Floyd Gibbons and other top writers and producers.

Roosevelt opened by saying, "Gentlemen, we inhabitants of Earth are not alone in the Universe. First, there are other planets in our solar system inhabited by people much like us. I've personally been visited by one of these intelligent aliens. Second, but more unbelievable, are verified reports of terrifying looking creatures who have emerged from strange looking crafts at random airports. I feel we must tell the public! But the question is, how? Gentlemen, can you help us? What do you propose?" The President then polled those present for suggestions.

A committee of five men was then chosen by the Chairman of Radio City to work quickly with Roosevelt on a drama format. From 100 narrators and producers they finally chose Orson Welles, with his clear diction and ominous voice. At 8 P.M. on the evening of October 30, 1938, radio listeners tuned into the Mercury Theatre

Hour heard a drama of horrible Martians landing in New Jersey. The original H.G. Wells story "War of the Worlds," seemed prophetic. The drama as portrayed for radio had been given a dry run at the White House to members of the cabinet and other key citizens, fifteen days before the public broadcast. With this audience aware of the tentacled visitors and hairy monsters, and the ultimate terror they or future humanoids could inspire, Orson Welles and his drama group were urged to make the fictional Martian invasion of Earth more dramatic in its inducement of fear. The radio play finally produced was a masterful piece of emotional suspense and terror, but it was also propaganda.

In hindsight, the invasion theme and the real fright and panic it engendered was not an appropriate way to deliver a message on the arrival of friendly outer space beings. People went berserk. Eight jumped from tall buildings in New York, other unexplained suicides were recorded during and after the show, and state troopers performed Herculean feats looking for the "enemy."

Exit roads from Newark and New York were jammed as were bridges and tunnels. Panic-stricken listeners tried to escape to the countryside where they might hide from the mythical Martian Invasion.

Unfortunately, no station break announcements were made during the hour long show to explain that it was only a drama, and those who had never heard of H.G. Wells' "War of the Worlds" believed the adaptation was real. The grim voice of Orson Welles kept up a running commentary of the terrified human exodus of America's greatest city, New York.

Acting solely on the effects of this radio drama, the Executive Branch of the time decided that the American public could not now be told the truth -- that we were being scrutinized and surveyed by a race from outer planets with technological advances far beyond that of Earth.

The unwitting cover up had already begun to insulate North American minds from the horrifying possibility of contact with creatures unlike us from other worlds. The ramifications of the traditional concept regarding the singular majesty of man, made in the likeness of a supreme creator, could no longer be reconciled by those who had seen other creatures totally unlike us in appearance but equal to or exceeding us in mind and spirit. The question then was how many anatomical versions of intelligent life existed beyond our frontiers of space. And as a result of the panacea of an alien visit in 1936 of humanoid types, the United States took action to suppress future knowledge of alien visitations to Earth. President Roosevelt and his advisors were the guiding force behind the original movement, and a vigilante committee of 100 was formed to monitor future sightings from across the country and advise government on them. At the time no private agency or government body existed who were versed in such a unique problem. Those chosen were men who exerted powerful influence and included prominent bankers, educators, industrialists, railroad presidents, judicial people and select politicians. Among those selected were Henry Ford, the Presidents of Pacific Electric, General Motors, the Pennsylvania Railroad, the Chase Manhattan Bank and a Justice of the Supreme Court. Through government policy, the power of these leaders would increase yearly, and in 1980 the vast territorial boundaries of that private advisory group would still survive and be instrumental in most aspects of the U.S. government's outer space programs. It would also affect the political, military, science and educational sectors of our entire society.

The broad charter of NSA is in itself properly warranted. Its global intelligence gathering abilities keep American's military leaders cognizant of the subtle shifts in military aggressiveness at world trouble spots, notwithstanding the stagnant diplomacy of the foreign policy experts who make judgments based on NSA intelligence briefings.

Therefore, since the Orson Welles broadcast over 40 years ago, the reality of even one outer terrestrial visit and it's disputable effect on a large segment of Earth's population has not been tested because of severe intra-governmental censorship.

At the outbreak of World War II, much of America's brainpower was being expended to improve existing concepts of the round-wing plane. And, although American scientists continued to search and evaluate the new capabilities of its design and propulsion, industry's main thrust was quickly switched back to conventional war apparatus with which U.S. allies were more certain they could combat the enemy.

On December 7, 1941, when the U.S. entered World War II, UFO's were first sighted in number over the White House, and the U.S. Capitol Building. Anti-aircraft fire from guns located in the center of Washington sent up a barrage of metal that literally surprised the extra terrestrials. Thus, as the hovering UFO's took evasive action, an Air Corps radar observer noted a hit on one spacecraft, which left formation and was seen vanishing into a large mothership located at 35,000 feet. This event was the first of several incidents during the war when unidentified flying objects were seen hovering over various buildings in the nation's capitol. It was also at that time that a different UFO design of cigar shape was observed over several American localities. These craft required heavy electric power for their propulsion cores and were frequently seen stealing power while suspended above and attached to the center rail of electric streetcar systems. During one such Washington incident in 1944 the power drain was so great that all of the cities' streetcars came to a standstill. Power plants themselves became the fast feeders for what came to be known as the "juice hogs" which began to steal electric power on a large volume basis. These "unknown alien craft" continued to pilfer power as evidenced by the Eastern Seaboard Blackout in 1975, and the New York Blackout in 1977, the latter of which is documented by U.S. Air Force electronic observation on the site.

By 1945, when the Japanese surrender was signed, America still did not know for sure the identity of any of the UFO invaders or the reason for their presence. At the beginning of his tenure as Supreme Allied Commander for the Far East, General Douglas McArthur summoned the top Japanese officials to his office in the Mechie Building in Tokyo. He stared straight at the Japanese officers, "All right, you so-and-so's," he spat out roughly, as McArthur could do. "Where do you keep those round spy planes you have had over Washington during most of the war?" The Japanese looked at each other and smiled. "What round spy planes do you speak of?" McArthur cussed, and refused to believe their denials.

But for the time being America had the last laugh. At the Yalta Conference, Stalin asked Roosevelt and Churchill why the allies had kept the secret of the round-wing plane from Russia. Roosevelt and Churchill denied the UFO's had been produced in allied war factories. Stalin was furious, and almost left the conference. He hissed across the table as his cold eyes apprised the two allied leaders. "You English speaking people act together. But just remember I have spies throughout both your countries, and I intend to uncover the whereabouts of your secret spaceships that hover over Moscow."

Was Stalin really aware of the UFO's? Indeed, yes! United States intelligence (perhaps unknown to Roosevelt who overly promoted Stalin's friendship) had penetrated the heart of the Kremlin for a period of time and witnessed some astonishing things. The most enjoyable to American intelligence was the following incident: One day in 1943, Stalin received a visit by a being from outer space. The alien suddenly appeared before Stalin's desk and identified himself as an emissary from the government of the Universe. Stalin looked up startled, and replied, "I don't appreciate American jokes," and half rising told the "Yankee" visitor he was going to call his guards. Without further discussion, the alien then told Stalin to call his guards -- who promptly entered. The Russian security guards grabbed the intruder and before Stalin's eyes the ensuing scuffle left the two embarrassed policemen holding only each other. The being had simply vanished into thin air. Adolf Hitler of Germany had also received alien visits, but the discourtesy shown by Stalin marked the beginning of an antagonism between Outer Space visitors and subsequent Russian leaders that has lasted to this day.

It is obvious that by the end of World War II, international intrigue to discover the origin of the increasing unidentified objects became the order of the day in several nations.

But, although public knowledge of the UFO phenomena was slow to spread throughout the world, extensive military interest in it grew during World War II. Over Germany and its occupied territory, allied pilots reported strange lights and luminous balls of fire hovering in protective gestures over their aircraft formations. These peculiar objects were considered by allied airmen to be of unknown origin while uninformed German pilots assumed these same phenomena were perhaps of allied invention. Among allied airmen the name "friendly foo fighters" became a wartime slang that was well understood. And in the living quarters of allied airmen stationed at British airdromes, hushed voices at night whispered of the lights from heaven that sometimes flew in their midst and gave courage.

Intelligence agents of all nations preoccupied with World War II fighting began earnestly to explore the mystery of the "foo fighters." Typical is this account of Russian intelligence interrogating Lt. Colonel H. Sylvester Williams (his code name), a United States Officer in November 1944, who had just delivered a special dispatch, direct from U.S. President Franklin D. Roosevelt to Russian Premier Joseph Stalin.

The special American courier had completed the flight from Washington to New York, then to England, then by special plane across Norway, Sweden and on to his destination, Moscow. The next morning the American courier was carefully questioned by a Colonel Murisky as to whether he had seen anything in the sky in his flight from England. The questions and answers were as follows:

Q. Did you see a cigar-shaped object flying in the sky either alongside your ship or nearby?

A. No.

Q. Did you see any cylindrical-shaped objects at all; say silver or light bluish in color?

A. No.

Q. Sometimes during the trip your plane flew at low altitude; did you observe any shadowy forms on the ground other than that of your own aircraft?

A. No.

Q. Did you see any round saucer-shaped objects that seemed to travel at extremely high speeds?

A. No.

Q. Did you observe any enemy planes during your flight?

A. No.

Q. Were you followed, say by odd-looking objects?

A. No.

Q. Did you see anything strange at all?

A. No.

At this point, the U.S. officer was told to please be on the lookout for anything unusual on his return flight.

During World War II, there were many fascinating chapters of intrigue in the international guessing game of who owned the UFO's even after the alien visits to major governments. The problem of being unable to place a nametag on the aliens was too simple. They looked too human not to be human. That there were those nearly identical to us in other worlds, was considered simply too blasé an explanation.

Truly, major governments could not accept that these objects were extra terrestrial. Deep prejudices that Earthman was a superior creature living alone in the universe were ingrained through our educational and religious concepts. Therefore, at that time, much of the intelligence and military of the world surmised two things:

the crafts were presumed hostile and were of earthly origin.

Each country quickly developed its own methods of counter surveillance, but with few real leads and facts to give its agents. The
Americans, the British, and the Canadians cooperated, anticipating
that collective action would bring faster results.

Standing orders of some countries to their fighter pilots in cumbersome propeller planes were "Hit a UFO - if you can." Already
they had catalogued several varieties including the common saucer
variety and Coleman lantern types, the bell, the cigar or tubular
object, small 13" disks, and even square -- yes, square ones -- and,
of course -- giant mother ships, brighter than Venus, stationed 100
miles high and as long as a mile in length – cities in themselves,
about which the military was divided, as to whether they were illu-
sions or realities.

It's a wonder that American intelligence (Office of Strategic Services) did not become atrophied at its biggest task since General
William Donovan had founded it in 1942. But, with the help of
the scientists and major universities, composure was maintained
and plans developed as the government quietly and clandestinely
swung its efforts into the Age of Aquarius without informing the
press or public.

Science forums across the land, usually sponsored by some government agency, first addressed themselves to the questions:

1. Are we seeing visions or real beings with bodies like mortals?

2. Is it possible that the vibrations which apparently hold together
in permanent shape the atom structure of human bodies might on
a higher vibrating scale bind the structure of beings from other
planets in such a way that the beings are enabled to appear and
disappear?

3. Must visiting intelligent beings breathe an air combination as we
do to survive on earth?

And then it was asked, "What if the force of gravity were negated?" The answer the scientists gave was, "If gravity could be overcome in a localized area such as a space ship, the mass thereof would be weightless.

And finally addressing themselves to the problems of space travel, other groups asked: is it possible for a given mass to travel along earth's magnetic North-South grid perhaps faster than the speed of sound? "Someday, we expect earth ships to do just that, and even fly at incomprehensible speeds between planets on free magnetic energy," was the reply.

With these concepts accepted, Air Force intelligence surmised that true aliens were arriving from our own solar system and possibly beyond and were indeed policing our skies. Certain U.S. scientists hurried to review the age-old concepts of earth's magnetic energy fields and the electromagnetic forces operating between planets.

By the end of World War II, Caldwell's round-wing plane would be a first priority and hidden in a location where it would become approachable only through 100 miles of guarded mountain roads and tunnels. In this hideaway, the design and pertinent specifications of English-speaking peoples' future round-wing plane would be decided.

The rocketry race to the moon in the sixties was simply a continuation of that American goal to learn more of the stellar world. For reasons of national security, the main thrust of the plan to build a round-wing plane was to be kept hidden or camouflaged under newly devised security wraps until the propitious time to tell would arrive.

Today, forty years later, many in America's intelligence and military community believe it is now an appropriate time to open the door for the public to see the dawning of a new technology that will change the world. But many others, in over 30 secret government agencies, particularly NASA and National Science Foundation, consider that telling of the struggle, even in part, is premature.

Although it was not articulated to the rank and file in the services, the American Air Force went on record in 1966 that some of those UFO's appearing in North American skies were interplanetary. With that admission, a confidence was growing that the UFO sightings must eventually be explained.

In 1977, a four-star Air Force staff general who had served in various hush-hush research and development projects since World War II, explained to the authors the Air Force reasoning paraphrased as follows: Heretofore, we were unwilling to divulge the nature of our own development projects; because, outer space beings we had met were so far advanced metaphysically and technologically that should they or other aliens less well disposed to humanity try to destroy us, we would have been helpless. It was the same assumption as that held in 1936. The General didn't mention weaponry or counter weaponry -- he simply spelled out earth's dilemma, not in terms of retaliation, but confined his remarks and thoughts to effective protection on the surface of this planet. Beyond that official explanation of the 20th century problem, the subject apparently was closed.

While the world in post-war years hunted old manuscripts to find the answer to the riddle of the UFO's, America knew the answer, and each year would bury it deeper and deeper.

For the U.S.A., the haunting question was simply this: Could she develop counter airborne hardware quickly enough to protect her own skies from extra terrestrial invaders? And in trying to accomplish this super-human task before the years of World War II, could she also shield her endeavors from the prying eyes of earth adversaries such as the Germans and the Japanese, and even the Russians whom they called allies?

Chapter IV

United States Readies Round-wing Planes for Possible Conflict with Germans

Before World War II, the rise of militaristic regimes in Japan, Italy and Germany had alarmed the democracies, but the war policies of Britain and the United States had not yet been formulated. France built the Maginot defense wall, Britain preferred to appease the Germans by compromise, and prominent American politicians tried to pull a blanket of isolation over the national perspective. Whatever the response by which the democracies sought to resist the dictators, the Nazis, under Hitler, were encouraged to establish illicit and aggressive information gathering services abroad

Thus by 1936, a strong German spy apparatus had already begun to function in the U.S.A. The espionage system had been easy to implement. German nationals were able to hide their activities without undue suspicion by recruiting new members from organizations like the German Bund or by drawing sympathizers from naturalized German-Americans enthralled by Nazi ideologies. Notwithstanding the presence of those Nazi sympathizers on the fringe of certain German communities, the bulk of the German descendants disdained the advances of the Nazi adherents and spurned their racial philosophies. In fact, loyal German-Americans not only opposed, but also were foremost in fighting the Nazis at home and abroad, as intelligence files later confirmed.

Cognizant of this foreign espionage activity, the U.S. Army/ Air Force officers who first interviewed Caldwell in 1936 quickly realized that this young man was on the brink of perfecting the greatest aerial marvel in the history of aviation. Although the first Glen Burnie roto-plane flew slower than 100 miles per hour and operated with a conventional small two-cylinder four cycle air-craft engine, the design of the machine and the airflow it induced was totally different than anything ever conceived and flown by earthmen in their skies. A cumbersome but necessary rudder often caused unwieldy flight patterns in cross winds, and while the ma-chine still required a short runway for takeoff, it was apparent that its future potential in speed, hovering, and maneuverability might literally allow it to reach the stars if adequate scientific help were provided.

Political unrest in Europe had alerted U.S. Foreign Service watch-ers, and their observations of a new arms build-up had been passed on to the military. Gradually, there began a shift from isolationism to uneasiness. Following Hitler's occupation of Austria, and later in March 1936, he marched into the Rhineland. While watching Germany, France began to overspend on rearmament, and Britain and America began to show alarm at signs of German expansion-ism. War clouds were obviously appearing over Europe following what amounted to international failure to promote disarmament. A reliance on peace treaties became mere scraps of paper.

Taking a hard look at her research achievements in the air, the U.S. suddenly realized that although there existed on the market new scientific breakthroughs in destructive weapons, America herself had produced no significant aerial developments since World War I. The continuing use of the aeroplane as an effective weapon of war had not been obscured in the directives of the U.S. Army/Air Force advisors as they prepared reports on how Spanish towns were leveled by German dive bombers in 1936 or how the air-cov-er of Italian planes lent support to their troops and tanks in Musso-lini's 1935 subjugation of Ethiopia.

Thus, with prognostic military awareness of the possible evolu-tion of aerial warfare, there occurred top-level re-assessments of Caldwell's first rotoplane. National security advisors became doubly concerned about espionage, particularly by the Germans.

Orders went out from the executive branch to relocate the Caldwell program away from the potentially prying eyes of a wave of German spies.

The new premises, operated under the supervision of Caldwell, would be located at Wright Patterson Field, outside Dayton, Ohio. In a corner of hanger number 2, in December 1936, Caldwell began again. He first set up a small machine shop and was given a fulltime machinist and welder. Caldwell was also provided with an assumed name which he would change twice again in the years ahead. Also, added was the additional luxury of an office girl to complete the constant reports required in written communications with the new Army/Air Corps sponsor.

For Caldwell and his wife, Olive, there would be the protection of constant security police. The Caldwell children, a boy and a girl, both in their teens, complained that their dates and friends were watched and the backgrounds of the families of their new friends were checked. The privacy for which they so often longed was gone forever.

Under Caldwell's supervision, a new machine with modifications was begun in late 1936. Plans called for it to be 33 feet in diameter and to hold a crew of six. Emphasis would be on using the lightest weight components obtainable. The structure would be thin, steel tubing built around a center cockpit. Initially a silk-covered plywood veneer was intended, but that was rejected for a silk-over-cotton covering. This skin was used for the first new models tested until replaced by duralumin from a formula developed by Dr. Bolton B. Smith of the Massachusetts Institute of Technology. Rejection of this aluminum skin also took place when it became obvious that it possessed a too low heat point, making it unsatisfactory for high-speed travel. The skin finally perfected on the roto-plane covering was an outer layer of paper thin, stainless steel, bonded to an inside layer of duralumin with a film of glued silk between. The new covering would be standard specifications on all U.S. round-wing planes of the future, until outer spacemen would provide a perfect skin formula for American machines.

Caldwell gave all his time to the project. Each spare moment he thought on how to improve the craft. One night, while working late under strict guard surrounding his home, a knock came at his study door. Caldwell's own vicious police dog outside the door did not stir. As Caldwell opened the door, he saw standing before him a tall man in a silver space suit and black calf-high boots, waiting with an outstretched hand. The German shepherd looked up at the stranger and wagged his tail. As the visitor was invited to sit down in front of Caldwell's desk, the inventor, still uncertain of his polite intruder, covered with a book the diagram on which he had been working. The stranger spoke: "Don't worry about those plans lying under the book. The problem that vexes you is one of propulsion. Actually, the heart of the problem is not only one of design; rather it is mathematical." The stranger then handed Caldwell a folder with seven sheets inside, including a new carburetor design and fuel formula.

Caldwell offered his new friend a cup of coffee. They talked for fifteen minutes and the stranger explained how Caldwell could overcome the existing difficulty he was encountering in the new round-wing plane.

The spaceman departed, and as Caldwell reread the plans more carefully, he noticed a "formula of seven ingredients, which, when later added to the kerosene fuel for the jet engines then being tested, gave such an improved performance that the added horse power and mileage range were unbelievable. (Up to that time, there had been no need for a highly combustible fuel. The simple additive of lead to gasoline was adequate to run the piston engines.)

German espionage agents had lost the trail of Caldwell and his amazing machine late in 1936, much to the relief of security personnel. In their new Wright Patterson quarters, the Caldwell crew was free to come and go from their workshop, but their presence in the community of Dayton would, of course, ultimately be discovered. German agents, undeterred, were already searching the country for their lost quarry.

In the meantime, earlier work by Caldwell on a jet engine was now being completed with help from Northwestern University and advice from the outer space man. Caldwell's jet was an improvement on an earlier model invented in France. Plans were made to replace the conventional aircraft engine in the round-wing plane with the newly developed jet. (Early versions of Caldwell's jet plans were stolen by German agents and first installed in their new Messerschmidt 109.)

The scope of the project was enlarged when the full military application of the plane was recognized. In January 1937, Northwestern University provided physicists and contracted to do all the lab work in design, metallurgy and chemistry for the Caldwell project. Facilities in Wright Patterson Hanger No.2 began with a total of ten people helping Caldwell in the makeshift factory. The crew grew monthly. A governing board was appointed consisting of the officer commanding the airfield, plus two other officers, along with Caldwell as supervisor.

Caldwell had narrowly missed being killed more than once in flying his new contraption; therefore, two test pilots from Kelly Field, Texas, were brought in to keep the inventor on the ground. The name roto-plane was now dropped in favor of the round-wing appellation, and in official correspondence, the project ceased to be called the Long Island project in preference for the new code name JEFFERSON.

Jefferson quickly was placed under the highest security in the U.S.A. For the new personnel, their movements outside the hanger would be subject to closer scrutiny, and their social and family contacts would be monitored 24 hours a day.

But the new vigilance came too late. The German espionage agents had narrowed the Caldwell trail to Dayton. German agents reported their discovery to their military attaché, and quietly a plan was drawn up to catch the Americans involved in the Jefferson project in a way security authorities would never suspect. German espionage teams carefully laid out their new net.

By early 1938, Project Jefferson had covered 20,000 square feet of

Hanger No.2, plus an adjacent hanger. There were now 102 employees sworn to silence by oath, who operated under the jurisdiction of an expanded ten-man governing board. The employees were paid top wages and often were seen at a particular bar in downtown Dayton, where the best drinks were served and affable waiters and attractive decor made an evening at the cocktail lounge a most enjoyable event. For patrons who liked the thrill of gambling, the waiters would discreetly whisper that a special room was located at the back. For patrons from Wright-Patterson Field, IOU's were honored and inducements extended to bet heavily.

It was during this period that reports from the northeast began appearing at police stations, newspaper offices and air force installations of strange, unearthly looking aircraft that streaked across the horizons at unbelievable speeds, faster than anything ever seen in the skies before. (World records in 1938 for propeller driven fixed wing planes were in the vicinity of 300 mph.) And with the sightings of these novel craft, often there was also reported a bright luminosity. The light was purely reflective, the plane's surface being so highly polished as to show a mirror-like reflection in the moonlight or perhaps a blinding flash in the bright sun that obscured its shape. The planes took off and landed at Wright-Patterson Field -- generally at night.

But now the Germans had competition in their American espionage activities. Just as interested in the new aerial phenomena were the Japanese. World War II was only a year away, and international military jitters were spreading around the globe.

Had the curious sky watchers known the truth, they would have learned that the newly seen night craft were American made. They were in fact almost totally new versions of Caldwell's first rotoplane. Of course, they were round, 33 feet in diameter, with a cabin on top in mid-center. The heart of the propulsion was now a kerosene-fed jet motor that could provide the plane with a top speed of 750 miles per hour. The jet sucked air into its chambers, heated it and dispersed it through a system of ducts that gave the sudden maneuverability in all directions which ground viewers had observed and reported.

Ten of these beautiful machines stood hidden in a hangar in Wright-Patterson in September 1938, approximately two years after Caldwell had flown his first canvas-covered craft the 45 miles to Washington. September 12 was a special day. Caldwell himself took the controls of one of the planes as it was wheeled out. Before daybreak, he took off after a dozen maintenance men checked out the ship and gave it clearance for departure. The jet could not lift the mass and weight straight up, but once airborne it could hover.

Up like an arrow shot in an oblique line of flight at 35 degrees, the round-wing plane rose into the covering darkness. Less than two hours later, as morning broke over Washington, D.C., alert onlookers saw a strange object hovering over the White House, stationary, and emitting a muted whine.

The appearance of the plane over the home of the President was a combined salute to the Chief of the U.S.A., President Franklin Delano Roosevelt, from Jonathon E. Caldwell and the Army/Air Corps, which had helped him build the world's first operational round-wing plane.

Not only were the American President and his staff watching, so was the German military attaché. After that 1938 recorded inaugural flight, there would be renewed interest by foreign embassies in America, particularly German, concerning the most unconventional aeroplane the world had ever produced. The Germans hurried up their scheme to obtain plans on the amazing American invention, an updated version of the 1936 Caldwell rotoplane.

It was less than a month after the Washington fly-over by the round-wing plane that the new, posh downtown cocktail and gambling lounge in Dayton was staked out by the FBI. Reports began coming in that gambling debts would be forgiven if indebted players of the games of chance provided information about activities at Hangers 2 and 3 at Wright-Patterson Field. It was soon ascertained that the bar was German-owned and was the trap by which they planned to obtain the secrets of the new American round-wing plane. Briefly, these developments of counter intrigue took place. Two FBI men, masquerading as draftsmen on the new round-wing plane, ran up debts in the German gambling room. The bar was closed and all personnel connected with the premises were arraigned and placed in jail under the severe statutes of treason; they were detained till further World War II emergency powers were invoked. Then, these spies were summarily executed. The last attempt had failed by which the Germans intended to obtain the revised plans to America's revolutionary plane.

The American intelligence authorities had learned a valuable lesson. From then on, all loose talk about the new plane must be stopped. Furthermore, the round-wing plane facilities must be relocated again, and this must be done quickly. Government and military apprehensiveness mounted.

The Secretary of War wrote Caldwell to expect a move in the autumn of 1938 to a new location. Orders were given to dismantle and crate the machinery and equipment. At a scheduled time, a long train pulled into Wright-Patterson Field where it was loaded, after which Caldwell, his wife, and teenage son and daughter boarded a Pullman car. Their family possessions were also packed. On a flat railroad car went Caldwell's canvas covered personal automobile. Railroad men along the line called it the "X" special because it moved with the same priority as a Presidential train, requiring all other trains to stand by on a siding till the "X" train passed through. All switches along the route were spiked to prevent tampering, and armed soldiers guarded key points.

Well before the year 1938 ended, on October 23, Hangers No. 2 and 3 in Dayton's Wright-Patterson complex were emptied and closed, and only the ghosts of Jonathon Caldwell and his builders of a new aerial empire lingered behind.

The next location selected for continuing development of the round-wing plane was in a military town near the continental divide in New Mexico. At an army center, near the town of Los Alamos, the complex was hastily made ready. A railway spur line was run in and new facilities added for the elite company of men and women about to arrive.

As the special "X" passed through Los Alamos, the engineer found himself riding on newly laid track. Cavalry units guarded the new rails. While the train pulled into the final destination site, the Caldwell entourage beheld a regiment of soldiers surrounding the enclosure. After the train was unloaded and vacated, the dining and Pullman cars were pushed into sealed sheds that then were filled with cyanide gas in case a spy remained hidden on the train. Such was the security surrounding the second move of the Caldwell group known officially as Project Jefferson.

The new headquarters were self-contained insofar as the life style that prevailed during non-working hours. Total security would be maintained in a setting of barbed wire and electric fences. Elaborate precautions were taken to prevent unauthorized outsiders from getting past the guards. Any truck or other vehicle leaving the Los Alamos installation from the moment of the Caldwell arrival would be thoroughly searched and torn apart if the security inspectors so decreed.

For the new inhabitants all amenities were provided, such as private tutoring and school classes, library, church services, films, restaurants, clothing, food. There was only one stipulation. No access to the outside world was tolerated, all outgoing and incoming mail was censored and telephone conversations monitored. The personnel of Project Jefferson were prisoners. And wherever Caldwell and his family went, their constant protection by Secret Service personnel would be greater than that required for the President of the United States.

In the year 1940, in the nearby town of Los Alamos, a group of merchants provided maintenance for the fast-growing personnel living in the adjacent area, engaged in production facilities for a fleet that was being hurried to assume a role in the skies should neutral America become involved in the European war which had broken out in September of 1939.

In addition to the merchants who provided station provisions, there moved into Los Alamos another type of resident. This was the dogged German and Japanese who listened for casual information about the close-by activities and whose high-powered binoculars and cameras scanned the clear skies for any unusual man-made phenomena.

Americans were unaware, but all the nation's industrial and scientific endeavors, including the Manhattan project, were now secondary to the deployment of the country's brainpower in the Jefferson Project.

Then in 1941, another trauma of defense consciousness occurred with the arrival of Japanese bombers over the U.S. mainland, after which it was feared the new Los Alamos round-wing plane site might be bombed. Three bombs had already been dropped in Northern California. Some Japanese field workers in Hawaii had been found guilty of espionage acts that had pointed a path for planes toward Pearl Harbor installations. Authorities asked themselves, "How vulnerable to air attack was the Los Alamos site and were Japanese espionage agents operating nearby?"

Although total military vigilance was maintained around the Los Alamos site, secret security personnel monitored the establishments that the soldiers favored while in Los Alamos. On one occasion, seven soldiers went into an "off limits" bar. As drinking increased, two of the soldiers began loudly bragging about their activities to the waitress. Within minutes, a squad of military police rounded up the group and they were returned to base. All off duty soldiers in town and at the site were also recalled. That afternoon, the two soldiers were court-martialed and sentenced. The same day they dug their own graves in full view of their regiment. A squad of 12 men was called out and a firing squad executed the two who had boasted about the project in public. Such was the sensitivity to secrecy built around the round-wing plane development that continues to this day.

A short time after Pearl Harbor in December 1941, traffic suddenly disappeared in and out of the Los Alamos complex. Dignitaries and visitors were seen no more, and bids to provide food and beverage were no longer asked from the merchants of the town.

Also missing were the bewildered foreign espionage agents.

High in the sky above Los Alamos one winter night in late December 1941, a fleet of over 60 round-wing planes with their trained combat crews of over 400 men disappeared into the blackness of the unknown.

By all evidence, the great American project surrounding the round-wing plane installations had been abandoned, to be heard of no more.

Of course, by the end of 1941, the United States was at war with the axis powers of Germany and Italy, and had declared war on Japan. Hostile planes had been sighted over San Francisco, and war in the air was potentially closer to home.

As for the American war effort in the skies, all the public learned that year came from the mouth of National Defense Chairman William B. Knudsen, who said for the record: "The U.S. will soon double its present 900 monthly plane production of fighter and bomber craft in an air re-armament drive." The new aircraft fighter hope, apparently, was still a conventional fuselage with one fixed cross wing called a P-40, clocked across the Buffalo airport at 320 miles per hour.

Were the 60 round-wing planes that reputedly could fly at speeds in excess of 750 miles per hour too untried to mention? Or, were they classed as secret weapons being held in abeyance until America would enter the war and one day bring Hitler, the new master of Europe, to his knees?

Chapter V

Early German Development of the U.F.O.

The Germans shot down their first unidentified flying object in 1938, and thereafter, attempted to lead the international space race. Already tooled for war under Hitler's crash program, Germany's engineers and skilled tradesmen set out to duplicate the downed machine from Venus.

Upon hearing of the fortunate prize, Hitler directed his private pilot, Christina Edderer, to fly him to the site. It was during an interview in Munich in 1975 that the courageous Christina Edderer, perhaps unjustly imprisoned by the allies, showed the authors a collection of over 100 snapshots from her album of many famous Germans and the facilities involved in their round-wing plane production. One such picture showed Hitler, the German Chief of State, posed smiling, with one foot on the edge of the downed and tipped-over saucer craft that revealed a broken landing tripod.

In 1938, German research began in earnest on the implosion engine and the round-wing aircraft. One of the foremost early inventors of the implosion engine was a German-Swiss named Victor Schauberger who went to work full time on the project. With the downed UFO, the Germans created a new industry to duplicate the engineering and flight characteristics of the alien craft.

A hidden factory was tunneled out of the Austrian Alps, and the facility remained undetected by American or British reconnaissance planes during most of the war.

Genesis for the Space Race

The Germans began their research under a veil of secrecy more complete than similar measures of news suppression in America's Manhattan (Atom Bomb) Project. In Germany, death was the penalty for an unguarded tongue, and only a release from the Fuehrer, himself, permitted a worker to return to the outside world once he was taken to one of the hidden factories.

Few in the German Command were made aware of the round-wing craft development project, and Albert Spear in his book, Inside the Third Reich, fails to mention it, although for a time he was in charge of German War Production. German airmen throughout the war were also ignorant of the round-wing building and testing program. Like their American counterparts who asked questions, the German fliers, who saw alien UFO's in their skies, were told truthfully they were Extra terrestrials.

The Germans experienced several difficulties in recreating their version of the Venusian's craft that they had acquired. To say the least, the German version fell short of perfection. A major problem was in the field of metallurgy, the Germans being unable to duplicate the metal substance of the UFO skin. A lightweight alloy, thought by Germany to be superior to anything in the Western World, was finally rolled out in the Krupp mills. But it was a poor substitute, and the Germans knew it. Another hurdle they couldn't overcome was to reproduce the craft's electromagnetic engine. The coil was duplicated as faithfully as German technology could provide, but the hard, unknown, metal substance used for the craft's skin was also necessary for certain parts of the propulsion coil. The formula for this metal continued to remain elusive.

In 1941, an American soldier of German descent enabled Germany to evaluate what the U.S.A. was doing in the advanced field of aerodynamics. For $5 the German, Edward Gunther, bought the patent description of Caldwell's 1936 Rotoplane. He resold it for $50,000. The German government eventually paid $1,000,000 for the patent drawings and description. In June 1943, the first German spy, Gunther, was apprehended, convicted and sentenced to be shot as a spy. The story was kept out of the news media although a high treason conviction was handed down by a Military Tribunal Court in Judiciary Square, Washington, D.C. Roosevelt reversed the convicted traitor's sentence of death by firing squad, and death came in the electric chair at Sing Sing Penitentiary.

American newspapers of that period mentioned the affair, but the reading public did not learn the complete facts because of government censorship.

A total of eight people who were involved in the theft received death sentences and died in Sing Sing's electric chair under contract between the State of New York and the federal government. Two of the spies were Julius and Ethel Rosenberg as well as a clerk in the New York patent office. Also participating were other German nationals beside Gunther.

The Rosenberg involvement is said to have begun prior to their espionage activities in the Manhattan Project. Once the Caldwell plans had been acquired, they knew they had in their possession the hottest aeronautical invention in the world. The plans were first offered to Japan, which refused them. Then the Russians were approached and they also turned the Rosenbergs down against the advice of their military attaché, who had watched Caldwell's Roto-plane through field glasses fly over Washington.

Subsequently, the Germans heard that the Rosenbergs were peddling the Caldwell plans and, recognizing their military value, acquired them through a German agent.

The name Long Island Project was used to designate the stolen Caldwell plans because a German submarine had surfaced off Long Island at night to pick up the plans of the revolutionary plane. Within ten months, the Germans had made and flown their version of Caldwell's Roto-plane.

German engineers gained enough knowledge from the American invention to produce their operational models of the Roto-plane -- which gave them a breakthrough, but they needed more time to perfect their Roto-plane, more time than the emergencies of war would allow.

Undeterred, German technology continued serious work on propulsion of the Caldwell craft and using the implosion engine, determined to place a round-wing plane in the air for use in the final month of World War II.

The Germans finally produced a design prototype combining the alien UFO and the stolen "American" patent of Caldwell's.

In late 1942, Adolf Hitler gave orders to those in charge of research and production to produce an airworthy round-wing plane by 1943. In March of that year, in compliance with the Fuehrer's orders, the country's first earthman version of a full size round-wing spacecraft was wheeled out for testing.

The craft could best be described as resembling a spoked wheel, (like Caldwell's Rotoplane) with spokes actually being adjustable fins that moved from a horizontal to vertical position. In the center of the wheel was a rounded hub for the Schauberger implosion motor, over which the craft's operators sat. The whole operation from a distance somewhat resembled a bowler hat with a wide brim.

We interviewed one of the three occupants of that craft in America, and he corroborated the story of the ensuing test flight.

Uncertainty dominated the takeoff. The three occupants were strapped into a heavily cushioned interior, and the craft was catapulted into the air. The machine was then taken to an altitude of over 10,000 feet. However, the first German UFO pilots were disappointed in its lack of speed and maneuverability. Shortly thereafter their disappointment turned to fear.

In addition to ground observers who tracked the craft and accompanying conventional chase aircraft, the Germans suddenly became aware of another presence above them -- an aerial craft similar in design to their own.

After determining the position of the alien craft, occupants of the German plane realized they were locked in the power of the plane above them. The German pilot tried to take evasive action and change his craft's position but was helpless to do so. This strange, celestial experience thoroughly bewildered the young Germans.

Then, as they sat in quandary, a voice came over their radio in perfect German. "Don't be afraid. We are here to help you."

The voice introduced itself as a Venusian! He stated that his people had watched German progress since the day the disabled Venusian craft had been taken by the Germans in 1938.

"I'm here to instruct you," the voice told them, "and to get you back safely to earth which you would never make without our help. We are, at present, holding you safely in our tractor beam which is an embodiment of the magnetic principal you are trying to unravel."

He then explained that as superior as the ship's metal alloy was, it was unsuitable. The alloy would burn under the friction of re-entry from space into earth's atmosphere. He explained the metal was still too heavy, and subject to deterioration from stress. "Also," he said, "your propulsion must be changed."

German engineers had tried to reproduce the Venusian's magnetic coil but rejected it in favor of the more conventional implosion engine when the magnetic coil failed to provide controlled lift.

The stranger knew of this failure, and he told them that before they again used a magnetic core, their metallurgists must produce a metal that would be magnetized only at those precise times in which a low voltage was passed through the coil. "Whereas," he continued, "in the earlier prototype which you abandoned, the magnetic field was sustained for a time after current was turned off and the craft, therefore, failed to respond immediately to your control.

"Without such a change in your power core, your craft will always have propulsion difficulties regardless of design." The alien spaceman addressed the young Germans in perfect calm.

"Free electromagnetic energy is the agent that holds our solar system in place. This force can also take manned vehicles into space faster and more quietly than the conventional petro-chemical or new solid fuels derived from the earth. Someday your costly earth fuels will be depleted, but the free energy of the planets is everlasting."

The stranger admonished the Germans. "You earth people don't fully understand the cosmic marvel of this energy of which I speak. I repeat, it is free to all who seek it and is a gift from the Supreme Being or Godhead. Harness this basic force for peaceful purposes, and it will become your servant -- as it has been the servant of other planets for millions of years. Harness it for war and you can no longer count on our cooperation -- or tolerance."

The Germans were asked to cut their power and rely on his space ship above, and thus, locked onto the UFO's magnetic field, the Germans would be lowered safely. "Otherwise," he cautioned, "you will crash, and all of you will be killed. Trust us," he continued.

"I promise that we will appear before your engineers and teach them how to make these improvements to your craft. Your time is short. For the present, there should be no delay. "Now let me tell you of the future! I shall meet two of you again in America when Germany and the U.S., now at war, are once more friends."

The spaceman said farewell. His final message was to prove prophetic.

The space stranger told two of the German plane occupants they would be involved in America's space program after the war. To the third occupant, he foretold that he would remain in Germany and continue his work there.

The German flyers were debriefed on landing. Observing ground forces had seen the two ships descend as though connected by an invisible beam, whereupon the upper alien ship took off.

Today an American scientific spokesman describes the invisible magnetic ray as a "tractor beam," i.e., a magnetic pick-up force generated from one spacecraft over another. The use of this magnetic beam has been verified in the following documented cases: Rescue of one space ship by another -- the capture of an American helicopter according to Naval records -- abduction by friendly alien space ship of an American missile which had gone, off course. Earth nations today are working feverishly on their various perfections of the tractor beam, because its application in a number of aerial requirements, both civilian and military, would be worthwhile.

When the three young German spacemen told the story of their aerial encounter with the Venusians, the German officers in charge of the debriefing were incredulous. The interrogators at first refused to accept the apparent manifestation of alien aid from one ship to another.

From then on, the academic search to find an explanation of the strange encounter 10,000 feet in the air spurred German attention and explanations were sought even in the occult, the paranormal and psychological communities. But, like their American counterparts, many Germans remained perplexed as to the reality of the voice visitation from another world. In any event, the Germans decided to delay their final conclusions.

If the alien or others like him were able to appear again to help them perfect their spacecraft as he promised, the Germans would accept that there existed a higher wisdom that they had yet to learn. The phlegmatic German scientists waited and hoped. They knew they needed a miracle to meet Hitler's timetable for craft completion. They were not to be disappointed. Eventually a number of aliens appeared in their engineering departments to instruct them in new metallurgy and chemistry techniques and provide them with a partial electromagnetic breakthrough.

The German staff apparently continued their all out effort to turn the tide of war, but their priorities changed. Late in 1943, many of their best scientists and skilled workers were transferred from the round-wing plane project to the same mountain area for work on solid fuel rockets. It was anticipated by the General Staff that these secret weapons could be deployed quickly and in strength over London to make the British surrender. A longer-range rocket version also was being drafted for use against New York. This shift to rockets was due, in part, to German anger for the mass destruction of their cities by allied air raids and the ultimatum by their non-earthling helpers that the round-wing plane could not be used against the enemy. The rocket project therefore delayed German deployment of the round-wing plane by six months. So German industry at that time switched to quickly mass-produced rockets with conventional warheads, as opposed to overcoming engineering deficiencies in their round-wing plane.

Recent evidence from captured German records suggests that their round-wing plane project also was deferred for other reasons. By 1943 they had not incorporated a sophisticated laser ray weapon system into the craft to suit their engineers, and although they believed they were ahead in the international race to build a viable round-wing plane, they elected to keep their product under wraps, for use in the future when Germany would use it again. But the most compelling reason for deferring military rise of the new round-wing plane was the Venusian's threat against Germany if it were so employed.

In the coming months the Germans projected that allied bomber-force capabilities would increase while German strength declined. The German Air Force already knew the value of the round-wing plane and how space weaponry in the form of laser rays could be used in conjunction with it. Their military reasoning was based in part on events stemming from the Munich Stadium rally in 1936 while Hitler was delivering a speech. A huge, wingless, cigar-shaped object that hovered menacingly high above the sky downplayed him.

Attempting to buzz the intruder, all the engines of a protective fighter squadron went dead, forcing the pilots to land on feathered props in nearby fields and airports. A beam from the UFO (witnesses interviewed by the author) had disabled each of the German airplanes.

Hence, seven years later in 1943, German scientists were mindful of Venusian threats and also that without advanced space age weaponry to fight enemy marauders the secret of their round-wing plane should be kept under wraps. As promised, the aliens ventured to help them in their revised plans but only in a limited way. Mass production of their new plane and new weaponry, therefore, would be delayed until that particular period when it could properly take its place in Adolf Hitler's grand scheme to continue the Third Reich and pursue his conquest of the world.

That period was not far off and the allies were totally unaware of it's dawning.

Early in 1944 Germans in the environs of one underground Austrian round-wing plant saw the "saucer" activity gradually disappear from the skies above, as did the piercing humming noises associated with the craft.

Large trucks moved out the machinery as well as two unfinished craft, and the mountain forests were returned, in part, to their primeval solitude.

In the five years of German effort to duplicate an alien spacecraft, they had made several significant breakthroughs combining alien technology and Caldwell's patent. They had begun with a conventional liquid fueled aircraft engine while solving problems of rotating balance and guidance in the plane's "design." But the machine was ponderous and slow. According to one of their test pilots living in America, this first version, like Caldwell's, was a vertical lift propeller machine, indicating it was a very elementary version of their later designs. The design and functional improvements in their prototypes came as a result of direct outer terrestrial help in 1943-4 that enabled them to overcome their prolonged failures and build a round-wing plane with limited capabilities. Albeit, when the Germans secretly started their exodus in their five 30-foot round-wing planes, somewhat similar in design and propulsion to the alien one shot down in 1938, they were sufficiently airworthy to load and depart under their own power. Two unassembled planes were also removed. During the closing years of the war, entire German factories mysteriously disappeared. When the allies accepted the surrender of Germany from the substitute leaders, the former enemy had already removed to unknown regions of the world those round-wing plants that were to enable them to continue research and production, undetected by the victors of World War II.

Of course, along with the UFO factories, standing orders had been issued that scientists, engineers, and personnel who had worked on the latter UFO program, would also be sent abroad with the secret shipments of UFO manufacturing paraphernalia. Thus, thousands of such German experts were swallowed into a natural refuge which the allies never surmised was in existence and which will be described later. American and British intelligence units had deciphered the German round-wing riddle prior to the surrender, and it only remained for those teams to seek out the evidence of German production. Working on slim leads, the Western powers uncovered what remained of German UFO plants and personnel. Meanwhile, the Russians concentrated their search on the rocket factories. In all, the Russians forcibly removed over 3,000 German science and technical experts in rocketry. With this inflow of German brains and industrial resources, the Soviets acquired the post-war lead in the field of manned rocket flight.

The English-speaking allies would assess German accomplishments by sifting through reams of top-secret German files and transporting German round-wing machinery to Canada and Great Britain for examination. They would also enlist the help of 183 German round-wing plane technicians brought to North America after the war on a voluntary contract basis, and 100 other German experts under Wernher Von Braun to work on missiles and rockets.

But in spite of the favorable status given the German experts, there is some uncorroborated evidence that a number of Germans, by necessity, surrendered their freedom in North America as did the native son, Caldwell.

It is recalled that Hitler had asked for an operational version of the first German round-wing plane in 1943. Allied Intelligence now maintains he was carrying out a long prepared plan to divide the remaining German resources, including its manpower, in order to continue the struggle elsewhere beyond the reach of allied bombs. The reader will realize in the succeeding chapters that no other explanation can exist for the vanishing German personnel and their round-wing technology in the last years of World War II.

Chapter VI

USA Shares Secret of New Plane with Allies

As World War II began, allied intelligence speculated that the Germans also had developed the round-wing plane. No one learned if the enemy had turned out ten or 1,000, nor when or where they would strike. The worst was feared, and the U.S. geared itself to produce a counter force with plans calling for a preponderance of their own round-wing planes in answer to the German threat.

The ultimate military advantage of Caldwell's new aerodynamic invention had been realized by government authorities as far back as its discovery in 1936. President Roosevelt had shared the secret with Prime Minister, Mackenzie King, of Canada, outlining the gravity of keeping classified the development and testing of the new round-wing plane.

In 1936 the Canadian Prime Minister, on hearing the difficulty of security and the need to challenge the Germans in case of hostilities, had arranged to place a hidden valley of central British Columbia on Canada's west coast off limits to settlement. The 300 square mile valley was so remote and without road entry that only a bird would be able to enter this wild refuge undetected. The hideout was designated to become the new home of the round-wing plane endeavor and, in a far-sighted act of wisdom, President Roosevelt decided to give the project national priority and share the development of the round-wing plane with the Canadians and

British. Thus in 1936, the impenetrable inland hideout in British Columbia saw hundreds of surveyors and planners break solitude for a new industry and town. By 1938, roads were being built and a three-mile tunnel for a two-track electric railroad was cut by hard rock miners through the mountain into the valley domain. No one guessed the reason. In the valley proper forests were felled, heavy roads and airstrips were built, town and factory sites were laid out, and the world's first spacecraft manufacturing facilities were feverishly erected.

By January 30, 1942, the Caldwell group had arrived from Los Alamos. Foreign espionage surveillance would again be without their quarry.

Two top U.S. scientists, John S. Pershag (structural design) and John B. Meyers (instrumentation) were assigned to Caldwell's staff; and also John B. Adams of whom records do not give country of origin.

A separate, international team assumed special scientific tasks also. This team included Colonel Charles Hadden of England, who had done yeoman service in the Royal Air Force defense of London. Hadden had formerly taught physics at a British university. An American of German descent, Felix S. Essen, was also part of the team. Canada sent Steward L. McLane, kin of Prime Minister, Mackenzie King. McLane had taught advanced mathematics at the University of Ottawa.
This team of engineers first built models and tested them for stress in wind tunnels. They also worked on aviation fuels for the new jet motors. Throughout their terms of service, Hadden and McLane chaffed to get out of the round-wing engineering functions into conventional military combat but were refused permission to leave. (See Epilogue for their awards for achievement).

Northwestern University's lab also became a part of the British Columbia operation. President Roosevelt had authorized Russian scientific participation, but the Chiefs of Staff in the U.S.A. and Great Britain refused to endorse direct Soviet participation. Russian advisers were therefore sent to the U.S.A. but were never given visas to the heart of the project in Canada. New workers were recruited to run the various enterprises and facilities. The Caldwell venture, which had begun in an abandoned barn in Maryland, U.S.A., became a state within a state in British Columbia, Canada. Maximum security would guard the greatest invention of mankind, and any aeroplane flying into this forbidden air space would be shot down or escorted by fighter craft to an outside airport from which its occupants might not be freed if their stories did not suit the authorities. The combined intelligence of America, Canada and Britain would make it certain that plans and development of the round-wing plane would never again be stolen by a foreign power.

The fact that the Germans had acquired the original Caldwell patent and drawings had never ceased to anger and embarrass United States intelligence. But in 1943, some providential information about the German round-wing plane development enabled the Americans to retaliate. The task would be to steal people. Allied Intelligence headquarters in London revealed that three of Germany's top scientists wished to defect from Hitler's round-wing plane program. Their skills were: metallurgy, chemistry, mathematics, and a profound understanding of electronics, a new technology in the 40's. All of these sciences and skills were useful in several areas of construction that the allied space program in British Columbia desperately required.

Five Americans were dropped at night into Germany amid intense ground fire from the secret installation against which the raid was conducted. Under the quiet and unassuming leadership of OSS Colonel Williams, nicknamed The Fox by the Germans, the group cut their way through barbed and electric wire into the camp. Two guards were silently garroted and the American infiltrators, three of whom spoke perfect German, entered the building where the defectors lay sound asleep. Once identified, the German scientists were wakened and before they could exclaim in surprise, their mouths were taped without incident. Each was given ten minutes to fully dress in the darkness. Back through the fence the American OSS men and their willing hostages crawled to the outside as two Yanks lingered to repair the electric wire with jumper cables so the current would flow undetected.

Four miles away from the camp, the eight men followed their map co-ordinates off a main road down a narrow dirt path that dead-ended.

Suddenly two camouflaged jeeps were seen indistinctly and a cheery English voice called out: "I say there you chaps, we wondered what kept you!" Colonel Fox grinned. Three days later, traveling only at night and hiding in pre-arranged rendezvous, the group reached a lonely Swiss border post that opened as if expected. Stopping at Berne, the British and American agents disbanded. The three Germans, each on a different plane began their trips that eventually took them to the pulse of the English-speaking world's round-wing development located in a pioneer town far away in British Columbia, Canada. In the months that followed, one of the Germans provided invaluable help in perfecting the electronic gear of the craft. Another's immediate contribution resulted in a vast improvement to the craft's former lethargic lift-off, and the third German defector used his mathematical ability, along with that of the metallurgist, to redesign the framework.

(Following the war, the families of these German scientists joined them, along with 183 other German round-wing technologists who were later recruited. Many of them live today in British Columbia and California.)

By mid 1941, employment offices throughout North America were set up in such points as San Francisco, Detroit and Toronto, and special skills were sought. Drafted labor, generally bachelors, was enticed to move to British Columbia with its special amenities in a brand new town. Each was carefully chosen for his stability and reliability. Before the end of the year, new production lines were filled with skilled men ready to begin turning out round-wing planes in a revolutionary aircraft industry. When the U.S. entered the war in December 1941, production was stepped up and the new valley town geared to become the Detroit of the Pacific Northwest.

The Caldwell planners, on the advice of the U.S. Air Force, decided they would produce a new pressurized 98 foot, long range ship, designed to be equipped with a successfully tested laser beam. They opted for a maximum range of 20 hours and 25,000 miles destination -- to Germany and return, or if need be, non-stop around the world. The new jet-equipped model would slice the air in rain or shine at 750 miles per hour cruising speed, above the range of the best German anti-aircraft guns.

Production difficulties were still being encountered and the planners wished desperately for more skilled workers in the new techniques required building the plane. Shortly after the arrival of the German scientists there also began appearing, as if in answer to the planners wishes, super-skilled tradesmen who, according to their applications, had been hired in various North American centers. These men all spoke English with the same unrecognizable accent. It was also observed that these people preferred to speak among themselves in an unknown tongue. The hiring personnel estimated there were at least 450 such strangers. Another odd thing noted about these workers was a preference for their own company. Whether on the job of tool and die making, or drafting, their craftsmanship was so superb that they seemed to have been pre-trained and thoroughly experienced. Furthermore their members often suggested techniques to improve manufacture, design, or production.

At a meeting in June of 1942, Jonathon Caldwell, aware of the new superior workers, called a top management meeting of the governing body. Rumors had been rife at the plant about the foreigners in the work force. "Gentlemen," said Caldwell, "authorities in Washington and Ottawa have alerted me that our plant work force has recently been augmented by the arrival of skilled workers, each of whom has identical vocabulary and accent. I have been told they all are graduates of a central, interplanetary language school located on another planet, namely Venus." That is how the final word was broken to the management that the allied round-wing effort was being aided from another world. Whether that word seeped through to the workers of earthly origin is not known.

The military had come to believe that the object of the friendly infiltration was to aid the Caldwell group in turning out a superior round-wing plane in such numbers and superior quality as to make the allied war effort invincible, for the day they would be used to crush the enemy. To the civil authorities in charge of key planning, it would be decided later which to deploy first -- the (Manhattan) atom bomb, or the (Jefferson) round-wing plane. If atom bomb tests failed over the Nevada desert, then most certainly the round-wing plane fleet would become the primary offensive weapon.

Unfortunately, the allied military, on accepting this advanced aid from another planet, had not understood that the visitors intended the allies to develop only a tactical superiority in the air by means of the round-wing plane. The aliens emphatically forbade its use destructively over Germany or Japan. This denial on the part of the Venusians for military use of the round-wing plane would be a moral problem that would frustrate the allies during the entire war.

The governing board in the British Columbia space center, known as Project X, was not prepared for the next extra terrestrial shock that befell them in mid-1942. Production kinks had been cleared up and a new plane was being finished every thirty-six hours. Student pilots from Kelly Field were arriving to take further advanced training in the new planes and the valley complex grew steadily each month.

In the late summer of 1943, a strange space ship dropped out of the sky and stopped in a clearing near Caldwell's office. As a crowd began to gather a tall, dark-haired stranger stepped down carrying a black suitcase. His introductory words were: "I wish to speak to Jonathon Caldwell. I bring something necessary for the improvement of your new round-wing plane."

After some confusion and delay by security forces, the unannounced visitor was eventually taken to Caldwell where he introduced himself, saying simply he was from the capital city of planet Venus, wherein dwelt a sister race of planet earth. "Many Venusian workers and others of intergalactic origin are already helping you in your plant." Then asking permission to open the small suitcase, he lifted out a round device weighing less than five pounds.

He addressed himself to Caldwell. "We have been watching your progress for several months at this location. Some time back we (i.e. our solar system council) decided to send skilled workers to help the English speaking people working here, sponsored by the industrial might of the United States. The object of the aid was to expedite your production plans. I shall not give you our entire reasons for this help, except to say that our extra terrestrial foresight of world happenings is greater than that of Earthlings. In observing the North American beginnings in the design and manufacture of your new native-invented round-wing plane, we have not been disappointed. In typical American fashion you have built a fleet of planes that lack only a few modifications, or should I say breakthroughs, to enable you to explore space. The round-wing plane is the most impressive aircraft in your entire world." The stranger was interrupted. "But you, sir, didn't come to us to simply compliment our war effort," spoke up Caldwell.

"Definitely not!" said the visitor. "I have been sent here on a mission of aid. But first may I request that I be permitted to become part of your management group for a few weeks -- if you don't object. To show my good faith, I have been instructed to present a special gift before I explain my liaison. The gift from my home planet is this." The speaker then held up in his hand for all to see what he termed an anti-magnetic motor with which to power the largest of the new planes. "It will take the place of your excellent jet motor," he added.

More than one of his listeners smiled. All knew the jet motor and its accessories weighed at least 1,000 pounds. Another looked at the device held in the alien's hands and laughed. Ignoring the interruptions, the stranger continued: "Of course I know you think I'm joking. Therefore, to prove my credibility we will test this motor in one of your completed 98-foot ships. We will do it today if you don't object. Then, if you are satisfied," he said turning to Caldwell, "I will remain long enough to show you how to modify your existing ships and set up facilities to build the motors for future production."

Someone said, "It looks like it came out of a refrigerator or washing machine," as the motor was passed around for examination.

The stranger smiled politely. Caldwell knew what his advisors were thinking: Up to 40 per cent of the power generated by a conventional motor was used in moving the weight and mass of that motor before it could lift or move its pay load.

Next day, on Caldwell's instructions, the new five-pound motor was mounted temporarily on a round-wing plane, the jet remaining in place. Electric circuits were shut off on the huge jet motor and Caldwell himself entered the ship along with the pilot and other executives as the Venusian spaceman took the controls. The motor was turned on and like a toy ship, the huge craft lifted silently straight upwards.

In a moment, the group was looking down on the valley from several hundred feet. An astonished Caldwell eagerly took the controls. When the craft landed a few minutes after the anti-gravity lift test, the being suggested they hover over a Sherman tank and attach a steel cable from the tank bolts to the round-wing plane. The tank weighed several tons more than the plane. Attachments completed, the plane slowly rose as the cable became tight. Ground onlookers yelled as the round-wing plane with the five-pound propulsion, anti-magnetic motor imported from Venus, rose into the air and carried the tank aloft as though it were a leaf from a tree. The tank, in fact, had become weightless. Turning to the crew, the alien mentioned that it would be as easy to lift a 10-story office building. He explained that when the iron chain was placed around the tank it also became an electro-magnet by repulsing the Earth's magnetism as did the plane itself, i.e. the object (tank) lifted and became an integral part of the ship.

(The original motor described above is now mounted and stored in a glass showcase in a U.S. Air Force underground vault in Kensington.)

The visiting alien later unfolded plans for motor manufacture on the site. In the future design, the small anti-gravity motor would provide ascent and descent propulsion, operating in conjunction with precise magnetic points of fluctuation in the plane's perimeter for horizontal flight. A panel computer would handle all combinations of horizontal and vertical flight patterns. The electromagnetic energy of the universe would run the planes from now on.

Furthermore, the round-wing plane capacity would not require space for the big jet, and another third of the interior capacity would be freed from fuel storage and converted to equipment installation or cargo. The great power of the new motor would also enable the engineers to reinforce the lightweight girder frame of the craft with heavier, load-bearing materials.

Before the visitor settled down he had another surprise package, for which he went back to his ship. When he emerged, he carried under his arm what looked like a roll of plain, pewter colored wallpaper, but much thinner. In the next few days the Caldwell staff discussed the application of the new material. It had been brought fresh from a Venus rolling mill and the Earth engineers were told there was enough of the paper-thin substance to cover at least six key ships if applied within the next seven curing days. A craft just off the assembly line was set aside and the man who still insisted he came from planet Venus stretched and cut the material to cover all exposed surfaces. Six ships were covered. The new material would be case hardened and ready for flight in a year.

"When you roll these six craft out in September of 1944," the alien explained, "you will be able to circumnavigate the globe in an hour if you wish and their impervious skins will not overheat."

By the end of 1944, there were 500 round-wing planes with new motors (three model sizes 98', 60', 33') stored in the British Columbia valley. The skilled workers presumably from Venus had gradually departed in unaccountable ways after training a labor force that had become their equal. Also by late 1944, advanced versions of Caldwell's craft and their crews were training daily in formation flying over the Pacific Northwest. Increased speeds far beyond 3,000 mph had eliminated the obsolete rudder. The alien advisor had also left plans for a new battery and an improved landing gear with self-propelled castor bottoms. Also, the planes could now hurl themselves from a great height to ground level by reversing the motor from magnetic repulsion to attraction. Near the point of ground impact, the motor again automatically reversed to repel, at which time the landing tripods were electronically lowered to earth. The crews referred to this technique as "ballooning the ship to the ground." Pilot jargon for setting down the ship and cutting the motor was called "peaceful landing."

Regarding gravity, the reader should abandon his present concepts and rest assured that in such a landing the crew would not feel the elevator effect of either a free fall or lift-off. There are no gravitational forces exerted on the human body in such a balloon landing or sudden lift-off from ground level, because the entire crew becomes part of the round-wing plane itself -- and therefore does not have to overcome gravity. The crew and their plane make use of the properties of attraction and repulsion in magnetism in order to function with gravity -- rather than trying to overcome that force.

The small motor size and stronger interior also permitted a doubling of crew from six to twelve, if necessary, for a military mission, or more passengers if used as a passenger carrier. Also important, most new models were downsized to 60 feet in diameter when free magnetic energy made unnecessary extra storage space for the liquid fuels that formerly fed the jet motor. One day in September, the alien requested that Jonathon Caldwell assemble all the governing board and other executives. He complimented the Earthmen in the valley for use of their small, radio-controlled drone planes, used for testing the aerodynamic possibilities in later full-scale models. "You people here," he said referring to the valley complex workers, "are way ahead of any Earth nation in development of the round-wing plane, first invented by your native son Caldwell. That is why, among other reasons, we advanced people of this solar system decided to lend you some help. I beg of you, however, don't misuse that help we have given you!"

Then the polite stranger dropped a bombshell on his listeners. "Your leaders have already been told that we would not like you to use these new planes in this war except on a limited basis. Any thoughts you have in mind for punitive action should be dropped." Looking at the U.S. Air Force liaison officer he said, "Although I loathe war, I must trust in your military superiors to heed my advice and not use this new machine as a weapon but rather a conveyance to expedite the ending of this present, unnecessary worldwide conflict. This entire solar system is watching your tragic world war. We do not want you to use this new invention to deliver to an enemy your latest explosive device (he referred to the atom bomb) that you are now perfecting.

"We have already provided you with new motors. We shall withhold the formula for the skins. Thus, without that formula to prevent overheating of the ship's outer surfaces, ultimate speed necessary to leave and re-enter planet Earth's atmosphere must be carefully controlled. Someday when the time is ripe, we will help you in this regard also. In the meantime, be content with what you have."

He ended by saying, almost apologetically, "On our planet, as in this entire solar system, war is outlawed. More important than this technological help I have brought with the blessings from our nation is the fact that war on Earth must also be outlawed. When war on earth is over, then Earth men will be shown how to use their own resources of men and materials to venture into space."

The Venusian had stayed four months. He constantly gave his directions to Superintendent General Caldwell who in turn comprehended their significance in production techniques and passed on the alien's suggestions to the Earth planners. The new team functioned smoothly as the guiding genius sent from another world sat in the councils of the Earth developers of the round-wing plane -- and together they built a fleet of marvelous craft. The alien, who was known simply as Mr. Lewis, one day said good-bye to his new compatriots. Taking the hand of Jonathon Caldwell, the alien said softly, "I salute you, sir! You are the man who first was called out of your country to point the way forward for people of the Earth. You showed men how to fly without wings." As the stranger said good-bye to a host of friends, a ship dropped out of the sky, and he departed aboard it. In a group photo taken before departure, the place where the alien stood was blank.

Chapter VII

Allied Development of Round-Wing Plane During World War II

Nineteen forty-three was World War II's turning point. As the year ended, hostilities in Europe continued with Germany still appearing to be strong, but enemy reverses were occurring. German confidence began to ebb as American entry into the war helped roll back German armies in North Africa, Sicily and Italy. On the Eastern front, the Russians, with vast amounts of American Lend Lease equipment, were starting to counter attack after a long period of German mauling.

In December 1943, a new Commander, General Dwight D. Eisenhower, was appointed to lead the western allies, and the same month three thousand British and American planes bombarded the French coast in a single night and a day, while another fleet of bombers sent Berlin sirens wailing. Seven months later the enemy on the western front would be in retreat, and Paris would surrender.

Control of the sea-lanes also proved to be as decisive as the winning of land battles. Thus, 17,000 merchant ships were dispatched by the U.S. to keep the life-line open to England, Europe and Russia, and the conflict's balance of power tipped in favor of the allies despite staggering losses to U-boat action. Britain had held the breach till the American industrial colossus flowed over the Atlantic onto European shores and turned the tide against Germany's short-gain fortunes.

By late 1943, growing numbers of round-wing planes from the

Canadian valley had been appearing over Europe. The round-wing pilots were graduate aviators of the Technical Training Flight School located in the B. C. valley. General Caldwell was also the officer in charge of this manpower training as well as superintendent of the entire manufacturing complex.

A wartime aircraft crew consisted of six airmen, and on each round-wing plane, a combined operational group always included one Britisher and one Canadian along with the American personnel. Scattered among various crews were Australians and New Zealanders, as well as a handful of Norwegians.

The new ships now boasted sleek and smooth silhouettes with the flaps and outside surface controls not distinguishable. The new pilot class could execute intricate patterns, either singly or in formation that made those sighting the airborne ships gaze in wonder. Day and night over England and Scotland the great bomber and fighter armadas heading for the continent often reported the presence of vanishing lights thought to be extra terrestrial; they would be seen one moment and gone the next. According to the viewers there was one common denominator in all sightings. The strange and aloof phenomena showed an apparent affinity to watch over and protect the allied planes.

Jonathon Caldwell and his wife loved their children, but each was particularly anxious about their son who had volunteered as a B-29 bomber pilot and had flown several missions over Germany. Olive, Caldwell's wife, kept praying their boy would be safe. On one such daytime bombing raid, young Caldwell felt a presence he could not explain. Looking above him, he saw a huge, round-wing escort plane sailing along at his same speed, like a mother hen. The round-wing craft wobbled in a friendly way. It flew on and then repeated it's wobbling which seemed to say hello to the American fixed wing bomber below. Guessing it was a salutary signal, the bomber captained by Caldwell dipped its wings, and young pilot Caldwell smiled and raised his hand in a V for victory sign. Reaching target area over a heavy flak region, the round-wing plane on occasion dropped below the bomber and took some direct hits. But it continued unflinchingly through the danger zone. When Caldwell got home that night he took his wife aside and assured her, "Everything's all right. I flew escort with our son today!" When the young Caldwell got a furlough, he came home for a visit and told a story. "Dad, I must tell you about the friendly round-wing bird that protected us on a raid. At times I pretended it was you out here, dad, but I know you're too old." (Caldwell was 45) The parents smiled.

Unknown to the allied airmen, these lights seen weaving among the formations on each mission were operated perhaps by friends they knew back home in Kansas City, Halifax or Manchester. The illusive sky visitors that resembled luminous balls of fire at high speeds were nicknamed Foo Fighters. These round-wing planes were not out just for practice or pageantry or to confuse regular aircraft pilots and observers. They had a purpose. They acted as a guardian system to a target, often relaying information back to London, allowing allied planes to take evasive action. They also took composite pictures of targets before and after raids. When not busy, the planes occasionally buzzed German formations, and in a more serious vein, they also observed the flight directions and numbers in enemy formations headed for Britain. Of course, they were not available during the heroic Battle of Britain that broke the back of Goering's Luftwaffe.

A brisk Atlantic traffic of diplomatic and scientific personnel was also transported via the planes, and the round-wing Technical Air Command provided President Roosevelt and Prime Minister Churchill with a plane should occasion demand.

But an unforeseen misfortune, quite apart from technology or enemy threat, was to fall upon the valley complex. The problem was Caldwell himself. His innovations and leadership abilities became drained because of his wife, Olive. She was on the brink of death. In fact, her doctor finally told Caldwell recovery was hopeless; Olive was terminally ill. At best, she had a week to live. Caldwell's spirit flagged, as had his supervision for some time. Others took the matter into their own hands when Caldwell (a Protestant) demanded that a priest be sent to say the last rites for his dying wife (a Catholic).

The U.S. Army Air Corp liaison chief sent the urgent request to his Washington headquarters. The matter of security was so touchy, the U.S. Air Force requested help from the O.S.S. The O.S.S. moved immediately. One of its top European agents, a graduate of West Point and an ordained priest, who had been recalled to America for a new assignment, was contacted. He was known only by his code name of Father John, a devout but tough Christian, as well as a soldier.

Father John was flown to Seattle where he boarded another military plane. He alighted at the B.C. valley in the uniform of a Brigadier General, carrying a black, flat briefcase initialed Father John, S.J., inside of which there was a bible, a note book, and two gold crosses. A nervous Caldwell met him.

On seeing a military man, Caldwell exploded, "I asked for a priest not a soldier." Quietly Father John sat down his brief case. "I am a Christian first, a priest second, and a Catholic third. I serve a living Savior." Caldwell calmed down under the charisma and confidence of the big 6' 1" priest.

When they reached the bedroom where Olive lie dying, the post's medical officer was standing by. He confirmed that she had but a few hours of life or a day or two at the most. She was in a coma.

Father John unfolded from his bag the smaller of the two gold crosses and hung it at the head of the brass bed. The doctor and Caldwell stood at one side of the room. The silence was deep as Father John gave the ritual of the last rites, anointing Olive's forehead with a mixture of blessed olive oil and salt. Tears filled Caldwell's eyes. His wife had been part of the round-wing dream since he had been a young man. She had sacrificed everything to stay by his side when he had spent all his abilities on the plan's reality in later years. Now, the one person who understood him and whom he needed most was dying.

The soft-spoken words of Father John could again be heard: "Father God, I have done my priestly duty to this soul who is speeding on to her eternal rest. Father God, I beseech you in the name of Christ to delay the return of this soul to Thee." Father John's voice grew louder.

The priest then took the larger cross and placed it before her eyes. "Evil spirit! In the name of Jesus the Christ, I command you be gone from this child of God!" Suddenly, the woman in coma jerked her head from the pillow and threw an arm over her eyes to resist the gold cross. In a moment her body trembled violently and she sat up. The evil spirit had fled. Father John helped her to sit on the side of the bed, and in a moment she put her feet to the floor.

Beads of perspiration showed on Father John's forehead and his eyes turned upwards. "We praise and thank Thee for thy faithfulness, Oh Christ," he repeated.

No one moved as Father John stood erect and waited. Suddenly, for all to see, there stood at the foot of the bed a full-size, three-dimensional figure. All knew instinctively He was Christ. Seconds went by as a soft light, brighter than day, bathed the room. Olive Caldwell looked around and exclaimed, "What are we doing here?" The Christ figure faded but around Olive there remained a glow. The spirit of a living and healing Christ had filled her.

They all went into the living room where Olive served coffee and cakes to Father John and the doctor. She beamed all over. "Please stay with us tonight," she begged Father John. But the big American priest of Scottish descent excused himself and affectionately said his farewells.

As he left, he cautioned the Caldwell's, "Don't make that room or this house a shrine. We serve a living Christ; He is not confined to a room -- He is everywhere."

(The record of that visit is among the O.S.S. papers of Father John, located in the National Archives. See Epilogue about Olive Caldwell's recovery and retirement years.)

The valley complex was back to normal and Caldwell's vigor

returned. The glowing success surrounding the performance of the new round-wing air arm caused people in high places to respond. Towards the end of the war, the allied round-wing complex had two memorable occasions that came close to being called holidays. The first of these events occurred in late December of 1943, when President Roosevelt and Prime Minister Churchill visited the aerospace complex along with their host Prime Minister, Mackenzie King.

The three personages had arrived in the private railway car of President Roosevelt after crossing into Canada at Winnipeg, Manitoba and proceeding west into the British Columbia Valley. An American band met the train and played the National Anthem and Hail to the Chief. A British band, the Royal Fusiliers, played God Save the King and ended up, along with the American band, playing the anthem, O Canada.

The leaders stayed a day. On addressing the airmen, President Roosevelt touched each of their nerve centers when he told them they were not the forgotten men of the war about which they had been grousing. The President dropped a secret: "You men are being trained for what is intended to be the most secret and decisive project of the war. Stand ready," he said, "for that moment when we shall call you to deliver the greatest rebuke to the Nazis on behalf of your countries. For on that day, when you are called, be ready to climb into your new round-wing armada and cross the top of the world to destroy the enemy in an hour's time!"

When the cheering response quieted down, Churchill rose and, with a few apt phrases, said he agreed, on behalf of his nation, that the men of the valley had not been forgotten but were actually being trained "for one quick knockout blow of the iniquitous Nazi scourge that has taken over Germany."

The idea to destroy Germany in a single round-wing strike is attributed to the planning of Roosevelt and Churchill.

Later, in speaking to one of the station's top executives, Churchill is said to have remarked, "Into this valley with its awesome power of round planes, we English speaking people have placed all our hope for shortening the war -- in case everything else should fail."

President Roosevelt had caught that vision of the military relevance of the round-wing plane back in 1936. He shared it with the British and Canadian heads of state. Later, it was that cooperation between the three nations that enabled Jonathon E. Caldwell and his staff to make President Roosevelt's dream become reality.

On September 18, 1944, Station Commander General Caldwell ordered a full review of his 3,000 airmen at 8:00 a.m. The unsuspecting airmen assembled, waiting for a routine inspection. Suddenly out of the sky one of their own 98-foot craft appeared and the attention of all the airmen was riveted on the descending machine. As it touched down close to the formation, right on a prescribed circle, a thousand voices murmured in unison: "Peaceful landing."

Then out from beneath the round-wing plane the assembled airmen saw emerge the figure of a tall, smiling, immaculately dressed soldier covered with ribbons. As he left the shadow of the craft, a cheer went up from the ranks of men. The flight officer yelled "Attention!" As General Eisenhower shook hands with Station Commander Caldwell and other officers, the entourage moved to the assembled troops. Three thousand allied airmen saluted their chief in honor. An airman boasted later that the cheers could be heard in Vancouver. Before "Ike" had reached the troops, he was joined by a second figure in a black beret that, because of his victories in North Africa, had recently been made a Viscount. He was Bernard L. Montgomery, and he came forward to join the Commander-in-Chief of all the allied the military scattered throughout Europe. The British airmen took up the cheer again, and quickly the Canadians and Commonwealth buddies added voice as the Americans in final crescendo raised the roof of the valley. Montgomery addressed the airmen in an overlong monologue. Eisenhower summed up his own thoughts in less than half an hour. He told the assembled airmen, "The moment for which you have been trained, the time when you will be called to strike the enemy -- is not far off."

The allied war leaders later toured the giant aerospace facilities.

As General Eisenhower talked informally with Caldwell, a young genius in his mid-forties, General Eisenhower praised him: "There is no way we can adequately express our thanks for what you have done for the allied cause and for freedom."

The allied leaders had left a station in Britain before daylight Pacific coast time. By way of Iceland, Greenland, Baffin Island and Hudson Bay they had flown non-stop watching the sun rise over Port Churchill, Manitoba and racing ten times faster than the speed of sound to their destination. They sat down with friends for a Canadian breakfast of ham and eggs over seven thousand miles away from the shores from which they had departed.

Upon leaving they would be back in London, England on a leisurely trip of about two hour's time.

Another momentous occasion arose at the end of 1944 almost a year after the visits of the allied political leaders. The valley's air station had been on constant alert in late December. Something was imminent.

On the last week of the year, the huge fleet of 500 round-wing planes took off early one morning for Germany. The preplanned targets were "strategic German cities. Roosevelt had vetoed an earlier attempt that month by Allied and German generals, including Eisenhower, Patton and Von Runstedt, to end the fighting in the west. Now, the round-wing air arm was on its way to execute the end of hostilities in Roosevelt's own way. The terrible lasers had not yet been installed in the new round-wing planes but in their holds several of the planes carried the new atomic bombs while the others carried bomb bays full of blockbuster explosives.

As the planes appeared over German skies in mass, several squadron leaders saw a long cigar-shaped craft as it watched from high above. The first targets were reached and orders given to prepare bombs and finally "bombs away."

But not one plane could release its cargo of destruction. All electrical circuits connected with the bomb delivery were dead. Radios, too, were silent. Finally, in consternation, the fleet followed the lead ships and turned back to Canada. They landed without incident, and maintenance men examined the planes. Then, as if on cue, the entire fleet became electrically functional again.

High above, a cigar-shaped craft of giant proportions moved off into the unknown.

Allied intelligence sources say the Germans under Hitler lost earlier technological blessings from the aliens when the Nazis embarked on a plan to use their five round-wing planes to bomb major American cities including New York and Washington. The enemy intended dropping new instruments of mass destruction called atom bombs that the Germans had produced at about the same time as the allies. Their first Hiroshima was to have been New York. Hitler himself is said to have ordered the raid. The planes left Germany. What happened thereafter is unknown.

Did the extra terrestrials prevent the planned deaths of so many countless humans and the mass destruction of cities? It seems most likely. Here is why:

The alien who visited Roosevelt in 1943 had told him the extra terrestrials were totally aware of the new round-wing plane then being developed by Caldwell and group. The alien reminded Roosevelt it could be used as a blessing or an evil. He warned the President not to use it for evil purposes. Reminded of that warning while authorizing the German strike, President Roosevelt replied, "Let's forget the aliens! We now have the round-wing planes -- we intend to use them."

Just as important as the words of the extra terrestrial who visited Roosevelt in 1943 is the warning of the alien scientist sent down to earth's aerospace valley in British Columbia. When he departed in 1943, he reminded Jonathon Caldwell and company, "Don't try to use the new round-wing planes to destroy your present enemy, the Germans! It will turn out that your ultimate enemy has not yet been revealed. For the present, the round-wing planes are for your protection only."

On May 6, 1945, World War II ended in Europe as Germany, in the absence of Hitler, surrendered unconditionally. Even as the allied generals accepted surrender at Eisenhower's Rheims School Headquarters, at 2:41 A.M. French time, May 7, a fleet of 500 round-wing planes dropped down from 60,000 feet and plummeted to a 3,000-foot elevation over beleaguered Berlin. There, in mile long letters executed by the round-wing planes, German civilians and Russian troops below stared up at the huge lighted sign which spelled out in English the word SURRENDER. The Germans had capitulated after five years, eight months and six days of the bloodiest conflict in history.

Neither side had been able to use their round-wing planes for destruction of each other -- neither the allies 500 planes or the Germans' five.

Earlier on the evening of May 5, when the surrender was first announced over the BBC radio, allied soldiers and English men and women had jammed downtown London. Trafalgar Square teemed with masses of singing people; the lights came back on, and in front of Whitehall huge crowds shouted impromptu for Prime Minister Churchill. As the Prime Minister appeared on the balcony, he stuck his cigar trademark in his mouth and raised his hand in a V for victory symbol. Then the cheering crowd stopped as all heads turned upwards. The entire London sky, as in Berlin, was filled with strange speeding lights. Unquestionably they spelled out one word -- V I C T O R Y. In his first public admission of the aerial phenomena, the British Prime Minister tried to explain that the formations above were one of the secret weapons the allies had chosen not to use in winning the war. As the heavenly lights disappeared across the English countryside, they left in their wake a mystery -- a mystery no one on the allied side spoke of again.

Across all Britain the airborne formation flew in slow parade. As the round-wing plane assemblage moved on in silent tribute, the huge word VICTORY blazoned over the home towns of many young Scottish, English, Welsh and Irish pilots and crewmen.

From the countryside below, jubilant Britishers occasionally saw packets attached to small parachutes flutter down from the strange birds. Retrieved, the finders noted the packets contained dozens of letters on RAF stationery with British stamps affixed to the envelopes. Each packet was wrapped in a special binder that said: "Finder, please take to nearest Postmaster!"

The next few days, across the British Isles, the letters from the sky were being delivered to cottages and flats by the score. On opening one such letter a lonely Englishwoman, worrying about her son, might have read: Dear Mom . . . Sorry I've been away so long. But soon I'm coming home . . . Love, your son.

During the next week the jubilant British sang, danced, paraded, and worshipped as each in his or her own way threw off the shackles of years of war-time regimentation. Quietly, the British War Office had planned another surprise that to this day has never been told except to those in the know.

In the early morning blackness of May 15, several giant round-wing planes dropped out of the overcast and hovered above a field on an island off the Scottish coast. Bright lights shone down on the turf as the machines sat quietly down, each on its tripod legs. And from the stairs below each craft, young Britishers stepped down with their few belongings and moved silently away into the darkness.

Shortly thereafter, twelve assembled fishing boats took aboard over 480 young men and headed for the mainland. The fishing boats normally hauled "goods vans" southward to major coastal cities. But the skippers had been called by the Ministry of Fisheries for a special task that morning. Sworn to silence, only the skippers knew they had been asked to pick up nearly 500 war heroes. As the young men huddled on the cold deck of one of the ships, an old Scottish fisherman, obviously trying to goad the young passengers into revealing their point of origin, remarked slyly, "Aye, mon! I've seen everything now. All you lads spending your days on that forlorn island while the rest of the world was busy fighting a war."

Above the boats, over 20 strange craft blinked their lights in farewell as the young airmen looked up and smiled with nostalgia for
their air-training home in far away Canada.

In the morning, as dawn broke over Scotland's most northerly
village served by rail, a long Royal Scot steam train stood slowly
puffing and waiting. The town's industry, a nearby cannery, had not
yet opened. Meanwhile the young warriors who had manned the
world's greatest World War II inventions assembled at the station.
The wail of the bagpipes was heard, and this music to Scottish ears
came in a medley of homecoming tunes played by the band of the
Scots Guard from Edinburgh castle. The band had come up on the
train. As the last "all aboard" was sounded, the engineer called
to the fireman, "It's a three hour run to Edinburgh. We'll have
an hour's stop while these passengers stretch their legs and get
the biggest and best breakfast the city of Edinburgh can dish up.
All other trains take second place, even if we meet up with King
George himself!"

But London was waiting for the special train. Prime Minister
Churchill was on hand. And so was King George VI, accompanied
by His Majesty's Coldstream Guards. As each man disembarked
from the train, they lined up and received a handshake and a medal
from the King. On the medal were inscribed the words: FOR
VALOUR BEYOND THE CALL OF DUTY.

The demob officer had already spoken to the young heroes. "For
the remainder of your lives, you men must be content to know of
the courage with which you served the cause. Remember, you can
never share the secret of the round-wing plane with anyone, as
difficult as this order may seem to be. Someday, in the wisdom of
the top brass, perhaps somebody will be allowed to tell. I hope we
are still alive by then." The Britishers melted into the crowd and
headed for their homes. Each carried a paper giving him a choice
of honorable discharge or re-volunteering for the Round-wing
Plane Service. In Canada, the airmen were discharged at Ottawa;
the Americans were taken to Tacoma, Washington. Today the
identities of those pioneer airmen are not known, but on the wall
of the Canadian Air Minister is a plaque referred to as the Silver

List. Engraved there are the names of approximately five hundred Canadians.

The Regiment of Royal Fusiliers, who had been employed mainly as security forces in the B.C. valley during the war years, got home to Britain in 1947. Some of them had left Scotland by round-wing plane but all were returned by train to New York and then by ship to England.

The United States emerged from World War II as the world's undisputed superpower. Before the war ended she had become the world's leading shipbuilder. She had supplied the allies with more shipping tonnage than both Britain and the U.S. combined possessed in 1939.

Expansion of conventional air power enabled the allies to dominate the European skies. The United States had trained and equipped twelve million armed men deployed with over 50 allies on various fronts, while still providing the Russians with massive shiploads of Lend Lease armament. When the war was over and rebuilding of the continent began, it was the American Marshall Plan that got the Europeans, including the former enemy, back on their industrial feet.

From 1941 to 1945 the U.S. War Council had managed to divert scientists and technicians to the Manhattan bomb project while still carrying on with the manufacture and delivery of conventional armament. In addition the War Council recruited the brainpower required to research and produce the (Jefferson) round-wing plane, a project that eventually filled a small city. The costs were shared between the three allied powers based on population ratio.

The audacious total American wartime achievements had been burdensome in taxes. The national debt rose from 50 billion in 1940 to over 250 billion dollars in 1945, nearly nine tenths of this amount expended on winning the conflict to liberate Europe and the Pacific.

Quite apart from the manufacture of conventional war apparatus, the industrial miracle of the allies, shared mainly by the U.S.A., was that a revolutionary air arm of round-wing planes, with crews, had been developed in secret, and without disrupting the effort of the country's six million men and women in the military labor force. (Inevitably, the secret was not perfectly kept, but leaks in every case were plugged before serious breaches of security could occur.)

Although the war ended in victory for the allies, the Americans were always acutely aware that, if need be, the scales of justice would have been tipped in their favor had they introduced the advanced, round-wing plane and its awesome laser power. Yet, in spite of the disastrous war that bled America and the world of so much of its valuable resources, she still managed to carry herself and the globe into a new age of free flight that, before the century ends, may become the prime mover of people and commerce.

Canada's beloved scientist and World War II General A.G.L. Mac-Naughton said: "Isn't it ironic that it took a war to bring about such scientific achievements?"

Winston Churchill called it the "unnecessary war." President Eisenhower agreed.

To the young English boy who asked his grieving mother, "Who won the war in which daddy was killed? She replied, "No one -- everybody lost." Sixteen million fathers and sons never came home. Nearly ten million innocent civilians who died in the flames of war would have agreed had their voices been able to cry out.

Chapter VIII

Fatherland Evacuated in New Aircraft and Giant U-Boats

In the summer of 1943 the French underground suddenly began advising London of nightly troop trains traveling over secondary French railroads toward the Spanish border. The French estimated that each train carried 500 German troops. Allied intelligence was perplexed. There were several reasons.

The enemy had been defeated in Africa and was bogged down on the Russian front. Therefore, Supreme Allied Command was desperate to know if the Germans were starting a second front or planning to invade North Africa from Spanish bases. Was there some truth to the continuing rumors from allied agents, that the elite of the German army and her top scientists and technicians were preparing to evacuate their European homeland -- and, if so, to where? Even more disquieting, the British and the American OSS had learned that Hitler had put much of Germany's scientific effort into a new type of round-wing plane which was perhaps laser equipped to destroy London or New York in an hour. The American OSS knew precisely the horrible possibilities of such a German breakthrough. The question was asked if the Germans were building those planes in some remote area of Spain or South America.

Allied headquarters in London sent 12 top agents into Germany, France and Spain and asked the American OSS to infiltrate these troop trains to ascertain German intentions. Three Americans were chosen; one of German decent and a graduate of Princeton Law School, and another an ordained priest who later became Director of the C.I.A. They all spoke fluent German.

A fourth Spanish speaking agent was sent to neutral Spain, where in Seville he established himself for three weeks to listen to Spanish railway men and observe Germans in Spanish uniforms, changing trains for a coastal destination. Two of the agents managed to get their messages to London in spite of being caught, and Allen Dulles got behind enemy territory and back without detection. This story of American espionage on German troop trains is said to be legendary in intelligence circles. For sheer heroism it is one of the bravest and most dangerous wartime episodes ever recorded.

In an Atlanta restaurant, late one evening in April 1976, the author sat with three survivors of the four original agents who penetrated the German railroad evacuation plot. The former agents, a Catholic priest, a Presbyterian and a Christian Scientist, ate slowly. They talked and relived their train ride with the German troops. After the meal, the priest, then a Cardinal, placed a bottle of wine on the table. Allen Dulles had brought it back from the 1943 episode on the train. Each year they would have a reunion, and to the last survivor would go the German Wine. (In September, 1978 the heroic clergyman died in Rome.)

The reports of these agents began seeping back to London, and within 40 days the allies were piecing together a mystery.

Germans were cleverly executing a contingency plan for their troops and certain civilians to evacuate Germany for a second stronghold after battle defeats in Europe were no longer reversible.

Although the war tide had turned in favor of the allies, they had also been caught napping about alternate German intentions. Then, perhaps, never before in history, had an army suffering defeat made contingent plans to abandon its homeland and revive the military venture elsewhere.

The collective reports from the American, British and French agents confirmed that crack German troops were being withdrawn from all fighting fronts and shipped to Spain. Furthermore, the three agents who had infiltrated the German troop trains reported that personnel on board comprised the essential manpower needed for a colonization attempt. These agents had identified a diversity of professions; business experts and workers disguised as soldiers. The agents had actually spoken with doctors, dentists, teachers, architects, toolmakers, machinists, etc., whose new oath, on being verified for the train evacuation trips, had required "unflinching and everlasting loyalty to the Third Reich and its Fuehrer."

The last stop for the German troop trains had been Hulva, and Aymonte, Spain. It would take another espionage effort for the OSS to determine just what was happening at these Spanish ports, and on this requirement allied intelligence would focus next.

In the meantime in 1944, the reports of other agents, verified by aerial photography, also indicated unusual activity in German Baltic ports. Huge quantities of industrial equipment for overseas shipment were beginning to appear at these docks. The allies wondered if the Germans were shipping their new round-wing planes abroad for later use to strike from hidden bases. About this time the Allies learned of a secret meeting held in Strausberg on August 10, 1944, wherein it was decided to remove all the gold and precious metal reserves from Germany for overseas shipment. Overseas, but to where?

Despite tight German security, the American OSS began to discern some obvious intentions. One, that there existed a German master plan to evacuate personnel and wealth from the fatherland to parts unknown during the height of the war, and two, that secret weapons were being shipped out, including an unconventional aircraft which the enemy had not committed to the fighting. Those assessments provided by allied intelligence left a major question unanswered. Why? What secret weapon, or weapons were so advanced or devastating that a determined Germany would not commit them when she was losing the war? Were they so advanced that she could safely gamble her future on them?

As the Allied Command also pondered German intentions in Spain, it was aware that although Spain was neutral, General Franco, because of German threats, was under the German thumb.

London, therefore, concluded that Spain's importance to the enemy lay in the use of her Atlantic ports.

It was in conjunction with these intelligence summations that the first reports arrived regarding a new fleet of giant German submarines approximately 400 feet long and several decks high. Agents reported sightings of these subs in the vicinity of Aymonte and Halva, Spain. They were also seen at Baltic and Norwegian ports.

In 1944-1945 it was confirmed that the loading of these subs at Baltic ports with unusual machinery and equipment was secretly being carried on. The Norwegian underground picked up the super subs' trail. These reports, pieced together, told a tale. The giant underwater megaliths had left Germany, thence to Norway and along its coast northward to avoid Allied shipping lanes, and then west from Narvik toward Iceland in the North Atlantic. From a point below Iceland, the subs steered an oblique southerly course that eventually took them to the Atlantic ports of Hulva and Aymonte, Spain.

At last the Allied command had solved the 1945 puzzle of the disappearing Germans. The answer was obvious! The German troop trains puffing through France and Spain at night were eventually disembarking their passengers and other cargo at Spanish Atlantic ports, where from another direction, German ingenuity had brought together undersea transportation. Once the Germans had boarded the subs they were swallowed up quietly by the sea.

By V-E Day, the allies estimated that over 250,000 Germans had evacuated the country by various means, including air, submarines and even, by merchant vessels flying American and British flags. The enigma of where the un-apprehended Germans were headed still eluded the Allies.

In April 1945 the world press was preoccupied with the forthcoming German collapse. In a political agreement made by Roosevelt and Stalin at Yalta, Allied armies were forced to mark time on the Western front while Russian troops took Eastern Europe and half of Germany, including Berlin. The German armies, on the western front under Von Rundstedt, fought delaying actions, their local commanders knowing that the end was near. Rumors were rife among the German High Command that Hitler was about to unleash secret weapons that would annihilate the enemy. A similar German story circulated, that the Western allies would link up with the Germans at the Elbe and together join the German army on the Eastern front and race for Moscow to contain communism.

All of these rumors of anticipated happenings, circulating among the desperately besieged Germans, had a ring of truth. In another way, and at another place, one of the supposed fantasies became a frightening reality.

As usual, the Allies were unprepared. When the tragedy occurred (gathered in 1977 from British and German sources) it bridged two eras. From that moment on, World War II became the last great chapter on mankind's history of conventional armaments. As a result of the tragic incident that followed, World War II may well be known as the last of the lengthy super land battles using explosives and gunpowder.

Involved in this terrible drama was one of the giant German submarines. She was one of those built secretly in 1944, and it carried a cargo of top-secret German plans, documents and proto types of new inventions. The sub was in the North Atlantic at an approximate position of 35 deg. N and 14 deg. W when her oxygen supply gave out due to malfunction of equipment. Unable to stay submerged, the leviathan slowly ascended from a depth of 2000 feet and its 12" thick hull of steel broke surface of the cold Atlantic at midnight on 23rd of April 1945, within a mile of two British cruisers. Up went flares as the British ships opened fire on the German sub. Eight-inch shells straddled the huge craft to get range, as an odd-shaped German gun appeared on the sub's hull. A pencil beam of laser homed in on the cruiser Cambden.

There was no battle thunder or fury from the sub. The ray silently pierced the air, and in seconds a 20-foot-diameter hole was cut from port to starboard through the first surface ship. Like a toy boat suddenly filled with water, the cruiser sank horizontally with a hissing of steam from the white-hot steel hull. Then the beam moved onto the second cruiser, Hanover, and as another 20-foot hole was opened, she burst into flames and settled down in less than 30 seconds. Most of the ship's complement never reached their battle stations. Those on deck duty jumped overboard. In less than two minutes only some oil slick, air bubbles and flotsam appeared where the cruisers had stood. The German sub moved into range of the cruiser's former positions and machine-gunned the survivors. The British flares settled into the sea and blackness again enveloped the area.

The German "U-boat" Captain left his bridge and went below. Putting his head in his hands he bent over and sobbed. An officer consoled him with the words: "It was the enemy or us! Otherwise, we were to scuttle!

At dawn the next morning, in the same area, a British fishing trawler spotted three men on a piece of wreckage. The sailors, numb from exposure, were hauled aboard and three days later were landed in the Hebrides Islands. That day, at Allied headquarters in London, a telegram was received from the Hebrides at British Naval headquarters that shortly thereafter reached the OSS General, Donovan. As General Donovan read the graphic story of the German laser that cut holes like a can opener in the British cruisers, he put down the cryptic message and said, "My God! Oh, My God!" A new war age had just been born. As a result of the naval engagement, the joint chiefs-of-staff asked the question: "Where are the missing German round-wing planes that disappeared out of Germany, and are they also equipped with lasers?" And from where was the enemy intending to strike with his hidden fleet of devastating new aircraft?

At combined Naval Operations in London, Allied Intelligence pondered where one of the laser equipped monster subs might strike next. Everything afloat on the sea-lanes was now vulnerable.

But the enemy could not wait.

The German plan had already been released -- they would use another of their twelve super subs in a devastating naval engagement that, if it were successful, might bring the U.S.A. to its knees.

An "accident of fate" would alter the German plan.

Here's how the story unfolds. Unknown to the allies in late 1944, the secretive and orderly German evacuation was proceeding well. Her top personnel, who were needed to continue the Third Reich elsewhere, were being removed by round-wing planes and super subs, the chief vehicles used among several withdrawal methods. Germans like Von Runstedt from whose area round-wing planes were evacuating key personnel, refused to give travel priority to those Nazis responsible for Jewish exterminations. The truth is that most of the regular German general staff had disdain for those Nazis who were not wanted in the new Germany destined to rise in another part of the world. Furthermore, German embarkation officers in the Hulva and Aymonte ports also refused to place key Nazi killers on board the super subs.

Major Otto Skorzeny, Hitler's tough deputy, had gone personally to Von Runstedt in December 1944 and demanded seats for himself and his top henchmen on the departing round-wing planes.

Von Runstedt had refused and so had Von Schusnick, the chief pilot. Thus the Nazis had to find their own way out of Europe to escape allied vengeance in the coming Nuremberg War Trials.

The architects of the German evacuation plan forgot Nazi interference until April 18, 1945, when, on that day, the Nazis made their moves and an encounter occurred in Alexandria, Egypt between German Nazis and German Naval personnel. A new super-sub that had left the Island of Bornholm in the Baltic in early February lay off Alexandria. Egyptian tenders had ferried out regularly chosen escapees under the sympathetic eyes of Egyptian officers, Abel Gamel Nasser and Anwar Sadat, each of whom despised King

Farouk and the British protectorate forces stationed in Egypt.

The giant war sub was full, and sealed orders were opened for departure to the southern hemisphere, when a German Nazi, Major Hauptman Schaemmel, came aboard and put a gun in the ribs of Lt. Commander Hans Meyers. He was ordered to disembark the 500 men. Another Nazi officer warned the naval commander that his wife and daughter were being held hostage in Bavaria to be killed immediately if the sub commander refused to obey. That night 500 German emigrants were replaced by an equal number of Nazi Germans who had made their way from Germany to Egypt via Italy by various escape methods. By morning, the giant sub had slipped away and headed out through the Straits of Gibraltar to the open Atlantic. She was not alone. As the sub commander piloted his ship deep under the surface of the Mediterranean, he was kept under watch. Above, on the surface, two British destroyers followed the underwater transport by sonar. As the sub neared Gibraltar, the British made no attempt to stop it. More ships joined the surveillance, and together the giant sub with the German navy crew under the duress of nearly 500 Nazi masters headed out across the Atlantic -- revised destination, New York. Its silent overhead British escort followed. The sub's new mission, un-authorized by the German Admiralty, was to be the most aggressive act of war the Nazis had devised for their final hours.

On the sub's foredeck was a long artillery piece with a 12" bore that could fire shells at the rate of 30-second intervals. It was claimed that explosives in the warheads (a triumph of German research) would pulverize the city of New York quickly and destroy a large part of its population. From New York the sub's new directions were to take it into Chesapeake Bay where Philadelphia, Baltimore and Washington would be leveled, and then to Halifax or Miami to complete the destruction. There was only one problem: the sub commander had not been told of the plans; although British intelligence was privy to the scheme from the moment it began shadowing the sub out of Egypt. The dash under the ocean to the U.S.A. went as planned. When the underwater giant reached American waters over 100 surface ships were waiting. Across New York Harbor stretched a bronze net, and underwater bells with searchlights were suspended from barges. The net held. The lights shone down on the sub. Depth charges fell astride her thick hull. Impregnable even from the depth charges and torpedoes fired from allied subs, the 376 foot long monster backed off and headed out for deeper water.

"Where to now?" asked the sub commander, under the gun of Nazi General Osker Dirlewanger.

"To Miami. We'll shell it off the map from far out in deep water." The sub commander replied, "Indeed! And how do I surface to man the deck-gun when depth charges are tumbling onto our hull every minute?" Deeply submerged, the sub quarry headed south into the Straits of Florida, but she could not lose her 46 surface hunters, including American, British, Canadian and French vessels out of Martinique.

Fifty hours later, the giant German submarine was still being tracked in a channel that narrowed quickly. From fear of being trapped, the commander attempted to turn around. Depth charges had dirtied the water and visual directions were impossible to determine. Reverberations against the hull were continuous. Suddenly, the underwater ship stopped, unable to move. She lay to for several hours. Outside explosions ceased temporarily. An examination by divers showed she was down 200 feet and washed by turbulent currents. The long barreled gun specifically fitted to destroy the coastal cities of America was jammed into a crevice under the roof of a shark infested coral shelf. The divers' final words were: "The sub can never be freed." In a few moments the word spread through the ship.

The depth charges became intermittent. The enemy above had abandoned the chase. The sub was unmovable. The 500 Germans began to reflect on death by starvation or lack of oxygen in a craft that had become their tomb.

The commander made five trips out of the sub in the next three days. Each time, he took off a Nazi, deposited him on shore, and returned with provisions or medications provided by collaborators.

The entombed men were beginning to succumb. Some of the Nazis screamed obscenities while others had nightmares. Murders were committed to steal rations for survival. On the commander's fifth trip back to the sub, some of the victims were reduced to crawling. Water and rations were almost exhausted.

After a conference, it was decided that in order to save lives, the commander and one top Nazi should surrender to the American authorities. As strategy discussions continued, Nazi Major Schaemmel slipped away and relieved the guard in the commander's control room. As the first guard departed, Schaemmel put a gun to the head of Commander Meyers and articulated forcefully: "You are my hostage. Obey every word or I'll kill you! Move in a normal way to the lower escape hatch! You and I are going to leave -- alone!" So Lt. Commander Hans Meyers and Nazi Major Hauptman Schaemmel left the tomb on the small two-man escape sub. They were never to return. Within ten hours the two had beached their sub off Elliot Key, surrendered to an American naval unit, been transported to Key West under guard and had boarded a plane for Washington. Time was running out for the sub commander. One of the five escaped Nazis whom he had taken out a few days earlier had, on separating, threatened: "You deliberately steered us into this trap. When I get to a short wave radio, I'll signal our people overseas to kill your wife and daughter. They are still my hostages."

The first morning after their departure from the German sub, on April 29, 1945, the two Germans were in the White House under guard flanked by Navy Intelligence officers.

In front of them sat the President of the United States, Harry S. Truman, in office since April 13, 1945.

The sub commander spoke. His sad blue eyes told of the human cargo left on board that would die if the Americans (whom they had been sent to kill) did not rescue them. During the interrogation, the commander explained his predicament: he had about 500 men with supplies exhausted; he had no passenger list. He explained that the first sub load had been bumped in Alexandria. Regardless, the sub commander asked that all lives be saved. As President Truman deliberated, the Nazi, Major Schaemmel, asked to speak without the presence of the sub commander who was then led out of the room.

Standing before the Naval Intelligence officers (whose names are withheld for security reasons) and President Truman, the prisoner began to speak. Suddenly his diction sounded unmistakably American. As he continued, Truman's jaw dropped in disbelief. These are the words he heard:

"I am not Major Hauptman Schaemmel, a Gestapo agent. My official rank and name is Col. Walter Schellenberg, and my secret OSS number is 78. General William Donovan, head of the OSS will verify this. Please have an officer make contact." Then, as the amazed President and intelligence personnel looked on, the Nazi impersonator saluted the President and withdrew from his sleeve a list of almost 500 true names of the German Nazi personnel from the stricken sub.

"I beg you, Mr. President, these are the real names of those beasts in that God-forsaken sub. The sub commander is not aware what terrible substitution of personnel was made in Alexandria. Under direct orders from Hitler, I was responsible for rounding up these infamous men and placing them on that sub." "When did you infiltrate the Nazis?" the President asked. Col. Schellenberg replied, "In 1942 I was dropped into Switzerland."

President Truman strode around the desk before the OSS agent. "Only God could have arranged your being in front of me today with this information. Welcome home and let me shake hands with a brave man." Then the President read the partial list of those Nazis on the sub and handed it to one of the Intelligence officers. Some of the names and particulars are as follows:

No. 1. FRANZ NOVAK: Adolph Eichmann's Transportation officer. It was his job to arrange transportation for those undesirable Jews from point of arrest to place of execution and disposal.

No. 2. THEODOR DANNECKER: In charge of deporting Jews of France, Belgium and Italy to their places of execution.

No. 3. HEINZ ROETHKE: Eichmann's Deputy in Charge of disposing of undesirable Jews in Paris. He directed the others who arrested and deported the Paris Jews. He is supposed to have completely eliminated all known Jews in Paris.

No. 4. DR. ERNST WETZEL: He operated a gas chamber in Poland. The official name was Elimination Camp for Undesirables.

No. 5. WILHELM ZOEPF: In charge of sending Dutch Jews to the gas chamber and was in complete charge of this operation throughout the country. Boasted that he didn't leave a known Dutch Jew alive; he was thorough in his operations. He is known to have had over a half million Jews exterminated from Holland alone.

No. 6. HERMAN KRUMEY: In charge of Jewish extermination in Hungary. Known to have sent over 400,000 Jews to their deaths. In complete charge of operating gas chambers in Hungary.

No. 7. OTTO HUESCHE: Executed 100,000 Jews in gas chambers. Bragged about the number of Jews he executed.

No. 8. MAJOR GENERAL OSKER DIRLEWANGER: Before the war, a convicted criminal who committed sex crimes on young boys, spending five years in a Bavarian prison for this. In charge of the toughest S.S. men who in return were in charge of the extermination camps for unwanted Jews.

No. 9. LEOPOLD GLEIM: Chief of Gestapo in Warsaw. After the war he turned up in Egypt, was given an Egyptian name and was in Nasser's service. He was one of the escapees from the sub.

No. 10. LOUIS HEIDEN: Translated Hitler's "Mein Kampf" into other languages and served the Fuehrer in other capacities.

No. 11. HANS APPLER: Killed 100,000 Jews in the gas chambers. Escaped from the sub, was deported by the United States and rather than risk being tried as a war criminal, made his way to Egypt and is now believed to be in the Egyptian diplomatic service.

No. 12. WILLIAM BOECKELER: Killed over 100,000 Jews in the concentration camps.

No. 13. KARL HOLTER: A former Gestapo Officer who was in charge of the arrest and deportation of hundreds of thousands of Jews.

No. 14. ALBERT THIELMANN: A retired schoolteacher who joined the party after Hitler came to power and was responsible for the gassing of over 100,000 Jews.

No. 15. BRIG. GENERAL WARNER BLANKENBERG: Responsible for the murder of over 100,000 Jews in the gas chambers.

No. 16. HANS BOTHMANN: Was in charge of the elimination squad in Poland and all gas chambers there. Under his jurisdiction, over half a million Jews died.

No. 17. LT. GENERAL FREDERICH KATZMANN: Murdered 434,329 Jews in Poland alone.

No. 18. JAN DURCANSKY: In charge of all the Jewish extermination camps in Austria and Northern Italy.

No. 19. DR. F. W. SIEBERT: Invented and produced the six-pointed metal star that Nazis required Jews to wear. All who wore this were liable at any time to be seized and sent to an extermination camp.

No. 20. DR. KARL STAENGE: In charge of the death camps in Yugoslavia. Took over an old brickyard in Belgrade and roasted Jews alive in the kilns.

No. 21. FRANZ RADEMACHER: Exterminated 15,000 Yugoslavian Jews. Listed as a dangerous man.

No. 22. DR. HANS EISELE: Exterminated over half a million Jews in the Ukraine by having them thrown in pits, sprayed with gasoline and set on fire. After the fires died out, the half roasted bodies were used to feed the hogs.

No. 23. LT. GENERAL HEINZ KAMMLER: concrete construction engineer before the war. Later in charge of the round-wing plane plants. An expert on gas chamber construction. He perfected the gas chambers for a four-minute kill.

No. 24. DR. MAX MERTEN: In charge of Jewish extermination in Greece and under his leadership over 60,000 Greek Jews were killed.

No. 25. MATTIAS RAFFELBERG: Had over a half million Jews murdered in Russia and Poland.

No. 26. MAJ. OTTO SKORZENY: The most wanted man in Europe. Called the toughest man alive. A Hitler favorite who rescued Mussolini. Escaped from sub.

No. 27. DR. RUDOLPH MILDNER: The Gestapo Chief in Denmark, in charge of the elimination of Danish Jews. Had over 100,000 executed.

No. 28. DR. PAUL WALTER: Concentration camp commander in Poland. Was responsible for over a 100,000 Jewish deaths by extermination and experimentation. Performed amputations without anesthetics. His favorite expression on recording a death: "So what! Another Jew out of the way!" The authors read Walter's final page from his diary of a day's work written in Jewish blood.

No. 29. DR. WILHELM WITTELER: In charge of the gas chambers in Latvia, and collected Jews for deportation.

No. 30. KURT HEINBURG: Was in charge of all Jewish extermination in Serbia.

No. 31. HANS HOEFLE: Responsible for murdering over 100,000

Jews in Poland.

No. 32. WALTER CASPAR TOEBBENS: A Dutch Nazi who made millions of dollars by making Jews work free of charge in his factories. Those who became sick or incapacitated were killed on the spot.

No. 33. ANDRIJA ARTUKOVIC: Under his able administration over 80% of Yugoslavia's Jews were wiped out. The Jewish population of Zagreb was 12,315 before the war and 1,647 after. From Mostar a train took six carloads of Jewish mothers and children to the station at Sumaci. There they were forced to walk up into high mountains where they were thrown off steep cliffs. At Korencia, Jews were tied in bundles and rolled into pits, covered with gasoline and then burned alive.

No. 34. HEINRICH "Gestapo" MUELLER: A policeman who rose to be Bavarian Chief of Police. Later rose to be a Lt. General in the S.S. (Security Police). Organized the Gestapo on the model of the Russian M.V.D. His organization murdered most of Europe's Jews.

As the President perused the list his face turned pale. He hurled invective across the room: "Die, you evil bastards, and be buried alive in your own tomb of the damned! I hope your crimes haunt you through Hell!" Then he lowered his voice to a clipped tone of command and addressed a navy officer. "No attempt will be made to save that infernal submarine. The death of those decent young crewmembers may be accounted to me in eternity. God forgive me for their sakes!"

The Lt. Commander was brought back into the room and the President thanked him for his honesty. "We must detain you, sir," said President Truman, "but is there anything I can do for your comfort?" On that offer of aid, the U-boat commander blurted out the dilemma of his wife and daughter being held in a cave in Bavaria. Col. Schellenberg concurred. Capt. Meyers begged for help. He told of the threat to kill his family made by the departing German escapee.

Truman acted immediately. "Round up those German Nazis who escaped from the sub!" As he spoke, the phone call of General William Donovan, OSS chief, was put through to the President. He identified the American agent, whereupon the President ordered a parachute rescue team to land in Germany in an attempt to save the commander's wife and young daughter being held as hostages. Two nights later, with the sanction of Prime Minister Churchill, a combined American/British team landed in a mountainous area of Bavaria.

As the German waited under detention at a Washington officers' club, a messenger came to his room and requested to speak to the German in his own tongue. The intelligence officer began, "I have a message for you from the President of the United States: Your wife and daughter were rescued last night and are safely in Switzerland. There were several German casualties among those guarding your family -- but all our men came back safely. We must intern you, but someday we hope you'll be re-united." The U-boat commander broke down and wept.

Meanwhile, the cries of the damned in the beached submarine would rise for a few more days before they would be stifled in their underwater tomb off Florida.

American naval records, captured German records, interviews with the super sub commander and OSS files were used in preparing this episode. At the Nuremberg War Crime Trials in 1947, after 2-1/2 years in prison the commander was acquitted of any deliberate wrongdoing while on the sub of the damned. In 1953 he immigrated to America with his family.

Col. Walter Schellenberg was promoted to Brigadier General and awarded the Congressional Medal of Honor, the highest award for bravery given by the United States. Great Britain awarded him its highest honour for valor, the Victoria Cross. The French Ambassador to the U.S.A. pinned on him the Legion of Honour. King George VI asked Schellenberg if he would accept a Knighthood, but the American graciously declined. After the war he settled down anonymously in an American city with the abiding wish that he never again go to war.

Many other details on the OSS espionage action and the underwater trip of the "sub of the damned" have been omitted for the sake of brevity.

By World War II's end, the allies had enough information to comprehend Part I of the German evacuation plan, which, in effect, was the removal of the elite of their armies and technicians, from Europe. As mentioned before, by December 1944, enemy rail movements ending in the port of Aymonte, Spain, had been observed and verified. In the north, evidence of the super sub route was being carefully examined. Any allied doubts that the Germans had not returned to the Atlantic in undersea craft were cast aside after the British cruisers were sunk.

Logic evolved from the intelligence disclosures categorically sought the answer to this question: Where are the vanishing Germans disappearing to on their carefully planned exodus route? It was at this juncture in the Allied intelligence dilemma that OSS analysis from New York told of an expanding presence of Germans in Central and South America. From Brazil to Argentina unconfirmed reports began trickling out of the southern hemisphere of unidentified flying objects being seen in the air and on the ground.

It was too early in 1944-45 to be certain of German intentions, but General Eisenhower and General Donovan are quoted as wondering if the official surrender of German armies in Europe might be only a gesture -- and that the many Germans who got away would fight again on another day and at another place.

Subsequent to the actual German surrender many questions were still unanswered such as the whereabouts of numerous well-known German political, scientific and service personnel. Too many were unaccounted for to be lost in battle, displaced, or incarcerated in prisoner of war camps -- unless they had been taken to Russia. Also, while searching for the missing, it was noted that many German dependents and relatives failed to show grief.

"Somewhere," said General Eisenhower, "I feel another Germany is being born, and I would rather we were the confidants of these Germans than the Russians."

Another key remark by German Admiral Doenitz in 1943 almost
certainly indicated a mass German emigration. Doenitz declared: "The
German underwater fleet is proud to have made an earthly paradise,
an impregnable fortress for the Fuehrer somewhere in the world." The
phrase "in the world" was later to prove prophetic.

The authors have interviewed many key witnesses including several former Nazis, the German Embassy in Washington, and high intelligence
sources in America, and all agreed that the German Chief of State, Adolf
Hitler, left Germany alive. The only difference in telling of the planned
escape was the time of departure, the route, and the method.

On December 15, 1944, General Eisenhower called a most secret
meeting of the High Command in London, England. Present were the
Allied Chiefs-of-Staff including those from free France, Denmark,
Holland, Belgium, Norway, etc. General Eisenhower's purpose was
two-fold as he turned over the briefing to General William Donovan
and his assistant, who were asked to record and take notes. The assistant
was the same one sent to Spain for observation of German troop arrivals at Seville. General Donovan began: "Gentlemen, for several weeks
our agents have been watching secret movements of Germans through
France to Spain. Our first opinion was that the enemy was planning a
surprise attack on the coast of North Africa. We diverted divisions of
troops and kept them in readiness for this anticipated attack -- but, as
you all know, it never came.

"Now we are certain that these untold thousands of German troops have
used Spanish ports to disappear in a way still uncertain to us."

The General paused, looked around at the group of Allied Chiefs-of-
Staff, and then slowly continued. "Perhaps one of those Germans who
disappeared through Spain was the German leader, Adolf Hitler." The
room was hushed and the General's assistant looked up at a sea of astonished faces. Then several individuals rose at once to ask questions. The
General stated he would answer only half a dozen, and those who were
not satisfied could personally have a brief audience with him after the
meeting.

The first questioner asked, "Who's in charge in Germany" Answer:

"Grand Admiral Karl Doenitz is said to be the leader, but General Von Runstedt seems to be the one making the real nuts and bolts military decisions."

Another assertion was made that Hitler had been seen lately; therefore, would not the story of his departure likely be a case of German deception?"

Donovan's reply was cryptic. "A double is in Hitler's place. Our Berlin agents say so, and the British and Russian governments agree that an imposter instructed by Goebbels, Bormann and Ley, rules in Hitler's place. The man is not Hitler-gone-mad. He is a double under the control of others."

Donovan concluded the meeting by saying he believed the disappearance of Adolf Hitler was directly related to the dispersal of entire German armies. He told his cabinet that when the German armies were uncovered the real Hitler would also be found. The OSS Chief said he was convinced of Hitler's personal and family exodus. Our next task, he told them, will be to pick up the trail of the German leader and his troops in South America.

After the Allied briefing, General Donovan flew back to Washington. On arrival he immediately called a special meeting of OSS Caribbean Intelligence and his Brazilian Bureau. Donovan's earlier hunches paid off. Into New York, the wartime nerve center for America's western hemisphere intelligence, the coded reports of German arrivals throughout South America kept cable lines busy.

Today, a confidential report by the CIA concedes: "The body found in the bunker was not that of Hitler, for among other things, neither fingerprints, nor dental work matched Hitler's. Until 1974, the true Adolf Hitler, nor a corpse proven to be his had ever been located." The words, "until 1974," are significant. They will be explained later.

The story of Hitler's heroic last minute May 1945 flight out of besieged Berlin was a cleverly contrived German ruse, in the opinion of Judge Advocate General John P. Davis of the Nuremberg War Crime Trials. Although Christina Edderer said it was the real Hitler whom she flew to Norway, records of the Nuremberg trials state that Christina Edderer was a courageous woman, but an unsatisfactory witness, jailed for perjury under oath. When the authors questioned Edderer in 1975 they were not convinced that the story she told was valid regarding her version of the Hitler escape.

In retrospect, the reader should recall that Hitler's master plan was to win World War II. When this master plan was thwarted, the alternate plan was to move their national endeavor to another land, free from enemy intervention. Execution of Phase I in the alternate plan was begun seriously in 1943, and when finished in 1954 saw three million Germans and other resources successfully evacuated.

Regardless of the low esteem certain German Generals had for Hitler, he was revered and adored by the German masses. His hero and leader image was never seriously challenged. His ability to arouse all the patriotic emotions of German society was never in doubt. However, Hitler was also an idealistic believer in a new Utopia for Germany, and according to his close associates, that zeal to develop a new Germany was such an inherent part of his makeup that it never waned -- even when Germany's military defeat was obvious.

Therefore, Hitler was the key to the German evacuation, and this fact will later be proven to be true beyond any doubt. In addition to Hitler's prominent role in the evacuation another more human side of his life is perhaps as important.

Hitler and Eva Braun were legally married on April 29, 1945 but their first-born son, Adolf Hitler II, was born in 1940, five years before their marriage. Hitler was said to be the father.

Back in October 1944, a select German group, working from a schedule compiled on August 10, in Saltzberg, decided to implement operation "Get Lost." Hitler was to be the catalyst.

All the art treasures, scientific developments, and treasury bullion that Germany possessed were first scheduled to be hidden or removed. First to be safely removed, however, would be the Fuehrer. Over Hitler's protests he was asked to pack immediately his personal possessions and leave Germany for the new land. A double stood by to assume the Fueh-rer's role and he would continue under the tutelage and surveillance of Bormann, Goebbels and Ley.

The Fuehrer's party left Berlin by motorcade, traveling at night, and safe harboring during the day to avoid Allied aircraft. The party con-sisted of Hitler and his wife Eva, their four-year-old son, Adolf II, and a twelve year old adopted orphan boy, David.

Over wide track French railroads, still traveling at night, Hitler and his party reached Spain. They were transferred to narrow Spanish track rail-cars, eventually reaching La-Aljaferia Castle in Zaragoza. There, Hitler met his Spanish confidant who was to act as advisor and escort. (It is from this highly respected Spaniard, that the authors, while researching in Spain, verified how Hitler left Europe.)

Hitler was outfitted in a Spanish business suit, his moustache removed and his hairstyle changed. His wife, Eva, was outfitted as a middle-class Spanish woman, and the boy David became a Spanish youth.

Spanish tutoring complete, at 3:00 A.M. on the morning of November 5, 1944, Hitler and party vacated the castle by motorcar with his Span-ish confidant as chauffeur. Through Valencia and on to Seville they trav-eled, resting the first night in the Colon Hotel. The next day the trip was resumed to Hulva and finally, Aymonte where rooms were provided in another hotel. The following night, November 7, after taking leave of his Spanish guide and friend, Hitler and his family were taken on board a super sub, along with 500 other Germans. During Hitler's stay in Aymonte and, for three days thereafter, Generalissimo Franco had placed the area under martial law. (Allied intelligence never learned the secret of Hitler's departure until long after World War II.) As the super sub slipped beneath the water she headed southwest. For the next 18 days, in an 8 x 10 cabin, Hitler and his family shared living and sleep-ing quarters. Two leather covered chairs, four bunks and a radio for the Fuehrer and his family were the accessories. There were two doctors in attendance on board the submarine for the 500 passengers, submarine crew and Hitler and his family.

The Allies knew Hitler had fled. The Nuremberg War Trials had created an unspoken climate of official concern that he would return incognito to Germany to become a symbol for Germany's renaissance.

In 1945 America decided to go after Hitler. But the secrets they discovered in South America and the Antarctic were so fantastic, so seemingly incredible, that telling the details to the world was as difficult as explaining that men from Mars had already landed on earth.

Back in New York, more OSS reports told of additional German arrivals in South America. The Germans were flooding into Belem and other river ports, as well as airstrips in Brazil's Amazon Valley, Leticia in Colombia and Georgetown, British Guiana.

The Germans always appeared to be in transit. At that point, General Donovan personally went to Brazil to direct operations. American agents posed as rubber, precious metals and timber buyers along the Amazon and Orinoco Rivers. They learned an amazing thing. Germans were appearing from hidden staging camps 3,000 miles up the Amazon beyond Obidas and even Manaus. From here they were traced heading south toward the headwaters of the Amazon where their trail often led up the still navigable Maran River, a tributary of the Amazon. The trail went cold in the vicinity of Iquitos, Ecuador. As one OSS Agent's report from Iquitos said, "The Germans arrive here in local dress by the thousands -- but they are not seen leaving. They are literally being swallowed up by the earth."

Neither local Brazilians, nor the Indians could explain the "Kraut" vanishing act. While at Manaus and Rio de Janeiro, Germans in civilian dress also were seen departing by air for Buenos Aires and Montevideo where they again were observed leaving in private and chartered planes for the interior of Argentina. One agent reported in February 1945, "that these VIPs in their hauteur and arrogance were like a newly formed German General Staff."

But World War II would end, Allied troops would demobilize, and another two years would go by before it could be established just what had happened for sure to Adolf Hitler and a corps of hundreds of thousands of select Germans who vanished from the Fatherland.

Chapter IX

Vanishing Germans Discover the Mystery of the Ages

The international race to put a fleet of round-wing planes in the air went unabated by those Germans who started life anew in another hemisphere after they had abandoned their ancestral home at the end of World War II. The new frontier life seemed to stimulate the Germans with a perseverance that enabled them to survive and continue on. Their iron determination could be attributed to a twist of fate that had begun 400 years earlier.

To understand the significance of certain historical evidence relating to the continuing German effort to build a new country under the protection of the round-wing plane, the reader should become acquainted with the following true adventure. It is a kaleidoscope of German resourcefulness bridging the 16th and 20th centuries.

The explanation centers around 500 warrior-colonists who left Germany in the 16th century and were presumed to have perished 4,000 miles up the Amazon River. The existence of those ancient adventurers was forgotten. Allied agents searching for Hitler's lost minions in the late 1940s unknowingly found descendents of the 16th century colonists whose current presence in that hemisphere actually changed the outcome of World War II, an astounding revelation still kept hidden from press and public.

The adventure in question began in 1572 when a select and hardy group of about 500 German colonists originating mainly from the Dukedom of Sax-Coburg, and including recruits from Bavaria and East Prussia, were hired as soldier-mercenaries by Sebastian I, King of Portugal, to man a garrison up the Amazon River. The German soldiers were allowed to bring their wives, for after building the fort and doing garrison duty, they were to be given land grants in the interior of what is now Brazil. The families were mainly Lutherans that had been subject to Catholic persecution.

These adventurers set sail from Lisbon, Portugal in three 130-foot, lightly armed warships named Urcas. Their first task was to build a Portuguese fort on the upper reaches of the Amazon in a region of what today is the approximate border between Brazil and Ecuador. Upon completion of the fort, the Germans were to man the same against the Spaniards located on the other side of the river. By territorial aggrandizement, Pope Pius V had issued a Papal Bull dividing the interior of South America between the Spanish on the west bank of the Amazon and the Portuguese on the east bank.

The ships were destroyed at the end of the journey when the Portuguese crew and German mercenaries were ambushed by fierce Indians. In orderly fashion, the Germans and Portuguese removed cattle, pigs, chickens and a few horses, as well as valuable seed grains for fruit and vegetables. Taking to the jungle, the Europeans fought an enemy who attempted to kill them to the last man and woman. It was a battle of bows and arrows, deadly blowguns and spears against crossbow and body armor. It was a battle of survival for the Europeans who were quick to adopt stealthy Indian tactics of forest fighting, as opposed to open European massed battle formation.

Eventually, the white men stumbled upon a cave entrance into the side of a mountain. Fighting a rear-guard action, the German remnant was saved and also their livestock and possessions. Because the Indians were terrified of the cave spirits, they abandoned the siege and left. The hole in the side of the earth became a refuge for those white men. Periodically the mercenaries were able to make armed sorties out to procure fresh produce and game. Meanwhile, inside the cavity, the besieged people found fresh water plentiful, and by lighting fires, they learned to sustain themselves in a primitive routine. With ingenuity and skills, the group persevered, but they dared not establish themselves again in the dangerous world outside. Only their basic survival instincts kept them from total despair.

After agonizing on their dilemma, scouting parties explored the cavity's interior and reported that the cave of refuge was actually the entrance to a deep underground tunnel. They also found there was evidence of human occupation before them, perhaps accounting for the fear which the Indians had of the interior. The white men took to the tunnels, not knowing where they were going, but hoping the routes would eventually digress to the surface again where they could resettle among friendly Indians.

A documented story of this adventure was recorded in diary form on the ship's log that the group saved.

The German colonists endured the hardships for three generations, until they "emerged" in 1647. The episode is told briefly here because what those 16th Century Germans accomplished enabled the German Third Reich to continue after World War II.

Leader of the original survivors of the 1572 Indian attacks was a German named Von Luckner. It was he who also organized the tunnel escape and unknowingly led the remnants of his party through the fissures in groups of 30, deep into the earth where several months later they found a huge, faintly lit cavity of approximately 75 square miles. The ceiling was 300 feet in height and the floor consisted of soil with all the natural nutrients for crop growth. Here the Germans established their first community, free from outside aggression. Insulated from the surface world of headhunter Indians and an unfriendly jungle, they built a village that over the years became their permanent home. On their journey down, the Europeans generally had fresh water, at times icy cold that came in trickles and rivulets from above. The temperature remained the same as on the surface for approximately the first 100 miles; but in later years, as they penetrated deeper, they were to experience an increase in heat from 80 to 100 degrees. Subsistence was a daily problem but the raw elements of nature on the surface such as rain, cold, wind and predators were totally absent.

At that time these colonists were a lost civilization. As a group they would never return to the surface. Hopelessly, but with an instinctive urge for survival, they surrendered their old ties to Germany and took on a new identity. The cultural, linguistic, and religious heritages from their homeland remained strong. These assets they would carefully preserve and record for their children as they wandered in the tunnels and adapted to their changed life style.

Persistent stories have been told for centuries that white men were seen on Brazil's upper reaches of the Amazon. These tales we now realize are true. Their basis grew in part as the hunted Germans cautiously reemerged to the surface where they developed trading routes much like the French "Coeur de bois" in North America. Of necessity, the Germans had to barter with the Indians and, also, eventually trade with posts and forts which other non-Germanic white men had subsequently built on the river. The lost Germans kept their hideaway a secret. At all costs, they made sure that no outsiders would stumble upon the new camouflaged tunnel entrance leading to their habitation in the interior of the earth. Those who did never returned.

In 1980, that village which the Germans started still survives and bears the name of its original founder, Von Luckner, who was proclaimed first king in 1572. The habitation now has a population of over 30,000 souls.

As American colonists heading west in the 1700's broke through one natural obstacle after another, so the Germans inside the tunnel continued to explore and move on. From the first settlement of Von Luckner, a group under the leadership of a man named Wagner moved further into the tunnel. They located another cavity where a settlement was started under Wagner's surname. (Population in1977 was 60,000). By mid 1600, the Germans had developed a system of crude tracks and carts on wooden wheels. On this rudimentary railroad system, they were able to haul their farm produce and livestock. They began to grow crops (particularly barley) that adapted itself to the photosynthesis emanating from the rock glow. This faint natural light coming from the rock walls also enabled them to see and their eyesight adjusted to the dark. Further down the tunnels the Germans descended and eventually established six cities along their 3,000-mile crude wooden rail system. Their offspring survived disease and hunger.

Like an army, they established each base, and after consolidating it, moved on to repeat the conquest of the tunnel system.

One recurring ordeal confronted the colonists. To understand their trouble, it is necessary to explain that the original tunnel they followed meandered and wound through 3,000 miles of labyrinths. From the seclusion of the numerous tunnel offshoots, the Germans were frequently attacked by a subterranean race of creatures that tried to kill them, as had the Indians on the surface. At one point, these "evil ones" or "Sons of Satan," as the colonists nicknamed them, walled-up the community of new German arrivals. To break out, the Germans were forced to tunnel out through a mile of rubble. The inner-race dwellers strongly resented the newcomers and agreed to guide them back to the surface if they would vacate and leave. Germans who still dwell in these original interior cities say the interior of the earth's mantle is filled with many cities inhabited by the "evil ones." These Germans who have now lived in the tunnel cities below South America for over 400 years, contend that the entire mantle of the earth is filled with different races of rock dwellers who went underground for survival after different surface upheavals or floods which occurred during the former pre-Adamite and post-Adamite civilizations. They contend there are literally hundreds of huge cities located in pockets around the globe and under the seas, from 350 feet below the outer surface to many miles in depth. The German colonists of 1572 may have been the latest arrivals to wander into the earth's mantle -- like it -- and remain.

As the years passed, three generations of infants were born in the tunnel system. The German "Rock Moles" had established a chain of settlements named Hagner (population, 1977, 180,000) and Baron Von Brighttner (population 1977, 100,000), Sillisteen (population 1977, 12,000), and Archduke Von Kitchiner (population 1977,

62,000). Then, on the 75th year of their forced sojourn, their scouting parties broke out into the Promised Land. Emerging through a rock opening the advance party looked about in wonder. All of them had been born inside the earth's mantle but had been raised to believe there was another world. As the first guides looked about, they beheld unending sky, trees and rolling land. More fascinating, everything including them was bathed in light from a faint man-made orb that hung in a real sky. (Their arrival inside the earth's rock mantle was at a midway point below today's countries of New Zealand and Australia.) The Germans cheered, they prayed, and they laughed for they thought they had arrived back on the outside of the world again.

Hurrying inside the tunnel, they told of this new wonder they had discovered. More jubilant Germans from the tunnel system emerged. Sometime later, contact was made with the occupants of this new land who advised the German explorers that they had descended to the inside of the earth where hundreds of millions of peaceful people lived who shunned surface dwellers. The new Atlanteans, which they were called, moved through the air in magical, silent, round-winged craft and drove four-wheeled vehicles without horses or oxen. These people had an advanced civilization that the amazed Germans recognized was hundreds of years ahead of the surface civilization their fathers had left years before. Also amazing to the Germans, the new Atlanteans had an ageless longevity span, with no noticeable traces of old age in their bodies, no ancient furrows in their facial features and no senility in their mannerisms. What was missing was the presence of old people, the Germans quickly noted.

Yet another surprise awaited the tunnel Germans. The Atlanteans or Atturians called in advisors from another Inner World continent named Bodland in order to further apprise the new immigrants. As the Bods and tunnel Germans conversed, the tunnel arrivals exploded with excitement. The Inner World Bodlanders and newly arrived tunnel Germans from the Upper World had the same root language! Unbelievable, the tunnel Germans heard a story of how the Bodlanders some 30,000 years earlier had sought refuge in underground tunnels when attacked by a vicious race which had come out of the sky in space craft using superior weaponry to destroy their cities and kill their people by the millions. Only a few thousand survivors were left and they were pursued into mountainous caves. The calamity had occurred in what today are Iran, Pakistan and Syria, once peopled by a race of fair people who called themselves Bacchis later changed to Bods. Many years later the Bods reached the Inner World via tunnels and pockets in the earth's mantle.

The group of emerging tunnel Germans was then invited to visit Bodland, and it was soon apparent to the tunnel Germans that the Bods were the most advanced civilization they had ever seen. The Atlanteans, also called Atturians, agreed to permit the new German race to settle on a relatively unoccupied continent adjacent to Bodland in the southern hemisphere where the second race of Inner World Aryans began anew. Only one stipulation was required, the tunnel Germans must live in peace and friendship and never return to the outside world.

A new German race, therefore, evolved. Its roots began in Germany. Uprooted, they were established in the tunnel system that began in the underground headquarters of South America. From here they migrated over a period of three generations to the interior of the earth where, reborn, the 250 original couples grew into a nation known today as the Six Kingdoms of Saxony. In the intervening years, surplus people from the cities confined within the mantle were forced to migrate to the interior and take up new residence in one of the six inner kingdoms. Eventually, in the 1900's, each family in the tunnel system was allowed only two children as population density was dictated by the cavity size in which each city was located.

In the early 1700's the elder Germanic race of Bods was persuaded by members of the new German royalty to transport their eldest sons back to Germany for schooling in the universities.

These young men were first sworn to secrecy and flown to their ancestral homeland in Bodland aircraft in less than half a day. In Germany proper, these Germans from the lost civilization were introduced as sons of wealthy German plantation owners along the Amazon. For over 200 years in this manner, these German princes of a lost world received their advanced education in the arts and history of the Upper World at the leading universities of Europe. Upon return to their interior homeland inside the earth's mantle and the earth's interior, these young Germans showed merchandise and told of the technical advances in the outside world that they had visited. Thus, for instance, those below learned of such Upper World processes as the printing press made in Germany and first brought to the interior by the Crown Prince Von Luckner.

In spite of this isolation, German communities in the tunnels also heard that the outside civilization that their forefathers left had again been re-contacted. Since they had grown and thrived in their new tunnel locales, they decided to remain there.

The original migratory tunnel route hit many dead ends, and although substantial improvements were made by use of the single car on wooden wheels and track, the tunnel still followed natural fissures, many of which doubled back like a winding creek.

In 1853 the tunnel Germans abandoned their reticence toward upper surface outsiders and brought in a German engineer from the surface in order to improve the system. In one place he shortened a circuitous length of 273 miles by boring out a new three-mile stretch. Within this three-mile bore they struck a large room over a mile by three-quarters of a mile in area. In this cavity, they later constructed railroad shops, yards, storage tracks, buildings, etc. Continuing to bore the tunnel system, repetitive curves and bends were straightened and the old length of 3,000 miles was shortened considerably. Borrowing technology and materials from the Bods inside the earth, a single-track electric railway system evolved that the tunnel Germans improved annually. However, the tunnel entrance in Brazil/Peru border was kept a well-guarded secret.

For those Germans who had eventually settled in the center of the earth, the interior climate was hospitable, and by the turn of the 20th Century their numbers had reached ten million. Because of increased visitations, reports about the sojourning princes had seeped out in Germany proper. At that time, the German engineer had told of his work among the lost German cities in the tunnel. Finally, during World War I, the Germans in the tunnel sent a volunteer regiment to fight with their homeland cousins. At this juncture, in the renewed relationship between the subterranean Germans and the fatherland, the World War I regiment located many missing relatives from whom their forefathers had been separated 14 generations before. However, the Inner World Germans did not participate in the Upper World wars.

Did Germanic underworld cousins, visiting Germany during World War I, advise her to abandon caution, and reveal the existence of the underworld? The answer is yes, in part, plus other considerations. American State Department papers of December 1914 and January through March 1915, describing America's peace efforts to end World War I clearly outline the strenuous efforts by Germany to insure a free access route to their underground nation. One of their most stringent demands in order for them to sign the Armistice was as follows: "Imperial Germany demands free access through the Antarctic via the South Pole to the inner earth for the purpose of future colonization."

American Secretary of State Representative, Colonel House later showed this clause to British Prime Minister Lloyd George. He laughed and said, "Give the Germans that icicle land of seals and penguins. It's nothing but a giant icebox. The Germans have gone insane." As for the interior earth, Prime Minister Lloyd George suggested to Colonel House that somebody was pulling his official leg. Obviously, even in 1915 German foreign minister Count Zimmerman was more aware than the allies that planet earth was hollow in its center.

By 1930, limited contact and communications had again been established with the tunnel Germans, and a sparse trade evolved, but Upper World Germans had never been taken into the subterranean localities or to the Inner World. Despite their isolation, the presence of the lost German civilizations was being pieced together and recorded by German authorities in the Fatherland.

At the request of Adolf Hitler, officials in Nazi Germany carefully and meticulously gathered all these facts of the German Walhalla. However, Hitler's ambitions as a demagogue to place Germany on a war footing and move toward a total European conflict, of arms, if necessary had not gone unnoticed by the Germanic cousins of the Inner World -- particularly the Bodlanders who had been at peace for 30,000 years.

It was in 1936 that Hitler, prompted by immediate and unknown reasons, decided to send an exploration team to the Inner World (presumably by air). The Bodlanders from inside the Earth watched the upper Germans all the way and eventually invited the team to the capital city of Bod where Hitler's Upper World Germans were treated royally before returning home. The King of Bodland was invited to come up to Germany's Third Reich for a return visit and, in October 1936, the Inner World Bodland King, Haakkuuss III responded, arriving secretly in Germany via his private space ship. After talking to the Upper World Germans, he was impressed by their national spirit and drive, but he also recognized they were prone to war and had placed themselves in the direction of a total war footing. Taking Hitler and some of his officers aside King Haakkuuss said: "I warn you, as a long lost German brother, that you are on the brink of a colossal war that will lead Germany only to disaster. I urge you to stop this madness and reconsider before taking your nation down the wrong road a second time in this century. War is hate -- full of negative karma and national agony. Develop a peaceful policy in a positive way."

He then explained that his own intelligence indicated the American President was also power oriented and would like to rule the world. Russia's Stalin was also bent on world domination. Then the King prophesied that if Hitler pursued his dreams of German expansion by war, he would eventually end up being crushed by the armies of Russia, the United States, Britain and its allies. Hitler, of course, disregarded this sage advice from the ruler of another German nation that had not been at war for thirty millennia and had built the greatest nation on or in the globe.

Following the official visit of the King of Bodland, Hitler instructed his general staff to mount an immediate combined naval and air operation leading to the opening at the South Pole by which they intended to locate again the lost German civilization in the interior of the Earth. That 1937-38 search came to light in 1945 when American and British Intelligence officers in London began examining captured German records. Revealed were the intimate details of the German penetration of the Antarctic under Captain Ritscher whose exploration teams fanned out to unlock the secrets of the subcontinent -- once a tropic.

One German name, Kurt Von Kugler, an experienced mountain climber, stood out. He actually descended with his German crew through two miles of ice in the vicinity of a place called "Rainbow City," and found evidence of an ancient but advanced civilization older than all of man's measured past. The Germans spent over a month there, and in this oasis of hot springs found tropical trees, melons and other succulent fruits. This find spurred the German teams to expend greater efforts, and other lost valleys were located. The Antarctic database was developed. Allied officers read the 100-page report with 300 photos and determined this singular explorer's activity was an astonishing discovery. These records of the peacetime German conquest on Antarctica were eventually turned over to the United States where they were quickly filed in Washington's Polar Archives in the National Archives Building under the recent guardianship of Franklin Birch, whose twofold job is to deny that they exist and also to prevent public scrutiny.

The Germans had left maps with routes and aerial photographs. On finding these, America notified Britain of their find and sent Admiral Byrd into the Antarctic to retrace the German routes. Byrd's expedition was composed of Americans, British and Canadians, one of the famous Britons being Sir Robert Scott whom the authors interviewed.

In 1938 German teams composed of military specialists and scientists finally found the long valley at the South Pole. Both land and aerial groups began the penetration. As they entered the 125-mile-wide Antarctic opening, the mystery unfolded. Traveling on, the valley deepened and 500 miles later, as the valley floor continued to drop, the snow and ice disappeared. Eventually, without being totally aware, the land teams (supplied by air drops) were descending into the doughnut-like hole to the interior of the earth. A German air team flying a Dornier-Wal made the descent. The rest is history. They flew north into the interior and landed thousands of-miles away -- among a race of people who resembled the aerial explorers themselves and spoke an ancient German dialect.

The descendants of those German mercenaries, whose forefathers had disappeared up the Amazon of the Upper World in the year 1572, had been found. The captured Bonn records tell how Hitler's advance parties met their long lost relatives and were joyously welcomed. The jubilant interior Germans then allotted unpopulated adjoining lands to the Germans of the Third Reich and signed six treaties of occupation, one for each autonomous German Kingdom below.

A snag debarring total acceptance of the new political alignment occurred during the good-will visit. When the Upper World Germans visited the neighboring continent and nation of Bodland who were also Germanic in origin, the first settlers of the Inner World rebuffed them. The Bods categorically informed their upper world relatives that they would not be admitted below except through a singular treaty made with the Parliament of Bodland and that any lands to be allotted for future colonization of Upper World Third Reich people would be at the sole discretion of the senior Inner World Bodland power and no other nation. The ultimatum was plain. Any Upper World German immigration would be under the terms of another German nation, who over a span of many thousand years had developed a political structure of government that precluded war. If the Upper World Germans wanted to live in this chaste environment, they were told, they must be re-indoctrinated throughout the whole gamut of their existence from the relearning of the family, school and college perspectives towards a new outlook at adulthood life. Thus any Upper World immigration of the Germans planning another world war would require total renunciation of their basic destructive behaviorisms before they could become federated with the Inner World people whose constant objective was peace.

The German Dornier-Wal was refueled with a chemical superior to gasoline and the surface Germans flew home. They had found their ancient Thule, but they had not experienced the applauding adulation expected from their long lost kin.

The Upper World War began without respite. In September 1939, Hitler's legions of invincibility invaded Poland. Britain, France and their colonial empires declared war on the Germans. In 1940, the Germans had turned on the Russians and, in 1941, the Americans under Roosevelt had come in on the side of the allies. The prophecy for fulfillment of the 1936 warning by King Haakkuuss III was about to unfold. By 1943 Hitler realized he could not fight a war on three fronts against enemies with inexhaustible supplies of men and materials despite advanced German preparedness.

Therefore, the Third Reich altered its plan for conquest of the world. Early in 1943 Adolf Hitler dispatched a delegation of unknown emissaries below to entreat King Haakkuuss III of Bodland to sell some unsettled land near the Inner South Pole entrance. The King refused to sell them any territory for expansion but, as a brother German nation, he welcomed Hitler's people to come down and occupy semi-desert land without compensation, provided they agreed to sign a treaty of perpetual peace with Bodland and dwell quietly with the other nations.

The visiting Upper World Germans agreed, whereupon the Bodland King called a special session of Parliament inviting the delegation of Third Reich emissaries to attend. As the visitors from the Upper World listened, they observed King Haakkuuss open the special session of Parliament and deliver the following address that was televised to the entire nation:

"Citizens of Bodland: As you are already aware, a delegation of fellow German kin folk from the Earth's Upper surface is visiting the leaders of our nation. These visiting Germanic speaking people from the surface call themselves citizens of the Third Reich, have a common ancestry with us dating back 30,000 years at least when we existed together on the surface, where our history teaches we dwelt principally as a great nation in what is called Persia since former times (and currently named Iran). Our ancestors also occupied other adjoining lands in this area of the world including what is today called India, Pakistan, Afghanistan, Syria, etc., all of which are now peopled by non-Germanic peoples.

"The cradle of our race, of course, was in the Antarctic from which our ancestors migrated to Persia (Iran) when the Antarctic area slowly became frozen over with ice which is now two miles thick.

"But completing the story of our ancient history, you know our surface nation was destroyed and our people hunted and killed by the millions when a vicious race from another planet named 'The Serpent People' landed among us from spacecraft. Many of our ancestors were driven into caves for survival, where for many years they remained. They were never able to return to their native lands occupied by the alien invaders whom our astronomers believed came from a strange planet that intruded into our solar system and also caused the earlier ice age over our original lands.

"While our ancestors were in the caves and tunnels, a remnant of them became separated from Bodland forefathers and eventually this grouping arrived back out on the surface through a cave in what today is called the Black Forest in Bavaria. They became the modern surface Germans and their kin scattered throughout the northern hemisphere above. As you listeners will know, we Bodlanders are the other part of the Persian exodus who eventually migrated through caves and tunnels into the center of the Earth, coming out in these very mountains of Bodland through the tunnels of which we can still connect with hidden exits on the upper surface with our fast magnetic trains and cars. To conclude the capsule history, I would point out that the languages of the upper and lower Germans are today somewhat different but our root words and our customs and even our music are all identifiable with each other."

The King paused and the Parliament of ancient Germans and newly found surface relatives listened with solemnity. His Majesty then re-addressed himself to the vast listening audience throughout the nation. "Fellow citizens, the subject matter on which I address my main remarks is simply this: Our brothers on the surface are involved in a war that can only mean their annihilation as a nation, having been led into this catastrophe by one man -- a foolish leader (Adolf Hitler) -- whom I tried to warn of his wrong doing three years before the war began – but he rejected my advice. At that time, I predicted his downfall if he were to engage his nation in war because two other surface nations, whose leaders also wanted to rule the entire upper world, would unite and destroy the German leader. I refer to Franklin Delano Roosevelt of the United States and Joseph Stalin of Soviet Russia.

"Our brothers on the surface are losing the war. It is only a matter of time before most of the country of Germany as a nation will be defeated and destroyed according to the plans of their enemies. A delegation of our surface kinsmen is sitting in the Parliamentary visitors' gallery even today. They have come on behalf of their leaders, to beg for our help. Without our befriending them, their people above are lost.

"Their foolish leader, in spite of his evil deeds which are mountainous, still has the makings of a great man if guided in the right direction, and therefore he is part of my proposal, in that he be allowed to enter the Inner World as a catalyst to reunite the exodus of his people under the following conditions:

"That we deed our southern wastelands to them for new settlements.

"That we assist them in developing these vast lands into productive croplands and urban centers. (Eventually the Bods drilled 1800 artesian wells in the arid lands for the incoming German tide from above and also built the first railroads and laid out the new cities.) Later the newcomers may stay in peace or return to the surface.

"That we give all our services to nurture their beginnings as a great nation like ourselves. But before committing our brainpower and labour to help them, a charter must be signed by their leaders agreeing to renounce war and not provoke any conflict as long as they remain among us. Each new arrival would sign such an oath before being accepted as an Inner World citizen.

"That Bodland supervise all new construction and make certain that no war-like beginnings are started by them while on the allotted lands. Those among the Upper Germans who exhibit a war prone attitude and want to continue World War II at a later date would not be allowed to settle among us, and therefore any new war beginnings would have to take place on the surface of the planet, for which it is already infamous.

"That Bodland's government would screen all newcomers and this immigrant supervision would last for a term of 30 years ending in 1973."

King Haakkuuss finished his speech and a Parliamentary Committee worked out details of the Charter. Three days later the treaty had been drafted and passed by the Bodland Parliament for signature of the King. The visiting Germans were shown a copy of the draft in the language of the Bodlanders, but the Upper World Germans could not decipher the text. Placing a glass screen over the pages, the Bods showed their astonished cousins the same pages again. Through the opaque screen, the language was in modern idiomatic and precise German. The document was accepted without revision and shortly afterwards the signed text was made available in both languages. There remained a place for the signature of Adolf Hitler and other German signatories.

The treaty in effect welcomed the defeated Germans into the Hollow Earth under strict conditions imposed by the Bodlanders' Parliament. The arid lands were to be made productive in order to sustain the newcomers. Strict immigration factors would constitute entry acceptance. Those denied entry would be top Nazis, all personnel connected with concentration camps or those who had hunted Jews and other ethnic groups or political or ideological enemies of the Third Reich. The list of immigrant denials was extensive. Only those in the present Reich armed services with clean records would be accepted for continuing police and defense duties. The Bodland criminal law denied citizenship to murderers, sadists, rapists and kidnappers, aside from explicit treaty conditions.

The King took the Upper Germans aside and told them that if they broke the treaty by warfare, they all would be eliminated so quickly they would barely have time for their lives to flash before them, so quick and devastating would be their destruction by Bod weaponry.

When the delegation returned to the surface they presented the treaty to Hitler. He angrily fumed and ranted but signed the document. From that day on, a secret government department was established, answerable only to Hitler and three other unknown men. The task of this department was to prepare the Third Reich for migration into the Inner Earth to resettle in the general vicinity and under the watchful eyes of the old kingdoms of Germans and the strict surveillance of the Bodlanders who would control all facets of the New German nation for 30 years. Albert Speer's grand designs for the public buildings to be erected in a victorious post-war Berlin were to become instead the models for a New Berlin in the underworld capital as batteries of Bodlanders swarmed in to help the latest arrivals build a new nation from the ground up.

Beginnings of the construction of New Berlin were started in 1943 including the new Reichstag and a palace for Hitler. By 1944, underground water and utilities were laid out for a New Berlin. The Bods and new German workers had already erected temporary living and office quarters.

Two obstacles faced the Germans migrating from the Third Reich. The first was the descent into the abyss for 125 miles through a wide hole in the Antarctic. No land entrance over the ice-covered continent leading to the abyss had been revealed by the German exploration teams. Hence, conventional aircraft must transport all personnel or supplies reaching the earth's interior via the South Pole route in -- an almost impossible task even with naval and land relay depots.

One alternative later devised was to have the five relatively untried round-wing planes (powered by magnetic energy) flown to secret hideouts in the southern hemisphere to become the nucleus of a giant airlift. Two additional craft were later flown down (one in 1946 and the other in 1947).

The second obstacle was the antiquated tunnel leading to Old Germany in the interior. The original tunnel of 3,000 miles, of course, had been reworked in the mid 1800's, but was still old-fashioned by modern standards. It had been used more or less for interior trade of the various communities inside the mantle, and not for mass transit. An updated German survey by Bod engineers, therefore, recommended rebuilding the system. Involved was a shortening of the total linear miles -- more secondary lines to serve the local interior cities -- and a new monorail system with sufficient electric power to carry up to 12 cars.

As World War II unexpectedly deteriorated for Germany proper after 1943, communications with the interior Germans increased via conventional aircraft and the tunnel system. Sometime in 1941 the subterranean German settlements invited their surface brothers to help modernize the tunnel system according to the earlier decision, and to expedite use of its facility in case they had to relocate their emigrants to the interior. Unable to await reconstruction of the tunnel system and its train then nicknamed "the space elevator," hordes of defeated Germans in 1944 began coming through the Brazil corridor via the tunnel to their new homes below.

Germans were questioned recently about the attitude of the interior Germans toward those surface Germans defeated in World War II who relocated underground. They described the relationship as somewhat parallel to the British/American wartime relationship: "England, the older Anglo-Saxon race, was in trouble, and America, a brother offshoot came to her rescue." German sources, for the underworld reports, were also asked by the authors if the old Six Kingdoms of interior Germans, or the Bods, would amalgamate with Hitler's new arrivals. "Not so," said the German sources. Each of the interior Germanys continues to value its strong nationalistic pride which none will surrender. The peaceful political tone has been long established and ingrained in the Bod Germans and the newcomers are expected to abide by these standards, the source declared.

The pair of nations could be described somewhat like the U.S.A. and Canada. Each has an English common law tradition and a stranger would not recognize any significant social or political differences between Calgary and Dallas -- except for accent and nationalistic pride.

The German source went on to explain that the tunnel Germans whose forefathers began the exodus would remain economically and socially connected with the old six interior kingdoms of New Germany, but recent fraternization and trade was making differences less recognizable.

In 1943 the tunnel railway custodians named "Two World Railroad Company" were reincorporated under the "Inner Earth Railway Company." On the advice of engineers from Bodland, they sent for a famous Swiss-speaking German engineer named Karl Schneider to rebuild the tunnel on a five-year contract. Schneider's vast knowledge of railway tunneling came as a result of his experience in building the Simplon Tunnel from Milan, Italy through the Alps to Srig, Switzerland and also tunneling jobs in Russia, Australia and South Africa. (On July 1, 1977, he completed the north-south tunnel under the Potomac at Washington in three months time with three additional months needed for drying and hardening of the glazed tunnel interiors. As of July 1977, he had two more Potomac tunnels to complete under his contract with Metro.

Schneider's survey crew under the direction of Bod engineers took two years to survey the proposed rerouting of the "Inner Earth Railway Company." A total of 316 miles of new tunnels were opened by Bod laser and drilling, often through solid rock. Many additional natural pockets were discovered and these were utilized for freight and railway transit supplies.

After survey completion, Schneider returned to the surface where he hired 5,000 Indians who were familiar with underground mine labor. Schneider also hired experienced bilingual Indian overseers in charge of illiterate Indian workers. They were transported below to quarters located in a rock pocket.

The tunnel beginnings were cut in spiral-shapes for 32 miles, where the gravity pull was unchanged from that on the surface. Below the 32-mile earthen skin, the tunnel was changed from the spiral formation, and descended more vertically at an angle of about 32 degrees. As the Indians descended deep into the rock mantle, they were surrounded by a greater land mass and consequently were able to walk on the entire 360 degrees of inner tunnel circumference and not fall. They, therefore, were unaware that they were employed on a project that was going from the outside to the inside of the Earth's mantle and believed, as they had been told, that they were in a mine digging for gold. Correcting the tunnel at the interior side of the Earth's mantle required another spiral 32 miles from the interior surface. (Hypothetically, a stone dropped from the upper surface into a hole would fall straight through the planet's entire mantle, eventually spiraling to a point mid-way in the mantle, where it would cling to the side of the descending hole or tunnel in the mantle.) The tunnel was finished in 1948, and as a sidelight, Schneider moved enough gold from the project to pay all his expenses. Meanwhile, as new tunneling progressed, the trains continued to carry German emigrants to the interior of the Earth, landing them in the continent of Agraharta, where the original German colonists had first settled. Inner world surface trains and boats then took the emigrants to their new locale inside the Earth's interior in the southern hemisphere.

Trains upbound from inner earth and downbound from outer earth follow the regular falling gravity norm and use breaks and gears until point zero gravity is reached, midway in the mantle. Then, on the second half of their journey, the electric power source is used to ascend.

As the tunnel was drilled and allowed to cool, the monorail system now in use was incrementally installed. Upon completion of the tunnels, new electric trains were brought in from Germany capable of pulling 12 cars. The power source originates at a South Pole generating station inside the earth; the actual source being solar energy coming through the South Pole entrance. The train rides on a double-flanged bottom wheel over a single energized rail. The top of the train is held in place by another double-flanged wheel gliding under a top rail.

The made-in-Germany round-wing planes also had to prove their capabilities quickly. Demands to relocate personnel and equipment were soon begun, using the new planes. After the German equipment and tools for continuing the manufacture of the round-wing planes had been removed to the earth's interior via the South Pole entrance, the five planes were put into international service operating from secret bases in South America. The first industrial task started below was to build a foundry, and the second endeavor was a factory for production of a 120-foot diameter round-wing freighter, a model that the Germans had tested in 1942.

The test flight of the first round-wing freighter made in New Germany was completed in 1946. The giant UFO's first job was to fly to America and haul back six caterpillar machines. German buyers had purchased the machines in Detroit and shipped these earth-movers and their spare parts by train to New Orleans. Then, under cover of darkness, the "caterpillars" were taken on lowboy trailers to a remote farm where they were loaded on the huge, round-wing freighter. Piloted by Captain Eric Von Schusnick, the round-wing plane took off to Brazil to load other accessories and tools. On the second day after leaving the New Orleans area, and stopping over for 36 hours in a hidden Amazon airfield, the freighter landed in New Berlin and discharged its first cargo.

In much the same manner, the fleet of smaller German round-wing planes picked up such equipment as turret lathes, shapers, milling machines, cranes, etc., from secret locations in German and American depots. The American goods bought by Germans prior to the war's end were purchased by their New York office for shipment to Rio de Janeiro, but often were moved out of America by round-wing planes landing in sparsely inhabited desert areas. These goods were paid for by check from Swiss Banks in New York, where German gold was stored by the New York Trading Company.

In late 1944 and early 1945, the Germans also shipped many train-loads of supplies to Spain to be lifted by the round-wing planes or loaded on new super subs and older-class subs nicknamed "sea cows" for eventual delivery up the Amazon to interior ports. These subs were eventually scuttled at the war's end.

Another priority below was for tool and die making and foundry work. Each machine required was shipped below by round-wing plane in order to resume the various capital projects including a fleet of round-wing planes and other defense priority needs. In 1946, exploration teams in the interior had located excellent deposits of iron, copper and aluminum and these were now used in the foundry. Wooden products including finished plywood were shipped down from Brazil via the tunnel.

In the first few months of operation in 1944 and 1945, the Germans had proven the round-wing plane was superior to any conventional aircraft and would become the actual workhorse and front line military aircraft of the world by the year 2000. But in 1945, the total reality of the German evacuation had not been fathomed. The only clues of which the allies were certain were that masses of Germans, including Hitler had disappeared.

Hitler, after debarking from his submarine, had arrived in Argentina by way of a routing through Columbia and Brazil. His trip was deliberately unhurried until initial preparations and housing were ready below in New Berlin. King Haakkuuss of Bodland sent his personal space ship to Argentina to bring Hitler below. Upon arrival in the capital of Bodland, Hitler was told authoritatively the peaceful conditions of residence by which he and his subjects must abide in their new land. Hitler re-affirmed his acceptance pledge in what would ultimately lead him into an untried life of human co-existence.

Upon arrival King Haakkuuss told Hitler: "We have permitted you to emigrate because you will serve as the catalyst by which New Germany will be reborn. Your good ideas you should keep and develop. The bad must be eradicated. The hateful aspects of your character must never assert themselves here below and notwithstanding your heinous record of evil to fellow mankind, we believe you can channel your drive into a positive direction as a national leader." The King added, "But your Nazi cronies from above like Borman, Himmler, Goering, etc. can never come below. We (the Bods) will personally scrutinize each arrival." He concluded: "It will take three generations to correct your (Hitler's) past mistakes in wrongfully indoctrinating German youth, and six generations will be required to bury completely the national instincts of aggressive and wasteful war."

In 1945 and 1946, American OSS agents began closing their net on the Iquitos, Peru area. Here the Germans were seen departing for the interior via the Inner World Railway. The American observers were confronted now by a different German than those who had left Europe weeks or months before. Now the Americans, and other international agents, including the British and Canadians, ran into confident Germans who revealed openly their true Teutonic character. They were still secretive about their reasons for being in that part of the world. Camps of Germans were hidden in Brazil, Columbia, Ecuador, British Guiana and other outlying areas. These Germans were emerging when called to take the last train ride to their new homeland. People with skills and professions needed below were sent down in the first trains available, while those of top priority were flown through the South Pole entrance in German or Bod round-wing planes. Eventually 2-1/2 million Germans settled below. In 1944-45 alone, combined methods of transportation including the railroad and round-wing planes carried over 200,000 Germans below. No annual census was taken, but the population expansions into the interior increased yearly. By 1948, German girls from the homeland began arriving and marrying their sweethearts. Families, whose husbands had gone below in the first waves, were also reunited by various methods and routings. When completed in 1948 the "Space Elevator" was carrying up to 3,600 passengers weekly, most traveling down. Schedules ran three times weekly each way.

In 1948 the new train schedule made six stops for food, beverage and lodging, traveling up to 300-miles- per-hour between stations, and traversing the entire distance in less than a 24-hour period. Scores of smaller inner tunnel communities were built up in newly discovered pockets, and interior-based local trains that never surfaced served these new communities. In 1978, three to five-car trains carried only 300 to 500 passengers weekly, the remaining cars being filled with freight and commodities.

A large German community has grown up in the vicinity of the underground depot that once was only a hole into a cave in 1572 and for eons of time before that. Today Germans return to the surface close to Iquitos, thence to Manaus and via VARIG Airways fly to Rio de Janeiro. From there they travel by Pan Am to San Juan, Puerto Rico or Lisbon, Portugal and then by plane or train to Germany.

Currently, many of these interior Germans are coming back to the surface to retire in their homeland. Some of the Germans also elect to retire in various South American countries or the United States, Canada, Britain and Spain rather than go to their old homelands in communist held East Germany.

In 1946 while the Bods strictly supervised the building of a minimal aerial, navy and land force to be used only for New Germany's national police protection and defense, a setback occurred which was to test their survival. It was from an unexpected source.

On July 12, 1946, inner-world radar picked up an airborne invasion -- bogies coming from the north.

The New Germans knew an enemy might attack them from either the large 1,400-mile North Pole opening that the Russians had used, or the South Pole entrance. The Germans were psychologically unprepared for this particular confrontation. The bogies were not airplanes or rockets sent down from their former surface enemies. They were round-wing planes.

The old, inner-world Viking race to the north had been watching the Germans grow in strength. Disliking what they saw in this militaristic action on the part of the new inhabitants of the interior of the earth, and aware of Nazi occupation of Norway and Denmark, the Vikings attacked the new Germans. The German defense was to be their first attempt to defend their new land.

Radar picked up the Viking round-wing planes moving southward toward New Berlin and New Hamburg at 5,000 miles per hour, from a northern city in Vikingland called Kupenhaggen (population 3,000,000). A red alert was sounded and five German UFO's, the first ones made in upper Germany before surrender, took to the air.

The aerial vanguards of the 12-million strong Viking nation on the continent called Vikingland had challenged the small 300,000 fledgling German nation. The aerial battle had lasted sporadically for several hours when the Atlanteans (Atturians) delivered an ultimatum to the Vikings that if they didn't stop the attack, the Atlantean craft would join the fray and cut up the Vikings with advanced lasers. The Atlanteans reassured the Vikings that the Germans must be made welcome inasmuch as they were making unclaimed arid land productive. The New Atlanteans further told the Vikings that the New Germans (related to the Vikings) in peacetime were the most productive people on the face of the upper earth -- but in war could be the most destructive. Finally, the Atlantean ambassador to the Vikings stated: "Let the newly arrived Germans live among us in peace! We don't want the war from above renewed below."

Unbeknownst to the combatants or to the Atlanteans (Atturians) the Bodlanders who had been grievously watching the unexpected Inner World beginnings of a war, moved in with their own round-wing planes. Moving ahead and above the advancing Viking formation, the Bod craft repeatedly threw out what appeared to be a solid force field. The oncoming Viking craft, unaware of the invention, struck the barriers and were turned back. The beginning of a war of attrition was stopped. (As far as is known, the above account is the first mention of the Bod's involvement in preventing the New Germans and the Vikings widening that aerial confrontation in the Inner World.)

But the New Germans had no sooner tested their combat abilities against the Vikings within the earth when an old foe from above began to stir.

Chapter X

Admiral Richard E. Byrd Finds The South Pole Entrance to Inner World

"Hitler is alive!" Those were the first words Joseph Stalin said to President Harry Truman and Prime Minister Churchill when a discreet moment was available at the 1945 Potsdam Conference.

"The body in the bunker was not that of Hitler," Stalin said. "The hair, teeth and fingerprints do not match." Then he gave complete autopsy details to the Prime Minister of England and the President of the United States. At the Potsdam conference, it was agreed America would send the first expeditionary force to the Antarctic to look for the departed German leader and the missing nationals who had left Berlin and Germany by various routes in late '44 and early '45. It was also agreed that as soon as preparations could be made the United States would invade the Antarctic, and the old allies, including Russia would stand by if further offensive action were needed once the Germans were located.

Therefore, according to plan, the United States assembled its Russian and British approved South Polar expedition. Existence of the round-wing planes would remain secret, and only conventional weaponry would be deployed. The entire 1946-1947 operation was billed as the largest expedition ever sent to the Antarctic and was given publicity for the media back home, rather than attempting to keep the expedition secret. It was also intended to establish a permanent U.S. base in the subcontinent, a move that had been delayed when the temporary American bases of 1939 and 1940 were abandoned because of the war. Although Admiral Byrd was the figurehead of the expedition, his real role was disguised. He would lead "a search and find an entrance into the Antarctic continent" where it was assumed many German leaders and troops had retreated.

An accompanying naval force out of Norfolk, Virginia under Rear Admiral Richard H. Cruzen included thirteen war ships, nineteen planes, supply and transport vessels equipped with helicopters, an icebreaker to lead the way, and a submarine to aid in any type of underwater research or assistance. All vehicles were caterpillar tread type tractors as these would be required to tow overland the sleigh and toboggan loads of building materials, Quonset huts, warehouse, weather stations, abundant food, clothing and all accessories, especially fuel and oil to transport a 4,000 man force in a hostile freezing land where ice and snow was up to two miles in depth. The Antarctic adventure was a full scale naval and overland expedition and in a real sense was a continuation of World War II, provided an enemy could be located in the 5-1/2 million square miles of Antarctic mountains and vast snowy wastes.

At Christchurch in New Zealand a branch station was set up as the midpoint for communications between there and McMurdo Sound, 2365 miles away. Also, at Christchurch additional repair parts and supplies would be stored for eventual movement to the Antarctic where they would be required by the 4,000-man force.

Byrd had a final meeting with the military in the United States at which time, on orders of President Truman, he was forbidden to fly his own aircraft until he reached the Antarctic.

The flight to McMurdo Base departed from the Hueneme, California base February 1, and it carried Byrd's co-pilot (and navigator combined), radioman, and photographer representing the National Science Foundation and National Geographic Society. They set a course for Hawaii as passenger Byrd sat back reminiscing with his navigator.

The following day Admiral Byrd and his crew took off from Honolulu for the aircraft carrier where his Antarctic plane was waiting to take them on the last leg of the journey into the South Pole Region to find the whereabouts of the 250,000 Germans. On the fourth day after departure from Port Hueneme, Admiral Byrd arrived at McMurdo Base in the Antarctic where his fixed-wing plane would be observed from a round-wing plane of German origin hovering silently above the Sound.

Byrd's team had been the first to fly over the South Pole on November 29, 1929, and for him this updated trip, of course, was no mere polar exercise.

On this occasion he was resolved to find the missing Germans. The irony surrounding the expedition's concept, however, was that while some planners were told it was a polar training expedition, Byrd knew from three former expeditions into the Antarctic that this trip would entail untold hazards and perhaps a lot more than a hidden valley where rumors told of a German hideout, or last stand.

It was Admiral Byrd's May 9, 1926 aerial expedition in search of the North Pole, accompanied by co-pilot Floyd Bennett, that first fired his zeal to return again and again to the Polar ends of the earth.

It was Bennett who first awakened Byrd's imagination about the inner earth being hollow with possible entrances at both Poles.

Bennett had long noted an important similarity in all previous Arctic (North Pole) accounts. The weather became warmer the farther north a traveler went. For instance, the log of Dr. Fridtjof Nansen, 1893-6, seemed to show conclusive proof that the North Polar Region was not a frigid ocean of ice. Nansen's conclusions read: "We have demonstrated that the sea in the immediate neighborhood of the pole...in all probabilities lies in a deep basin, not a shallow one...the ice seemed to drift northerly, unimpeded..."

(In 1980, NASA maps confirm that the Arctic's ocean floor is a sloping depression beginning in northern Greenland and running about 2,200 miles. Actually the incline of the ocean bed begins about the 85th parallel and eventually becomes the throat of the Arctic that leads into the hollow Earth.)

The official released version of Byrd's 1926 flight from Spitsbergen to the North Pole is unimaginative and sterile. Byrd's log is reported to have recorded the following: "We reached the North Pole. After taking two sun sights and many pictures, we went on for several miles in the direction we had come, and made another larger circle to be sure to take in the North Pole."

Not disclosed in the official accounts is the following paraphrased but authentic record of that 1926 journey in its final hours. "Bennet urged Byrd to proceed at their existing altitude over an ocean devoid of ice, the horizon of which seemed to enlarge beyond the 85th parallel. As they continued, the compass became erratic, the tailwind increased and the sun's position sank lower. The tri-motored Ford plane continued only a short distance into this area of mechanical confusion and navigational uncertainty. Then Byrd, becoming fearful, decided to turn back and head for base." They had seen and felt the unknown. From that day on Byrd and Bennett (until his death in 1928) shared the same observations and determination. They had observed that the spherical earth was concave at the so-called top of the planet, and that the Arctic Ocean apparently disappeared into an unending black hole. Before they reached base, they had resolved to return.

During the following year, 1927, (the author confirmed) Byrd and Bennett flew again to the top of the world but this time they penetrated into the earth's interior. Their new sponsor was the United States Navy. They departed in secret from an unknown base at an unknown time, and to this day no official word of that flight has been made available to biographers or compilers. Byrd is reported to have flown a total of 1,700 miles, the most astonishing time of which was spent inside the earth's interior. His diary of the event, records sightings of what looked like prehistoric animals, green forests, mountains, lakes, rivers in a warm climate where tall, fair people waved to the fliers. Pictures of these interior locales were actually seen by the researcher.

Richard Evelyn Byrd, descendent of an old Virginian family and who served in the U.S. Navy prior to World War I and as an aviation instructor during the war, was to become illustrious – in a tragic way. The panoramic evidence of that historic 1927 voyage was never to be shown or admitted to even exist. President Calvin Coolidge on seeing the over 300 pictures and upon reading the log of the flight said emphatically: "No one! Absolutely no one will believe this report! Let's keep it quiet! If we release the information, we will become the laughing stock of the nation and the world." President Coolidge was a New England realist. The decision to withhold the story of Byrd's epic journey was not a contrived cover-up. There was no national security involved. Others beside the President who saw the pictures and read the log simply believed that the phenomena of a world within a world was so fantastic as to be preposterous. (A secretary to the late President Coolidge verified the official reaction.)

The pictures and log of that Byrd flight to the interior of the earth were sealed and immediately placed in a vault at the Library of Congress. They lay there untouched for 12 years. When World War II began, the secret account of Byrd's 1927 flight was reviewed and became classified under the name "White Sheet Project". In the second year of the war, American Intelligence and the executive branch realized the significance of another world within a world, especially when Jonathon Caldwell, on a training flight in a round-wing plane whose routing was over the North Pole, drifted into the black void which Byrd had come upon in 1927. Consequently, the Byrd flight, along with Caldwell's 1940 log was relabeled the "White Pole Project". When World War II hostilities ceased in 1945 the "White Pole Project" was placed under a new Navy department called Polar Archives, where it still operates in 1978 on the sixth floor of the National Archives. In the 1960's, NASA Archives became the repository for much of the Polar activities because of the intense space craft action and related world research at the polar-regions.

With the reader made aware of the foregoing background information on Byrd's early Arctic exploits, we can now return to the circumstances surrounding his 1946 flight into the Antarctic, about which this chapter is mainly concerned.

Before departure for that 1946 flight, the Navy allowed Byrd to add to his extensive first-hand knowledge of the Antarctic by perusal of newly acquired information taken from captured German records and books. Most believable to Byrd were the exploits and observations of German teams sent to the Antarctic from 1937 onward. These aerial and land teams had mapped and photographed much of the subcontinent and the reports on their Antarctic findings were an engrossing study that had stimulated naval curiosity. Byrd was instinctively aware that the Germans would have preferred that these classified reports had not been moved to the Americas, for they gave helpful clues and conclusions about German intentions at the South Pole. Not all the classified information regarding the probes on the Pole had been given to Byrd, but the facts he had assimilated assured him that regardless of how incredible polar openings to the interior of the planet were regarded by those to whom he spoke, an entrance to the inner earth could indeed exist, regardless of scientific opinion. The location of such an opening, if it existed, should be near the South Pole beneath a cloud-covered area, which Byrd had observed in 1929 but had not been able to check. That possible site was east of the Pole on a line of flight nearby the 171st meridian.

Reflecting again on his past Polar accomplishments and the frustrations arising from government bureaucracy, Byrd was cognizant that 17 years after his last aerial trip to the South Pole he and a new crew were now heading into the Antarctic again. His polar adventures might unravel the enigma of the sub-continent.

From McMurdo, Admiral Byrd and his crew were flown to the aircraft carrier 300 miles north in the Antarctic waters. A final briefing took place, and the flight was scheduled for the following morning.

Each man on the crew had taken an oath of secrecy. If they failed to return after a given period of time in the so-called Antarctic exercise, a massive emergency search was to be started. Regardless of the outcome, it was agreed not to inform the public of the true purpose of the excursion into the unknown.

In the wisdom of the Joint Chiefs of Staff, Byrd had not been told the secret of the round-wing plane which America then possessed.

Byrd and his men checked out the conventional aircraft on which they had trained in the United States. It was called a Falcon, but had no relationship to the 1929 Falcon built by Curtis Wright Aircraft Company. This particular aircraft had been specially constructed in 1946 for high speed and great endurance. The entire project under which it was conceived and designed by the Navy was rushed to completion under top secrecy. The airplane's speed is unknown but presumed to have been a good margin over 300 miles per hour. Its range was over 6,000 miles. The Pratt and Whitney engines were also carefully tuned and all unused space in the aircraft was filled with extra gasoline containers, each filled with 100 gallons and tapped into the main fuel supply line to the engines. Extra food rations, because of their added weight, had been kept to a minimum. In case of emergency landing, there would be no hope of survival, particularly in the rarefied atmosphere of the mountain range that barred their path to the area of search in the South Pole region.

For takeoff, the plane was over heavy. Even with catapult assistance the pilot had difficulty sustaining safe height. It became necessary to fly at 5,000 feet maximum for over six hours until extra fuel was used up and its containers thrown overboard.

The following are notes from the log kept by Admiral Richard E. Byrd on his exploratory trip to and beyond the South Pole and into the interior of the Earth. On February 5, 1946, the log begins: "Catapulted from aircraft carrier with full tanks plus extra tanks;

the carrier located about 300 miles due north of the McMurdo Base; clear skies, headed for the settlement there, reaching it about 6:50 A.M., circled the settlement; flew low, waving to those on the ground who waved in return. (Byrd's flight from McMurdo, 400 miles due west to the first mountain chain's rim was time-consuming inasmuch as it became expedient to burn off his aircraft's excess fuel. It was too overloaded to permit a sufficient gain in altitude.) Arrived first designated area at 3:00 P.M. our time, skies very clear, Coal Sack would be seen very clearly overhead, circled the area three times, dropped a small American flag outside the window to claim for the U.S.A. (Reason for circling area was because aircraft was still unable to attain sufficient altitude to cruise over the 10,500 foot pass of the Axel Heiberg glazier onto the central plateau where the supposed valley might begin into the planet's interior).

"Dropped the empty gasoline drums by means of ejection chute in aircraft floor. After several hours, gross weight was reduced enough to gain height and cross the mountain rim.

"4:20 P.M. -- Arrived at the edge of the valley, sun was still bright in the sky. We started down following the contour of the ground, taking note of the terrain as we descended. At first, slope is gradual then it becomes steeper as though one were going down the side of a mountain. (Navigator now concerned that too much excess was burned off.)

"4:30 P.M. -- Ice Cap beginning to get thinner, now beginning to see the exposed side of the mountain. Our outside temperature gauge has also recorded a 10-degree rise from 60 below zero, observed at the start of the descent.

"5:00 P.M. -- We are still following a slope down, the ice is now very thin on the rocks that cover the slope, see some black spots that could be coal, sun is still high in the sky, temperature continues to show a slow steady rise, it could even be tropical at the bottom of the valley, maybe even a Shangri-La only time will tell.

"5: 30 P. M. - - Altimeter shows drop of about one mile since we entered the valley. We have traveled some 300 plus miles in a down slope, sides seem to be gradually getting steeper.

"6:00 P.M. -- Ice completely gone, rocks now bare, temperature shows a steady rise, getting warmer as we go deeper, all of a sudden we seem to have hit a bottomless pit in which the sides slope straight down, compass gone completely crazy and is not working at all. We are now spiraling downward; the sun is still shining, but gets dimmer as we descend.

"7:00 P.M. -- We have been descending into the hole for almost an hour, air outside continues getting warmer, a few minutes ago we passed a small waterfall from which steam seemed to be coming, we circled so that our photographer could get a picture. As the sun was dim, we had to use floodlights to enable a good photograph.

"8:00 P.M. -- We are nosing down as if traveling on level ground, the compass now not working at all, altimeter has shown a steady fall, instruments indicate our ground speed has slowed to about 50 miles per hour. Why are we traveling so slowly?

"9:00 P.M. -- Calculate we have traveled down for at least 100 miles from the top of the hole, fuel is half gone, dropped another empty gas tank. (Extra gasoline cans hold 100 gallons each, made of aluminum 1/8" thick.) It fell horizontally toward the wall as if being pulled toward ground; readings are crazy here, haven't enough fuel to travel further into the earth. (Bell has sounded indicating fuel supply in main tanks half gone.) We'll turn back and properly explore on future expedition. Our fuel will get us back if we start now, radio is dead, no contact. (Crew was confused because though not weightless, they were able to walk up the sides and on roof of the plane, and remain perpendicular.) Four synchronized clocks on board plus crew's watches kept time, but, later it was shown all clocks and watches had gained seven hours.

"10:00 P.M. -- We are now traveling up at a faster speed than we went down, and it is as if we were traveling along level ground; no explanation of it. It is starting to get cooler outside as we move towards the surface.

"11:00 P.M. -- We are now getting near the top where the steep drop off started, have given orders to fly a right angle from our course to determine the diameter of the shaft, cold is starting to get intense outside again.

"12:00 Midnight -- We have traveled for about an hour and we have returned to approximately our starting point, navigator believes hole to be over 100 miles in diameter. We are now ascending and steadily gaining speed with wind in our rear, temperature outside gets colder, speed increases automatically."

FOOTNOTE: Byrd later made a special report on how his speed changed without pilot aid from 300 miles per hour on the surface down to about 50 miles per hour descending the hole or shaft. He also told how the temperature went from minus 60 degrees Fahrenheit on the surface to more than plus 60 degrees Fahrenheit at the point of return during his descent. (They also reported seeing steam coming out of more than one hole in the rocks and discovered cloud formations within the 125-mile shaft. Their instruments also recorded a steady stream of air corning from deep within the shaft that he felt accounted for their decreased speed in descent. The Admiral recorded that the feeling within the great shaft to the interior was uncanny, as if one were on a different planet.)

"1:00 A.M. -- We are now out of the shaft and going up on the slope; have the movie camera taking shots of all rocks and looking for signs of life or vegetation as we ascend, ground ice forming and getting thicker as we go up.

"2:00 A.M. -- We are now at top of valley and will fly across to record the distance. Can barely see the sun corning up in the north. At this time of year it stays up most of the time. About four hours of night.

"3:00 A.M. -- We are across the top, finally, navigator calculated it approximately 500 miles in diameter at the top of the funnel. We are now heading for home base and the carrier."

While in the throat of the funnel (or as Byrd called it, the spiral of the screw) the crew saw in the distance a formation of at least five UFO's converging from deeper in the interior. This sighting was also tracked on their navigational radar. As the UFO formation reached Byrd's unarmed plane, a craft positioned itself on each wing tip of the American plane. Byrd's photographer continued to photograph his silent pacers that revealed clearly defined German swastikas on their tops and bottoms.

Actually, the German circular winged planes made no warlike maneuvers nor did they make radio contact with Byrd on that particular expedition. Bold, but not foolish, Byrd's pilot was instructed to take no evasive action, and the photographer advised to continue photographing with the still cameras and automatics. Later, over 300 interior photos sent to the National Science Foundation and the National Archives, would comprise the evidence that Admiral Byrd and his crew brought back.

"1:00 P.M. -- We are now back on the aircraft carrier having landed with no problem. After a good rest, we will fly to New Zealand tomorrow for immediate return to the United States."

According to the clocks on board the Falcon aircraft, the flight lasted 31 hours, but aircraft carrier time showed the Falcon had been absent 23 hours. Upon his arrival at the aircraft carrier, Byrd sent a coded report to Washington; then the Admiral and his crew rested for three full days on the carrier. In addition to the coded report, a fast reconnaissance aircraft took special documents and film to Washington via Sydney, Christchurch and Panama. Upon Byrd's later arrival in the United States, the Admiral was immediately escorted to a top-secret meeting at the Pentagon with the heads of various armed services.

Extracts from his log were read and hundreds of feet of movie footage were shown and explained to the military brass.

(Today, the specially built Falcon is under wraps at Wright Patterson Field, Dayton, Ohio. When the Navy releases the facts of this expedition, the Byrd plane will go on display at the Smithsonian

Institute).

The log book of the Falcon, written by the navigator and signed by Byrd was formerly stored in a safe in a single room in the National Archives, used only for the custody of this historical document. It could not be seen without a presidential order. The authors briefly examined it in 1976 for one hour while two security personnel stood by. A second examination in 1977 was permitted with the help of Senator Lawton Chiles of Florida. In 1978, the log was moved to underground history vaults in the U.S. Air Force Kensington Tombs.

After the movie showing of the Byrd Antarctic expedition, a meeting of the Joint Chiefs of Staff was held with President Harry S. Truman presiding. Conclusions of that historic meeting were recorded. Immediate plans were made for Byrd to return to the bottomless hole at the southern end of the world, penetrate into the interior, and locate the German base with its round-wing planes. The date for re-entry was set for February 16, 1947. The American squadron would again ride against the Germans on conventional, propeller driven, fixed wing aircraft. As for Byrd, he was still not told of the Jefferson round-wing project.

Thus, there continued the cover-up of America's activities in the Antarctic that was to prevent the public from knowing the true intentions of the United States and its post-war allies.

Chapter XI

Byrd Stalks the Missing Nazis

On February 16, 1947, Admiral Richard E. Byrd led his squadron of eight propeller-driven Falcon bombers to the South Pole to test German resistance. Each plane was powered by four Pratt & Whitney engines and tuned with precision for the endurance flight into the unknown interior of the earth. The planes were fully armed, but orders from President Truman were that Byrd was not to fire on any German craft he met in the hollow earth.

As the squadron repeated the flight pattern executed the year before, Byrd and his crew surveyed the terrain. Only this time, besides his own crew, a total of 60 astonished combat veteran Americans were descending in a straight southerly line towards the interior of a planet that was presumed to be of a solid molten core. They carefully noted that the mouth of the double funnel or "screw" as Byrd called it, had a 500-mile opening in the bottom of the Antarctic valley that tapered down to a diameter of 125 miles. Through this opening they would fly for 800 miles towards the interior, before emerging again in a vortex-like aperture inside the earth.

Gradually, the bottom of the hole to the interior widened as it did at the topside until the squadron of Falcons found themselves entering into a hollow world within a world. Above the planes, the crew saw what appeared to be sky and clouds. Below was sea and land just as above the entrance. They were now in the interior of the hollow earth which Byrd in 1929 had described as "that enchanted continent in the sky - - a land of everlasting mystery". (Whereas on the outer surface of the planet a direct line of vision on the convex surface is seven miles, a straight visual sighting on the surface of the earth's interior would be ad infinitum except for air impurities.)

Compasses on the aircraft strangely enough returned to normal upon their entrance to the interior of the earth. They were now descending further inside the earth's sphere, flying in an atmosphere identical to that on the outside of the planet. The seas and land masses clung to the interior walls, and the void between was filled with clouds and light in which there were seen mirages of the sea and terrain below. As the outside earthlings sped on at 259 miles per hour every sight they beheld triggered new stimuli of curiosity. They were not flying into a molten mass, and the only heat and light energy source came from a diminutive misty ball of fire, an interior sun that seemed to hang suspended in front of them in the center of the globe's interior.

The land masses below were protrusions on the inside of the earth's 800 to 1,200 mile thick mantle. The flyers observed one major difference from the outside of their planet. The interior appeared to have a greater land surface, for as they continued south, their visions widened in this new concave world surrounding them. There were no celestial bearings, no Pole Star or planet Venus on which to take a dead reckoning. Each hoped their squadron could find its way out.

In this unbelievable world of fantasy, Admiral Richard E. Byrd commanding eight navy Falcons and 60 airmen went stalking Germans.

A bellicose nation from the earth's surface had broken into the interior in search of another Aryan race with which they had fought two world wars in the present century. Was the "enemy" here in this lair? And would he fight?

Byrd had taken his squadron further than he himself had ventured the year before. He was now recording a distance of over 2,400 air miles from base.

Still flying north at approximately 10,000 feet, Byrd's navigator, Captain Ben Miller, of Navy air arm, spotted what appeared to be an airfield. (Only hours before, Capt. Miller had joined Byrd's crew. He had temporarily turned over to his second in command the command of his carrier. It was the same carrier on which Byrd's original navigator had taken ill at the last moment.) All eyes of the American squadron peered down and confirmed the sighting. A closer scrutiny revealed various fixed wing aircraft lined up in rows and high-powered lenses picked up their identity markings; swastikas, the emblems of Nazi Germany, were clearly visible.

The American squadron flew on. They reached a point of 2,700 miles within the earth before the order was given by Byrd to return. The cameras on Byrd's plane whirred away as a pictorial account of his journey was made.

An hour later the planes returned over the same compass bearing. Down below they had seen rows of buildings on their trip north and endless planes at a particular bearing. Now these were gone. (The pictures developed by National Defense later showed the airport had been quickly camouflaged.) Suddenly, the Falcon pilots observed that they had uninvited company. Above them and behind on their tails, were five unmarked round-wing planes which the Germans had finally elected to expose.

Byrd had come to this new German world poorly prepared for decisions on the conduct of aerial confrontation. He was primarily an explorer. The Joint Chiefs of Staff had assessed his capabilities and at a last minute briefing Byrd was ordered not to fire on any Germans if he encountered them in flight. Those instructions exist today and were explicit. In addition, Byrd did not evaluate his squadron's vulnerability in the present air situation that the five round-wing planes controlled. And worse, he regarded the German-piloted round-wing planes his natural enemy with whom there could be no compromise. Yet, Byrd was not a combat admiral, and suddenly he was catapulted into making a decision whether to accept or decline aerial combat. Did he fail at that time to discern that his so called "enemy" had abandoned the propeller-driven or even jet-powered aircraft of World War II vintage? Certainly Byrd was cognizant from his experience the year before that the Germans now rode the sky in advanced design aircraft that made his conventional Falcon aircraft completely outmoded.

But, on the other hand, giving Admiral Byrd the benefit of the doubt, did he purposely intend to confront the Germans and make them show their hand? No one knows what illogical drive motivated him in his last moment decisions, but they were not the result of any wise on-the-spot military sagacity or desire for survival. The only thing that can be said on behalf of Byrd is that the round-wing planes were conundrums that in his mind produced a panic.

Byrd had already given orders to his own gunners to be prepared to fire (and his co-pilot reminded him the order should be rescinded). Therefore, all of his aircraft were in a state of combat readiness. Perhaps ten seconds remained in which the Admiral could have changed his mind.

Then Byrd received an unexpected message on his wavelength from outside his aircraft. "Admiral Byrd, this is General Kurt Von Ludwig, commander of the flying ships you see above. Our fire power has your squadron covered."

The same German commander, who was later interviewed to substantiate this episode, continued: "World War II is over. Leave us alone and return to your base. However, if you wish to land at our station in peace, we shall receive you Americans in peace, for you are not our enemies. Our aircraft and weapons are so superior to yours that I advise you not to fire on us. There is no chance for your squadron to survive our attack if you insist on fighting. I would also remind you that you are over territory controlled by New Germany and that you are here under our sufferance."

Commander Byrd listened but did not reply. When the German had finished speaking, Byrd gave his order in two words: "Open Fire!" His aircraft hardly had time to comply before the sky seemed to explode.

Those Falcons hit by the saucers' laser beams broke up and spiraled or nose dived to earth where the crews were killed on impact.

From what looked like hidden anti-aircraft gun sites on the land below there emanated pencil-thin broken beams of red light. An American witness in one of the planes struck with this ray weapon said, "the ray seemed to let us down gradually and our pilot was helpless to maintain control; we had to ditch. Those who could, bailed out."

Admiral Byrd watched his entire supporting aircraft plummeting out of the sky nearby. Suddenly, the voice of the German commander broke into his wavelength again. "Commander Byrd, you are a fool. You have sacrificed your own men. You were warned. Now leave this land and never return. Leave at once." Byrd was shaken and quickly went into shock. Miller took over the controls and pointed the aircraft for the opening that led to the topside of the world. Byrd had carried out his orders to find the Germans. He had entered the young lion's den; but he was no Daniel.

The scene that followed as the American planes crashed to earth was not reminiscent of a wartime landing in hostile enemy territory. American survivors picked up by the Germans were interviewed in 1977 to verify the German version of what took place.

The Germans immediately mounted an all-out rescue attempt in order to save the American airmen. Some of the crashed American planes were not severely disabled. From these the occupants quickly crawled out with their hands over their heads. They were met by Germans who immediately disarmed them and asked them to drop their hands, saying that they were in friendly territory. German crews hurriedly raced to the totally demolished American planes, extinguished fires, and removed bodies in an attempt to save lives. Twenty-six live Americans were finally assembled that day by the Germans as ambulances with doctors sped to the scene. Paramedics administered first aid to the surviving American crewmembers as the ambulances headed to nearby hospitals in New Berlin. At the hospital, German specialists set limbs and carefully stitched wounds and made the Americans as comfortable as possible. Occasionally, the Germans addressed the Americans in English, some quietly telling how they had taken their degrees at German and American institutions.

Crewmembers not severely injured were taken into the city. A sign on the outskirts said, "New Berlin". The "prisoners" were then given an escorted automobile tour of the emerging city that the Germans had secretly begun in early 1940. Examples of buildings designed by Albert Spear on the order of Adolf Hitler were shown to the visitors. Stunned by the cautious friendliness of the Germans, the Americans were given a meal and made comfortable in a hotel.

But not all the invading Americans were so fortunate. As Byrd's plane sped homeward to his carrier base, German morticians embalmed and dressed the young Americans killed in the New Berlin raid. Using I.D. cards, victims were identified; features restored when necessary and then redressed in their own flight suits. The remains were placed in sealed plastic coffins.

The German commander came in and met some of the surviving American officers. Introducing himself, he called them "heroic fools."

The next day was February 17, 1947. Open German army trucks had picked up the various bodies of the young Americans. The vehicles assembled and slowly the cortege bore the dead American airmen through the broad streets of the new city. At the convoy's head, a German military band played Mendholson's Funeral March. Behind the cortege German airmen themselves, in honor, marched in slow step. Escorted in cars, American survivors brought up the rear.

As the funeral procession moved toward the airfield, cannons were fired in the air; and all German flags on Government buildings flew at half-mast as the dead and living Americans were prepared for their trip home. For the Americans and the Germans it was the unofficial end of World War II combat.

At the New Berlin Airport five saucers sat waiting. The dead

Americans in unbreakable plastic coffins were placed on board another craft. The 24 walking cases were taken on board two other German craft. Finally, Commander Kurt Von Ludwig and his crew boarded the lead ship.

A squadron of five German UFO's rose silently and headed south to the hole at the end of the world to pay a regretful respect to 60 living and dead Americans.

Emerging from the South Pole funnel, the saucers took a northerly course from the Antarctic continent towards Australia. Approximately 1,800 miles southwest of Sydney, Australia, a U.S. aircraft carrier hove to at the radio request of the German commander. As fleet commander Rear Admiral Cruzen listened, flat top Commander Ben Miller, now back in control of his own ship, was hooked into the radio of the German round-wing plane. A friend of Commander Miller then spoke from the German craft.

The American survivor appealed to the commanding officer to allow the Germans to land on one end of the carrier flight deck to deliver American survivors. The German UFO's sat down as Commander Kurt Von Ludwig hovered above in an attitude of surveillance. Americans stood down. No guns were drawn. No orders were given. No battle positions were taken.

The walking Americans stepped out and then moved to the other German round-wing planes to remove the wounded. These were placed or helped on deck.

American sailors began to stand at attention and many officers stood at silent salute. No American word had been spoken. No German voice had been heard. When the last stretcher was removed, the German UFO's silently lifted and joined their commander aloft, and then suddenly they were gone.

Under sedation in the carrier's sickbay, Admiral Byrd had missed the last chapter of the tragic drama he had begun.

From below the carrier flight deck, an ambulance plane was hoisted. Within 20 minutes it too was airborne, headed for Honolulu, Hawaii, where Pearl Harbor was alerted to receive the injured.

The same night, over 10,000 miles away from the carrier, five round-wing planes appeared at 8:00 P.M. over Arlington, Virginia. They stopped in mid-air and hovered over the tomb of World War I's Unknown Soldier.

A German plane broke formation and landed in an open area near the tomb. The door of the craft opened and darkened forms brought out the bodies of the 30 American airmen who had perished two days before.

There is a spirit, believed to be that of the Unknown Soldier, which had appeared often in the past whenever a body lay in state under the Capitol Rotunda. Many at Kennedy's death saw it. It appeared when the body of President Eisenhower lay in state, and it also appeared on the death of Presidents Hoover, Johnson and other notable Americans. The night of February 12, as the Germans placed the bodies of the dead airmen before the Tomb of the Unknown Soldier, completing their task, they stepped back and surveyed the darkened scene for a moment before entering their airships. As they watched, the apparition of the dead doughboy of the American Expeditionary Force in World War I was seen again. It gave a brisk salute and then vanished. The Germans themselves swear this appearance took place.

What arrangements were made with the next of kin is not known. Nevertheless, 30 men of all ranks were buried with full military honors at the cemetery. (Today in a nearby building a bronze plaque reposes, inscribed with the names of the young heroes – and how they died in the center of the Earth. The plaque will be erected in the year 2000 A.D.)

From Arlington Cemetery three of the German saucers stopped above the Capitol Building and two hovered over the White House where the Truman's lived. Simultaneously, all five shone powerful searchlights on the buildings below. The Washington military was alerted. Then the German Commander spoke via the Air Force radio channel. He said: "This display of our strength is a warning. If we so wished we could destroy both your White House and Capitol with deadly rays and within five minutes both historic places would be only ashes. Send no more armed military expeditions below unless America wants full-scale war." the German warned.

"If it is war you seek, then we shall fight you, but as for New Germany, we prefer peace and the friendship of America." The voice finished by saying "the real enemy of both our peoples is Russia." All night the German saucers hovered over Washington. Little did they suspect the U.S. chose not to show any of its military strength from the arsenal of over 500 laser equipped round-wing planes hidden across the land. The German craft departed westward at 9:00 A.M. the next day in a burst of speed.

In 1948, acting independently of the Americans or other nations, the Russians, who had watched the 1947 Byrd foray in the Antarctic from an Antarctic base, sent a fully armed wing of conventional combat aircraft to the earth's interior at the north. The Russians were told of the Americans' 1947 reception by the Germans at the South Pole, but they were uncertain of the outcome. They elected to penetrate the North Pole entrance from their bases. The Russian planes were computer clocked by Americans passing Point Barrow, Alaska heading due east. Canadian bases on three northerly locations kept the Russian planes spotted. The American base reported 102 planes; the Canadian checkpoints reported 97 planes.

The Russians' first aerial encounter was with the guardians of the North Pole entrance – descendants of the Vikings whom the Germans call the "old race." The Russian planes at first were challenged by the "old race" but were allowed to proceed when they claimed they were on a mission to New Germany in the southern hemisphere. The Russian wing, still intact, continued past the man-made orb of light at the equator of the earth's interior and sped toward the southern hemisphere where, in the Germans lion's den, seven UFO's were now waiting.

No Russian enemy plane escaped German wrath. One hundred planes and their crews perished. Those Russian bodies recovered were cremated. In 4-1/2 hours, German UFO's were over Moscow, brazenly scattering the ashes of the Russian dead over the capitol. As in the Washington incident, the Germans broke into the military airwaves and taunted the Russians with the statement: "Here are the remains of your brave airmen you sent down to destroy us!"

Moscow's red alert sounded. And up into the skies went Russian MIG fighters to teach the invading Germans a lesson. One after another, the German machines easily disposed of all the Russian interceptors.

In defiance, the German Commander in his undamaged round-wing plane hovered imperially above.

Then, over the military frequencies that moments before cracked with Russian chatter of aerial combat there came a final German voice: "Next time we will annihilate you."

The Germans flew off -- intact.

They would taunt the Russians over Moscow, year after year, following that memorial victory.

That day, when the squadron leader Von Ludwig landed in New Berlin, he patted his plane and commented: "I shall name her 'Old Ironsides' in honor of today's fight."

Chapter XII

USA Peacefully Invades Inner World

Deep down hundreds of feet below a Kensington, Maryland meadow are stored the logs of Admiral Richard Byrd's tragic 1947 flight into the interior world. In another vault adjoining the Byrd records are some other historical American accomplishments of greater significance contained in 14 classified books listing the records of the U.S. round-wing plane development and the accomplishments of their inaugural flights from 1936 to 1960.

These books tell of men who blazed new trails into the atmosphere of the upper and inner world. Even in 1977, the names of these humble, Lindberg-like aviators must be kept secret because of the knowledge they possess.

In 1978 the authors were given an opportunity to review the logs and papers and make some valid judgments about the history of U.S. aerial progress in the 1940's. To understand the continuous interplay between the German and American endeavors in the attempt to conquer space via dual versions of the round-wing plane, it was necessary first to see the log of Byrd's last flight into the inner world and his unauthorized confrontation with a superior force of New Germans.

The Byrd episode after his 1947 flight into the inner world is continued. Upon his release from the carrier's sickbay where he had been confined while in a state of shock, he was flown to Washington and sent immediately to explain why he had fired on the

Germans and disobeyed orders. His last instructions had been to go armed but not to open fire in the inner world under any circumstances. Hence, on appearing before the Joint Chiefs of Staff after his return he was downgraded for disobeying a written order. But for purposes of avoiding publicity and breaking security, the committee voted not to court-martial him, though a Court of Inquiry was later called to decide on disciplinary action. After all, they argued, Byrd had taken in a squadron of specially built planes, with competent crews, and by his willful ego had sacrificed the lives of over 30 young airmen. Had the Germans not honorably saved the surviving American injured and returned them quickly to the surface aircraft carrier (as recorded in the committee minutes), the mood of the committee most certainly would have been to sentence Byrd. But the national security lid was still on the Antarctic foray. There is also an indication in the minutes that the image of Byrd created by his former explorations might be considered more important to future historians than his fiasco in the inner earth. Nevertheless everyone connected with the expedition considered it a tragedy -- except Byrd. An exhibit placed before the Court of Inquiry in 1947 contained five typed pages written by Byrd, telling of the "successful exploit." The Court of Inquiry read it in frozen disbelief. The navigator's brief one page resume told the real truth, along with witnesses on the Commander's plane and the survivors returned by the Germans.

The findings of the Court of Inquiry, which were forwarded to the Joint Chiefs of Staff, labeled Byrd "mentally incompetent." Furthermore, they recommended that he not be allowed further participation in the program of inner earth penetration, and without further review, because of his insistence in boasting publicly about the episodes.

According to the notes of Byrd's briefing for his 1947 flight, Air Force intelligence had advised the Navy not to take him into confidence on the round-wing planes built in America; because, in so doing, he might be forced to tell the Germans of them if shot down.

The Byrd chapter on the Antarctic was tragically closed. In the next U.S. Air Force book opened deep underground in the Tombs were laid out the original records of the U.S. attempt to correct the Byrd fiasco.

The Joint Chiefs of Staff elected to drop what had amounted to a devious approach to the new German menace located inside the earth. The next penetration of the inner earth would be with round-wing planes carrying competent commanders and trained crews. The new ships would be the sleek, 60-foot craft that had been redesigned in the last year of the war. Top speed of these latest models was over 7,000 miles per hour and they were filled with sophisticated electronic gear for control and navigation. Also built into the craft were long-range, precise photographic cameras.

That first ship left in April, Air Force reference number 16. The ship chosen for that trip could race the sun, beat the wind and chase the stars. One of the 12-man crew referred to her as the sweetheart of time and space. She was so fitted that cameras would photograph a 360-degree arc surrounding her flight pattern as she moved through the inner world. Her point of departure was Los Alamos, New Mexico, and briefing was at 3 a.m. If all went according to flight plan, at 6 a.m. she would enter the inner world at the 125-mile wide, South Pole opening.

The purpose of the flight was purely high level, photographic reconnaissance. The ship carried absolutely no armament. At the briefing, instructions were to fly through the South Pole opening's rock funnel at 5,000 miles per hour, proceeding on a course northward and emerging into the upper world through the North Pole neck of the Arctic Ocean. As the American craft flew through the inner world, three small 16-foot photographic scout planes would leave her hold and do reconnaissance of specific urban and military sites. These small scouts, nicknamed fleas, flew at speeds in excess of 7,000 miles per hour, and returned safely to the 60-foot mother ship before leaving inner earth's air space. Once out of the inner earth the American ship was to land in British Columbia, where debriefing would take place.

The aerial trip was unbelievably successful, and so fast and uncomplicated to the crew that it was described by them as almost uneventful. But the expedition was less so to America's military strategists when they examined the photos. For, beyond doubt, the pictures accurately gave the U.S. its first authentic aerial panorama of the entire interior world. When the photos were evaluated it was decided to send a second flight as soon as maps could be completed and flight plans made ready.

In early June, the second round-wing plane (Air Force reference number 18) took off from British Columbia for the North Pole entrance.

The plane commander was Major R. Davies. He had been told to proceed along the established aerial routing over the Beaufort Sea to a fix above the Canadian Queen Elizabeth Islands. At that coordinate he was to fly on his own reckoning at an elevation of only 3,000 feet. Flight instructions were simple up to the 85th parallel. At that map reference, the navigator was cautioned to keep the surface waters in sight at all times and establish constant elevation readings by radar. It was already known to the Air Forces of Canada and the United States that a real danger existed of literally flying off the horizon in that concave area of the Arctic Ocean where the waters flowed deceptively into the throat of the planet. Ground elevation was also important in that area where compasses and instruments became erratic. Jonathon Caldwell, on an earlier training flight in 1943, had stumbled into that northern void while searching for a route to Europe across the top of the world. The Caldwell log and a subsequent interview with Caldwell by Davies had prepared the crew for any disorientation, panic or confusion which might occur to the uninitiated venturing into the Earth from the top of the world. The journey into the interior of the Earth was, of course, made long before the age of satellites. But today, NASA labels the geographic North Pole as imaginary -- the neutral zone or dead center of the Earth. In this center point of the 1,400 mile wide opening is the location of the imaginary North Pole or the end point of the northern latitudes. No sea or land area exists between the 90th and 85th degree latitudes; it is a gaping hole. Eighty-five degree latitude is located approximately on the edge of the opening to the hollow interior of the Earth. (The true magnetic North Pole starts at 86-degree East Longitude over the TAYMYR peninsula of Siberia.)

But, in 1947, there was no navigational chart on how to reach
the top of the world at the edge of the gaping hole that led to the
interior. With all his sophisticated gear, an airman flying the throat
of the ocean had to do so in airman's parlance "by the seat of his
pants."

At 6 A.M. U.S. Air Force round-wing plane number l6 struck the
throat of the ocean at 500 miles per hour. Speed was corrected
to 750 miles per hour as advised at the early morning briefing.
As the plane descended into the ocean's abyss, she accelerated to
the unbelievable speed of 5,000 miles per hour. All cameras were
turned on as the craft began the 1,200-mile long and deep descent
that would bring her out at the other end into another world. Still
traveling at 3,000 feet elevation, the plane from the upper surface
of the planet came into the interior over sparse settlements of Eskimos, much more advanced than their upper earth relatives. The
American crew had already observed and photographed, to their
astonishment, islands within the ocean's steamy throat that seemed
to support animal life -- namely dinosaurs, extinct on the surface
for an estimated million years. Now, in the Eskimo lands, they
noted herds of seals off rocky outposts.

Following a southeasterly course they soon encountered another
land mass and different civilization. Shortly thereafter they knew
for an historical certainty the territory over which they were flying.

The ship's radar picked up the bogeys. Then visual sightings
confirmed the presence of strangers coming up to meet them. This
would be Major Davies' first test of will and diplomacy. The Major
knew the object of the expedition was primarily exploratory, to
obtain as much low level, photographic evidence as possible, and
that the second reason for the journey into the earth's interior was
to determine if any people encountered were warlike. Another primary objective was to obtain all the information possible about the
establishments of the New Germans.

The investigating ships were round-wing planes similar but smaller
than the United States machine. Suddenly these eight to ten un-

identified bogeys were upon the intruding ship from the upper world. Major Davies pressed a button. Across the bottom of the U.S. Air Force plane large green letters spelled out one word: PEACE. The word flashed on and off as an attention-getter to the rising planes below. The attacking planes came on. Then a voice in excellent English broke over the American intercom. "Identify and establish purpose of air intrusion over Vikingland!"

Major Davies replied: "Our intrusion of your territory is not deliberate, or war-like. We are unarmed. Our intentions are peaceful. This is an American craft and we have come into this land solely to observe what the New Germans are doing and if they are warlike." The reply apparently satisfied the Viking Commander. He replied: "You say you come in peace. Go in peace. But leave our air space at once! Should you wish to visit us again officially, contact our surface intermediary, the Icelandic Government, and the request will be referred to proper authorities!" Major Davies flew away and took his next random bearing on an observed orb of light suspended in the center of the interior. As they sped south, the cameras picked up cities and towns that were similar to those on the surface. They also saw cattle and horses and flocks of sheep tended by shepherds. They beheld it all, the urban and the rural. On high seas they even observed sailing ships and noted the steady north to south trade winds.

The craft still had 2,000 miles of reserve power that he had not used. Unarmed as they were, if attacked they would rely on this reserve speed to develop evasive tactics or leave the scene of confrontation. The crew hoped if they came upon a hostile ship that it would not fire first and ask questions later -- too much later.

Within two hours over a zigzag course the ship came upon a new arid land. They had been told when they reached such an area to expect to meet New German round-wing planes. The pre-flight briefing proved to be correct. Looking down they saw soldiers drilling on the ground in an unmistakable goose step fashion. Many barracks and construction camps were nearby as well as visual evidence of a new railroad line being laid.

The picture was almost serene; when from below anti-aircraft shells began bursting. The pilot shot up to 60,000 feet and re-marked, "I'll bet those shells have 'made in Germany' stamped on them." But the shelling was not maintained for long. On the bottom of the American ship the large green letters PEACE again flashed on and off. The anti-aircraft flak stopped. Helmeted German soldiers stared upwards at the ship that spoke in a language they understood. Continuing its random search, the American ship then flew over a large settlement with an established airport. Breaking into the American wavelength a voice in German asked for identi-fication and flight plan. Major Davies knew a second critical point had been reached in his reconnaissance of the inner world. The flight officer handed the mike to a lieutenant who spoke German, replying to the tower as follows: "We are a lost surface craft origin USA. We can't explain how we arrived here after our compasses went crazy. Instruments now working O.K., but navigator cannot identify landmarks. Can you give directions?" No German round-wing plane took to the air. The cameras on the American craft con-tinued to whir away at the city and its environs below. (Later study showed the city to be New Berlin.)

The German tower operator paused, as if in consultation. Then he replied, giving an explicit bearing on how to depart to the surface. The American craft, still speaking in German, thanked the tower and left the scene on a northerly compass bearing as directed. After flying over the city at 3,000 feet, the American craft began its northerly track and later turned back toward the equator of the interior where a diminutive ball of light acted as a marker.

An hour later speed was reduced as they came up to the interior sun. The light was not intense nor did it hurt the naked eyes. As they approached the huge 600-mile diameter orb, they noticed it resembled a gigantic China lantern, around the circumference of which there went a railed catwalk. Plainly visible were huge doors leading to the interior where it was apparent the source of the diffused light was located. Closer aerial inspection did not reveal how the man-made orb was suspended in mid air. The crew noted that one side of the man-made sun was covered by a shield that, in slowly turning, provided daylight and darkness to the inner world.

It provided periods of light similar that of the outer sun.

While the American craft studied and photographed the scientific marvel, a third confrontation was occurring. From high above another squadron of unidentified Atturrean round-wing planes descended on the lone American ship, which was strictly out of bounds in the inner sun area. The PEACE sign in green was again flashed on and the ship turned for the newcomers to see the sign.

The challenge came abruptly. "Identify presence near sun and explain." The American commander quickly responded. The commander of the Atturrean ship then asked the surface craft to leave and his police squadron escorted the intruding ship back in a northerly direction towards the entrance at the top of the world.

In their flight of fantasy through the inner world the ship cameras also photographed a waterfall that dwarfed Niagara Falls. Nearby was a hydroelectric station. At another location in the continent where the Atturreans dwelt was seen an immense geyser of water throwing millions of gallons of steam and hot water into the air and forming a giant lake. From the reservoir a network of pipes was seen leading to cities many miles distant. The crew were now accustomed to various and changing environments. They came to the conclusion the inner world was not as densely populated as the upper world, but the next primitive tableau was unexpected. For in an unoccupied land in which there were no signs of civilization, the cameras came upon a time frame that went back into ancient history. In this area they actually saw a primitive tribe fighting an enemy with spears, bows and arrows. There is nothing new under the sun, even a man-made sun.

Unhindered and undamaged, the American round-wing plane and her crew of six finally re-entered the air space of the Arctic Ocean. At the top of the throat to the outer world they took a bearing when compasses were stabilized, and the round-wing plane headed for the secret air station in British Columbia. Eager officials would be waiting to hear whether the crew of the peace mission had succeeded in displaying the nation's strength with honor. If they had done so, the shame of the year before would have been nullified.

A new universal word PEACE had been flashed to all nations in the interior, whether the inhabitants spoke German or Scandinavian or the old language of the world. But even then, on reassessing the outcome of the journey to the interior, American leaders knew there were nations on the surface who would have come up to fight had their territory been violated, even unintentionally.

On landing, the flight crew noted they had been nearly 24 hours on the mission. They were quietly welcomed home. The Commander explained briefly that the mission had been successful. The crew devoured breakfast and fell into their beds.

The exposed film was removed from the ship and taken to the processing lab. Twenty hours of photographs would be the visual result of the cameramen's skill. After the film was edited, the meteorological data studied along with the record on the navigator's tape track, and the radio confrontation dialogue assessed, the U.S. would be provided with its first graphic understanding of the world within our world that had been kept hidden for millennia.

The pictures showed the inner atmosphere of clouds and rain and even a massive thunderstorm where bolts of lightning flashed in the same frightening way they would have done on the surface. The debriefing took several days, and experts from across the United States and Canada were called in for discussion.

In summing up the success of the flight to the hollow earth, the consensus of opinion was that (1) the races located in the interior of the earth were not hostile or warlike, and (2) the New Germans were now aware of America's round-wing capabilities and probably had "not rebuilt their air force sufficiently for any renewed aggression against their old enemy. Perhaps more important, it was noted that the New Germans, who were really the upper world Germans in a new setting, had not exhibited any hostility to the unarmed American visitor which they had surely recognized. Perhaps a new day was dawning.

The next question to which the U.S. would have to address itself would be not military but political. When and how would it be most feasible to open up a bilateral relationship with any or all of the nations in the inner world?

Thirty years would pass before that problem would be worked out.

Chapter XIII

Byrd's Aerial Disaster in Hollow Earth Establishes Post-war Posture of World War II Nations

A renewed military vigilance of the World War II allies developed from Byrd's 1947 escape from New Germany, and his subsequent landing on the American aircraft carrier south of Australia.

On board was American military brass of all services plus the brass of British, Canadian, Australian, and other nation's armed forces. Following the briefing by his military advisors, President Truman was sufficiently alarmed to persuade the principal allies of World War II into making a decisive commitment toward the future outcome of Planet Earth.

Twenty-three days after Byrd's debriefing, the President's yacht was at anchor in Biscayne Bay, Florida. Here, in utmost secrecy, the world's leading nations and their chiefs-of-staff met to map strategy on how to react to an enemy that had not been defeated after all, and who might be renewing his air force in order to gain a tactical advantage over the entire world in aircraft superiority and weaponry. All present believed that German military ambitions were continuing, and the British, French, and Americans openly surmised that a crisis existed in which democracy might have to fight another battle with Hitler's dictatorship.

The Byrd presentation of the New German fortress being built inside the earth was made to startled military guests. There followed proposals and counter proposals by which it was agreed that preparations for defense of the outer world should begin in the continent of Antarctica, both on and off shore. Alaska and Northern Canada, continuing in a line across Greenland to Russia also should be defended forthwith. Therefore, the defense postures formed during that period were related primarily to the Polar Regions.

In line with these various national outlooks, it was decided that the Antarctic discoveries of an opening to the interior of the earth and the German presence within the earth should be kept secret. The friendly outer terrestrials riding the skies would never permit confrontation against New Germany using the newly developed round-wing planes and their weaponry. There was also the question of what the outer terrestrials' response would be if the upper earth nations took war into the hollow earth or vice versa. Thus, upper earth response at the Polar Regions became conventional, and it was decided that the round-wing planes would be deployed secretly for surveillance only.

Henceforth, all nations agreed, the new allied military presence in the Polar Regions should increase and would be disguised under various names. There was Canadian Operation Pine Tree, and DEW Line in the northern hemisphere. High Jump and the Geophysical Year, with their variety of logistics and tactical exercises were held in the southern hemisphere. America's Greenland base at Thule would be a scientific ice station, and Canada's Baffin Island Station also would mock the truth. No mention would be made that the early warning stations were located within short flight minutes of the Northern Polar entrance to the interior. No one would admit that McMurdo Bay in the Antarctic was the headquarters for any projected entrenchment.

As a result of these post war decisions, there extends across North America today a line of Arctic defenses from the Bering Strait to Greenland. Russia had its own early warning system above its 70th parallel. The world's defenses begun in the late 1940's have continued to be improved and serviced since that time.

In the Southern Hemisphere manned stations have been in existence since 1959, occupied by those signatory countries that, by treaty, police the sub-continent. West Germany is not party to the northern defense system nor do they contribute men, materials or money. Nor are the New Germans one of the Antarctic guardian nations, notwithstanding the fact that the Germans in the late 30's and early 40's probably explored and mapped the Antarctic more extensively than any other nation.

Many nations committed themselves to keep the true nature of their polar activities locked up. But what was easy to hide from the public in 1936 was not so in 1946 when batteries of press corps and advisors were required by Canada, America and foreign governments to suppress the truth that a new aerial age existed, even those newspapermen who managed to wrangle junkets to Polar stations. As suppression continued, certain military government public relations agencies used the written tactics of fabrication and deceit to hide the secret of the ages.

In 1947 the government was inclined to believe that the American people would have demanded immediate war with the Germans, and the government wanted to avoid that. But in hindsight we now know that both the Germans and allies were tired of all-out war. As for the so-called flying saucers, most governments continue to believe that withholding the truth on so-called flying saucers would prevent mass hysteria. They pay science spokesmen to ridicule the existence of the round-wing plane. But there are nonetheless some in authority, particularly in the U.S. who believe that a gradual release of the facts would be propitious.

About the time Byrd himself was being officially gagged, it was realized by the World War II allies that the entire geographical discovery of an entrance to an inner world at the poles had been made more complex by German existence in that new land. For, if the existence of the inner world was publicly revealed, the military complications of the German presence would, of necessity, be revealed and vice versa. No one in authority in the United States, Britain, France, or Russia for that matter, cared to think of a New German war machine rebuilding a "Fourth Reich" which its founder had promised would last 1,000 years.

Whatever force it was that kept the polar antagonists checkmated, earth skies and particularly the Poles, were filled for years with alien ships probing the frigid skies at each end of the planet.

The aftermath of Operation High Jump and Byrd's expedition into the interior was tragic for Byrd and his family. He had already been shut off the air in Valparaiso, Chile, while making emotional remarks about momentous discoveries stemming from his polar exploration. A similar embarrassment later occurred over NBC radio in New York. Government sponsored denials of an Interior world were then put forth, and Admiral Byrd was told by President Truman that henceforth anything he said to the media would be censored. However, Byrd would not be silenced. He told authorities that he planned to write a book on his experiences at the Poles regardless of the government's gag order.

One day in October 1954, Admiral Byrd went into seclusion. He spent the next three years in a private sanatorium near Tarrytown, New York, from which he did not communicate with those outside with the exception of certain relatives.

Numbed by the secrecy order for silence, the aerial adventurer, upon leaving the sanatorium, signed an agreement that he would never again mention his experiences in the hollow earth. This American explorer, first to spend a winter alone in the Antarctic, first to cross the South Pole by air, first to fly into the earth's hollow interior from the North Pole, was kept silent until he died in 1957 at the age of 56.

As an adventurer, he had the daring and brashness that made him the equivalent of Sir Walter Raleigh or Francis Drake. But that same opportunism that led him on to new frontiers, along with his insatiable public ego, were the very characteristics that finally branded him unacceptable to his government when collective secrecy was demanded.

It is easy for an author to fix blame or formulate conclusions. However, there are still too many unknown contributing circumstances to totally comprehend the events of 1946 and 1947 and the attempts to keep suppressed the revelations of the inner world. As for Admiral Richard E. Byrd, his outstanding human weakness might have been that frustration caused him to die from a broken heart. No one was allowed to evaluate his contribution to his country and to mankind in general.

Post War Positions of Major Nations

Although Byrd's 1947 Inner World encounter with the Germans immediately hardened the polar defense posture of World War II Allies, the political events of 1945 and 46 also tempered attitudes and dismembered the wartime alliance even before the guns were silenced.

President Franklin Delano Roosevelt remained more intransient and antagonistic towards the Germans than Churchill or De Gaulle whose countries had suffered severe agonies of war. Roosevelt's animosity toward Germans was exceeded only by that of Stalin. In 1945 Roosevelt had called for maximum obliteration of major German cities by British and American bombers during the final weeks of the war. But Churchill, who was to concur, had deliberately put off sanctioning the scheme because he could not forget the needless deaths of over 36,000 Londoners during the blitz of the German V Bombs, as well as the destruction of historical English landmarks of monumental significance. The early Roosevelt/Churchill camaraderie had not fully blossomed into an abiding friendship as Churchill noted an increasing egomania and unnecessary military truculence on the part of the American president.

As World War II drew to a close, the most pressing need was to decide the fate of a defeated Germany. Hence the peace talks at Casablanca, Tehran, Cairo, Yalta, Potsdam and Dunbarton Oaks during the last years of the war.

Of particular significance to the story of the round-wing plane development, as well as the future of Europe and the world nations, was the Yalta conference that began in February 1945. That conference revealed frightening events that almost resulted in the western

Genesis for the Space Race

Allies being the post-war losers of World War II and the Soviet empire becoming the undisputed champion of the world.

Architects of the disaster formula were Joseph Stalin, the crafty evil premier of the USSR, and Franklin Delano Roosevelt of the USA, whom Churchill accused of having gone mad while at Yalta, as corroborated later by testimony of three American physicians before a congressional committee hearing. Therefore, the Yalta episode is briefly sketched herein to show how Roosevelt's tryst with Stalin at that conference not only influenced the defense posture of the English speaking allies and etched the boundaries of occupied Europe after 1946, but also hid the fact of the round-wing plane development under stricter cover up.

Roosevelt's departure for Yalta was arranged with panoramic secrecy far beyond precautions necessary for his safety. Under the code name Argonaut, not even Vice President Truman was told the presidential destination. And the special train carrying the 125 VIPs and over 300 staff advisors was broken up at its destination of Newport News, Virginia, when after detraining, the Presidential train was camouflaged and its locomotive tenders even switched to prevent identity. In addition, the train was repainted and the serial numbers changed before the cars were rerouted to different destinations. For years, writers alluded to it as the mystery train that vanished into thin air and even associated its disappearance with the Bermuda Triangle.

From the mystery train, the Yalta party under Roosevelt boarded the cruiser Quincy under command of Capt. Elliott M. Senn, and one of the largest escorts in naval history left port with overhead planes, sub chasers and surface ships. From Malta, the American party, bound 1,250 miles for Russia, left in an aerial armada of over 200 American planes including sixteen swift P38 Lightenings that would fly guard over the President's plane, flown by Col. Ray W. Ireland. In accompanying planes under the fighter umbrella would be dignitaries such as Secretary of State Stettinius, First Assistant Secretary of State Dean Acheson, Admiral King and Admiral Leahey and Chief of Staff George C. Marshall, special advisors to the President Mr. Harry Hopkins, Justice Jimmy Byrnes, Mr. A.

V. Harriman and Mr. Alger Hiss. President Roosevelt's daughter Anna, the wife of Lt. Col. Boettiger was also present as well as Press Secretary Steve Early who was required to leave his three pool reporters at Casablanca.

Except for press coverage, Yalta was the most carefully staged conference of the several held in the final days of World War II. There were no releases until Roosevelt arrived home in Portsmouth after the conference. As hosts, Russian intelligence rendered to Roosevelt all the hero worship of the occasion almost ignoring the Britisher Churchill. Vice Premier Molotov welcomed the US President as he landed on Russian soil at 12:10 on February 3, 1945 where an honor guard was lined up in the 40 minus F cold. The Russians had converted a jeep for the few minutes when President Roosevelt could inspect the troops to the tune of a brass band playing the Stars and Stripes. Later, in an American Packard, the Russian guest drove 80 miles to Yalta where honor guards lining the route saluted the American President every 50 feet. The dignitaries were housed at the grandest residence in the area, the 50-room Lividia Palace, built in 1911 by the last Russian Czar.

When the conference opened, Stalin continued his contrived flattery by demanding as host that the ailing Roosevelt be made Chairman. The two were soon calling each other Joe and Franklin. The British delegation, especially Churchill and Anthony Eden were appalled at the uninhibited familiarity between the American and Russian leaders. Top Americans also began to wince, but unknown to practically all open delegates, Stalin and Roosevelt were most communicative to each other while talking over the phones in their private suites.

Initially, the Russians under Stalin openly asked that they be given control of most of Europe including France, northern Italy, the Balkans, Greece, Crete, Syria, Palestine, 2/3 of Finland, the Baltic countries, Iceland, part of Greenland and even a return of Alaska. The Russians then planned to take Spain by force. In the Far East, Stalin asked for Port Arthur, and all of Manchuria, Outer Mongolia. He also proposed invasion of China by Russia to remove Mao Tse Sung, who was so independent that he preferred his own brand of Communism rather than become a puppet of the Soviets.

The British team, long wary of Soviet aims and their brazen disregard for the Western Allies, pressed for the division of Europe much as it is today. (Following Yalta, British armies under Montgomery threatened to team up with the Germans and drive on to Moscow if the Russians took one foot of territory west of the Elbe.) Eisenhower and other American leaders including Patton were in accord, but Roosevelt vetoed the plan. During the Yalta conference, Churchill consistently made his point that Poland should remain free of occupied Russian troops and that Germany should be dismembered, else it would rise again. But he remained adamant that France, though defeated and not a victor in the war should be left intact and unoccupied.

During the conference, the Roosevelt/Stalin attachment blossomed daily and the American president bathed in the ego build-up that Stalin and his aides showered on him. The Russian intelligence had long guessed what Roosevelt wanted most. It was not mainly concern over division of European lands, but instead, his declared nomination for President of the newly evolving United Nations, the founding of which the winners of World War II had been drafting during the war years. Stalin was also aware that to head the New World Order was Roosevelt's greatest dream, occupying his every moment of free thought. Therefore, Stalin recognized that Roosevelt would allow nothing to stand in his way to his becoming head of the new planetary body. As Stalin daily observed the frail and failing Roosevelt, he must have known that Roosevelt had thrown all his old caution to the winds in order to get support for presidency of the coming body of nations -- and he also must have shrewdly surmised there was nothing to lose by nominating Roosevelt whose life tenure appeared to be short. The crippling polio that Roosevelt had fought all his packed-full political life had left him a weakened man. So with time on the side of Stalin, he could not lose by nominating Roosevelt to be head of the United Nations in exchange for most of Europe plus other concessions.

The Yalta conference lasted five weeks, and by the third week the British, suspecting an ominous purpose beneath Stalin's pretext to befriend Roosevelt, tapped the telephone line going into Roosevelt's private suite in the Lividia Palace. Immediately Churchill was amazed to discover that Stalin and Roosevelt had made their own secret agreement for division of Europe regardless of the open negotiating sessions and also how the two conspirators regarded the new world of nations as they envisioned a revised constitution. As the conference continued, reverberations of the secret intrigue, which Stalin was surreptitiously conducting with Roosevelt, reached the ears of the Acting President of the U.S.A., Harry S. Truman, in Washington.

A bewildered Vice President Truman had purposely been alerted by two leading congressmen and another, then unknown source, that President Roosevelt was undermining the Allied cause at Yalta and that something had to be done -- quickly. It was at that point that William Donovan; President Roosevelt's choice to head the O.S.S. (forerunner of the CIA) was called by Acting President Truman. Truman's message to Donovan was crisp. "Meet me in Arlington Cemetery today at one P.M.!"

At the rendezvous, Truman confided his concern to the Intelligence Chief, and asked to be brought up to date on the Yalta happenings. Donovan, first of all, told the Acting Chief that on Roosevelt's orders, his intelligence team had not been taken to the conference, but nevertheless, an O.S.S. man was there in the disguise of a naval chaplain. Donovan said the code name of the agent was Father John, a bonafide Catholic priest. Then Donovan told Truman it was Father John whose reports had alerted him and other friends in Washington.

Donovan and Truman, at that meeting, agreed to add to Father John's reports and discover first hand what really was happening at Yalta. The acting president then asked General Donovan what was needed to get the counter espionage started on the Roosevelt/Stalin dealings and Donovan replied, five thousand dollars in my hands today and a fast plane to London. Truman went to his own personal account and drew the necessary $5,000 that Donovan would need for funding the trip to Yalta without government vouchers, and at Andrews Air Force Base, one of the five new American made jets was waiting for the OSS head. In London, the head of Donovan European operations was asked to stand by. He went under the code name of Major General Charles Lawson, a graduate of Princeton.

Forty-eight hours later, secret O.S.S. agent General Lawson had flown to Moscow via Leningrad. There at the American Embassy, a known O.S.S. agent confirmed that something wrong was taking place at Yalta between Roosevelt and Stalin. Getting a lift to Yalta in a Russian dispatch plane, the Russians thought Lawson was being called in by Roosevelt. To hide identity from Americans who might recognize him, General Lawson was billeted with a Britisher. Three hours after arrival at Yalta headquarters, the American OSS agent had tapped Roosevelt's telephone going into Lavidia Palace. What he first heard confirmed the rumors: Stalin, Molotov and Roosevelt were carrying on a conversation in English with Molotov interpreting difficult passages for Stalin. The Russians talked hopefully of a New World, with Roosevelt the global leader of the projected body of United Nations scheduled for its inaugural meeting in San Francisco sometime in 1947. Roosevelt showed his elation by the honor even over the phone. There was however, one small catch -- something the Russians wanted in return. Roosevelt knew all about returning favors, but even General Lawson was stunned to hear Molotov tell Roosevelt to lock all his doors from the inside that night and send out all personnel, particularly security people. At 12 midnight, Stalin and Molotov would visit Roosevelt and his daughter Sis alone in the apartment to discuss a contractual agreement. They said they would come through a secret passageway that ended at the wall of the guest apartment occupied by the American president and his daughter.

That evening bugs were planted in Roosevelt's apartment. General Lawson waited expectantly as 12 midnight approached. Precisely on the hour Stalin and Molotov were heard to arrive. The President's daughter Sis listened to the knock on the hidden panel and apparently looking at the wall, the agent heard her say: "Do come in, Gentlemen, the President is expecting you!"

Some small talk ensued as heard on the tape and then Stalin thrilled Roosevelt by extolling how he so expertly chaired the Yalta meetings and that he was Earth's best choice to head the forthcoming United Nations assembly. Stalin asked only one favor in return and he spoke bluntly in English:

"In return for our assured support of your desire to head the world body of nations in the post war years, we want the plans for your round-wing plane."

The Russians had made their bid. For what the Germans had paid a million dollars for in 1936 when they bought the crude Caldwell plans; Stalin now wanted not only half the World but also the plans of the round-wing plane.

There was a silence as Roosevelt paused, still reflecting the earlier Russian flattery to propel him into stardom as head of the world. Finally, the sick U.S. President spoke. "I see no reason why Russia should not share the secret of the round-wing plane. As Russia is to be our ally in a New World of one nation under the United Nations body which I would head, everyone should share the benefits of the great round-wing plane and its motor."

Stalin then withdrew from his pocket an agreement in English, which in return for the round-wing secret (which first was to be delivered by Roosevelt), they would use Russian influence to make him head of the New United World Order of Nations. Vice President of the new body would be Joseph Stalin and Secretary General would be A.V. Molotov. All three parties signed and Sis witnessed the signature of her father, the head of state of the United States of America.

The next day a smiling Roosevelt met Churchill and said in parting: "I think it's time to consider giving the Russians the plans for the American round-wing plane." Churchill glared at his former friend and replied. "Believe me! I well know you've been tricked by the flattery of that brigand Stalin." And looking squarely at Roosevelt, Churchill ended the conversation by adding, "And you, Sir, have gone mad!"

Within four days, General Charles Lawson would be back before

Truman, where he and key members of the Senate/Congress would hear the taped story of how Roosevelt agreed to give Russia without congressional approval or advice of the U.S. military, whatever part of Europe the Russians desired, as well as the secret of the ages, the round-wing plane.

Little did the members know that Estes Plateau, the visitor from another planet (Venus) who called on Roosevelt in 1943, had reminded him that his personal ambitions might some day place him in the same category as Hitler and Stalin.

Yalta ended. The Americans came home. And President Roosevelt proceeded to keep his part of the terrible Russian bargain. Plans of the latest round-wing plane were delivered to the Oval Office and placed in his desk.

One morning of late March 1945, Soviet Ambassador Andre Gromyko arrived at the White House for an audience with President Roosevelt. When the Russian left he carried an unmarked package that inside held the plans to the round-wing plane on which Johnathon E. Caldwell and thousands of others from America, Canada and Britain had spent their careers perfecting.

Less than ten days later Gromyko asked for a second audience with the U.S. President. The Russian, upon returning the plans of the round-wing plane to Roosevelt, told him that Russian engineers had un-mistakenly proved the blue prints were fakes and bore no relationship to the true design and motivational power of an operational plane.

The Russian diplomat was correct. On the night in which the plans lay locked in Roosevelt's desk, an unknown O.S.S. man entered with the help of Secret Service personnel and exchanged the authentic blueprints with fake ones.

The same day on which Gromyko brought back the doctored plans, Roosevelt called in Vice President Truman and explained that "plans of the round-wing plane he had requested had been substituted." Without explaining his own duplicity, the President asked

Truman to get the proper plans as soon as possible and find who had substituted them or drawn false ones.

Vice President Truman agreed to the order, but as part of the task he urged that President Roosevelt first take a quiet, restful vacation in his favorite spa, Warm Springs, Georgia. Truman promised that upon return the plans would be ready, and for the time being he believed that Roosevelt's absence would solve the immediate problem of preventing the round-wing secret from falling into enemy hands. Roosevelt thought Truman's suggestion a perfect way to recuperate after Yalta and he made ready to leave immediately.

On April 5, Roosevelt died in Warm Springs, and among the first to hear of his death and breathe a sigh of relief was Winston Churchill of England. Top U.S. Air Force officers were also pleased as were untold others aware of Roosevelt's perfidy. President Truman immediately sealed the Yalta papers of his deceased predecessor among which included the round-wing gift to Russia.

As the body of the late President lay in the closed casket guarded by four Secret Service men, Eleanor Roosevelt asked that it be opened so she could view her husband for the last time. The lid was lifted and for a few minutes she looked at the man whose vision had made the building of the round-wing plane on a friendly international basis possible, and who took America into World War II, but whose ambition in the final days of his illness lead him to try and give away the greatest invention on the planet, the round-wing plane. Had he not been stopped by the O.S.S. whose job it was to guard the nation's secrets, the military and science programmes that the Anglo/Canadian/American team had developed, would have been purloined by the Soviets, whose real goal was domination of the World.

When President Truman met Stalin the following year at the next peace Conference held in Potsdam, Germany, the bold Russian came up to Truman and spouted, "Roosevelt and I called each other by our first names. Let's begin by doing the same."

Harry Truman who learned to read the foibles of human character during his days with the Kansas City Pendergast political machine, looked contemptuously at the stocky Russian in knee high boots, baggy knee pants and khaki shirt: "I'll call you Marshall Stalin and you address me as Mr. President!"

Because of the new American hard line under Truman, the Americans and British kept most of Europe free from occupied Soviet control.

As a result of the military fear that the Stalin/Roosevelt agreement engendered, a tight cover-up prevailed over the round-wing apparatus in the U.S.A., Canada and Britain. Even elected congressmen in the U.S.A. and members of parliament in Canada and Britain, or those appointed to the U.S. Senate or the Canadian and British upper houses, were kept from the deepening secrets of the round-wing plane, whether of a military, science or technological nature. As the security ranks closed, it became an indictable offense in Canada and Britain to publicly discuss or write about the phenomena, while in the U.S.A. other punitive and secret measures of censorship were employed.

Thus the round-wing apparatus, which originally lodged itself in the security of the military and science worlds as a hidden technological process, gradually became a fortified position of mind power. The round-wing security division often degraded those who inquired about the phenomena; and those human beings who ventured to expose the truth became enemies within the state, to be destroyed if necessary. In short, by its covert composition, the guardians of the round-wing plane complex had to circumvent the laws of the state to survive and continue. The Freedom of Information Act eventually helped to right the wrongs of the cover-up by the round-wing plane establishment.

(For preparation of this chapter, 78-year-old CIA General Charles Lawson (not his right name) came out of retirement to aid the researcher and complete the book. When the OSS intelligence records were read at the National Archives (including the Stalin/Roosevelt agreement on the round-wing plane), it was evident why the Anglo American security ranks were closed more tightly after

1945. General Lawson is considered by President Reagan and present and past CIA directors as the greatest living legendary figure of World War II.)

PART II

The Inner World of the Extra terrestrials

Chapter XIV

Men From Atlantis

Nineteen eighty (the year of this book's publication) will be the first time that the people of the known world first learned that they were not alone on this planet. Over half a billion lost relatives of us surface dwellers live peaceably inside the Earth's center. Moreover, these highly advanced people occupy a land mass greater in area than the outside surface.

Their civilizations flourished thousands of years before Moses gave the Israelites their first code of laws. Their people were driving automobiles and flying in "aerial cars" when ancient Greece laid the foundations of Western civilization, and their commerce swept the interior oceans when the Mediterranean was but a Roman lake.

Yet these shy inhabitants of the hollow earth have remained incognito and free of war for 30,000 years. At what period this inner world was first colonized is unknown, but the existence of the largest group concealed in the earth's interior dates back 15,000 years -- 3,000 years prior to the sinking of their upper continent of Atlantis. They claim that that catastrophe is the deluge known to us as the Noah flood or Gilgamesh Epic.

But the oldest race in the inner world is of ancient Germanic origin, tracing its beginnings to the frozen Antarctic in the world above when that sub-continent was once an inhabited tropical paradise of unsurpassed riches and beauty. Their exodus to inner earth was 30,000 years ago.

Regardless of international government censorship, thousands of surface dwellers in several countries know something of the inner earth due to its recent enterprising colonization by modern-day Germans. But additional evidence is irrefutable that the ancestral races of the Lapps, Eskimos, Chinese, Scandinavians, Germans, Greeks and other large ethnic groups still live inside the earth.

First, lest the dubious reader wonder if this is the beginning of a chapter on mythology, it will be revealed that constant ocean commerce is at present being carried on (unknowingly) between certain nations above and (knowingly) by their counterparts below. Further, it is in various government records that over 100 of these inner-earth inhabitants work or study in the U.S.A., a similar number in Canada, and several hundred in Europe. When they come to the surface via Arctic sea routes they travel on Icelandic visas, but they also arrive above by means of at least three major train tunnel arteries, one being in the Western United States. The professional and technological "missionaries" from the interior who have been landing in such places as the United States, Canada, Germany or England for many years come only as friends without political or religious motives. They could best be compared to the American Peace Corps Volunteers to underdeveloped countries.

When Admiral Byrd flew into the interior of the earth in 1927 through the northern entrance, he brought back to the outside world the first authentic pictures of the lost people and cities to which this chapter refers, and the two 1947 flights of the American round-wing planes with their maps and photos amply verify the early Byrd record. (In 1965, NASA did a complete, detailed mapping of the interior world.)

But to understand the hollow earth facts and why they remain discredited, the reader should be made aware that a veil of international government secrecy has kept them under wraps for 50 years. In lieu of the truth, the fiery molten earth core hypothesis has been accepted as the current geological condition inside the earth's interior. Many scientific papers and books still expound this theory, and grade schools teach it. But such an explanation, while perhaps explaining the earth's formative beginnings, is outdated. Today, reputable scientists secretly scoff at the given story that is allowed to persist by such a prestigious institution as the National Science Foundation.

Several old chronicles of Scandinavian and Eskimo origin tell of people who were carried into the Earth's interior by ocean currents and returned years later to tell of it. But there were three projects developed by 20th century Germany that unraveled the reality of the Earth's interior with more discernment than did unsubstantiated myths. Those German endeavors to validate the existence of the hollow Earth and devise methods to penetrate it for colonization began, for all practical purposes, in 1913.

An un-named science faculty at Georgetown University sponsored a paper on this unusual scientific sea journey in 1977, and a West German national delivered the lecture. The lecture caught officialdom by surprise, and later all who heard the talk were instructed not to speak of it. The following narrative, except for the early Americans mentioned, is part of that lecture.

Perhaps the Germans know of the early theories of John Cleves Symmes of the U.S.A. Infantry that the earth was actually hollow and open at the Poles. Another American, Cyrus Reed, also held to this theory, though he was openly ridiculed. The hollow earth was written of in a book published in 1816 by James McBride, and in 1838 an American expedition actually left for the Antarctic after Symmes' admirers in Congress made it possible. Symmes' expedition, of which we know little, inspired Jules Verne to write his JOURNEY TO THE CENTER OF THE EARTH.

In March 1913 the German imperial pocket cruiser Moltke left

Keil, Germany on a top-secret mission to find a northern passage over the top of the world. Like attempts by other nations, the Germans were searching for an Arctic route via a northwest passage through the Bering Strait to the Pacific. War clouds made it necessary to keep the mission classified.

The ship was under the command of Captain Von Jagow, now deceased. Also on board was Lt. Von Tirpitz, grandson of the Kaiser and great-grandson of Queen Victoria. It was the son of Captain Von Jagow who was interviewed in September 1977 about his mission. With him at the interview was Lt. Von Tirpitz (now 81 years of age), who at one time was Grand Admiral of the German North Sea Fleet, as were his father and grandfather.

The Moltke under Captain Von Jagow steamed first towards Iceland, then past the southern tip of Greenland and northwest along Greenland's west coast to Canada's Baffin Island. It was late May when the ship anchored off the northern end of Baffin Island in the vicinity of 70 degrees latitude and 60 degrees longitude to wait for the pack ice to break up.

Within two weeks a navigable northerly channel appeared instead of the better-known westerly route in the Lancaster Sound area (referred to as the Northwest Passage and first recorded in 1903-04 by Roald Amundsen). The ice buckled and broke, permitting passage of the Moltke to open waters further north.

This was the first unexplainable situation. The open waters to the north were more extensive than the Germans expected them to be. As they moved northward on an apparently navigable course, the open water stretched as far as the eye could see. By the end of May, the crew was still sailing cautiously into warmer waters. Robins and bluebirds were identified and on islands they had passed there were reindeer and black bears, coming from the north. The German ship still maneuvered slowly further north, sounding the depth carefully. Daylight was continuous.

Then the captain became perplexed. The sun appeared to be low in the sky instead of above, and its position was lower the further they sailed. By the end of June the sun had apparently set or disappeared and the battle cruiser was sailing in darkness. The compass was erratic and the true north indistinguishable. The air became misty, the wind increased. Gradually the darkness lifted and a new light from the forward direction shone faintly. As they sailed on, the glow from the new sun's position never changed. The sky was now grayish to black. The navigator surmised they had sailed beyond the North Pole and were somehow headed south again on an unknown course.

Then they passed an Eskimo in a kayak who spoke a Greenland dialect of Danish. He said he had come from a place called Vineland located about 500 miles south where he had wintered.

For 300 miles Captain Von Jagow continued to steer a southerly course. A continuous chart and depth record of that voyage is today on display in the German Federal Archives in Bonn along with the ship's log.

Finally the ship reached a rocky island inhabited by Eskimos who canoed out to meet them. Some of these also spoke Danish and had been to and from Greenland on several occasions. One of the group said he was a Lapp from Russia. The next day was a surprise. The German log says they saw on an island what they believed was a species of supposedly extinct dinosaur. The dimension they had entered was too unreal to comprehend.

The Captain called an officers meeting. They were utterly lost and orders were given to reverse course. Fourteen days later, traveling at full knots, the true sun having reappeared, they found themselves back at the same bearing at which they had anchored in late May off Baffin Island.

It was then that Captain Von Jagow made a decision to explore the northern waters more extensively.

Drawing an arc, the ship directions were so given that the German battle cruiser actually sailed around the edge of the hole leading to the interior. On the outer perimeter of the circumference they ran into thick packs of ice and bitter coldness again. They finally (wrongly) calculated by checking compass movements that the elusive North Pole might be inside the doughnut hole leading into the Earth. Explorers before them had been fooled also.

On July 10, a course was set for Germany and on August 1, 1913, the German ship and her crew reached home.

A complete report was made to the Imperial German Naval Command, but its contents was not published. In 1922 one of the ship's officers, Lt. Von Tirpitz, wrote of the experience under the title "The Memoirs of Grand Admiral Tirpitz." From avidly reading this naval officer's account of the northern inner sea, Adolph Hitler became convinced of the validity of a northern entrance to the hollow earth.

During Hitler's book burning in 1936, one of the banned German books most sought was Von Tirpitz' story of the epic voyage on the Moltke battle cruiser to the inner sea at the top of the world. Hitler's agents confiscated all the books they could for public burning, but Von Tirpitz removed his copy from his own library and hid it elsewhere.

In 1924 the Imperial German Navy dusted off the old records of the 1913 expedition into the northern throat of the world. The expedition had not penetrated into the watery corridor beyond an approximate 400 miles but it had proven the existence of an opening. So, in the reasoning of German engineers, if there were an opening that led ultimately to the earth's interior, another such voyage would verify just where that northern doorway ended and the inside of the world began.

Information is indeed sparse on the cruise of the German icebreaker that was used on the expedition. What is known comes entirely from American Navy intelligence sources of 1924-25. In 1924 American Naval vessels followed the German icebreaker towards ice fields northeast of Greenland when the German vessel broke passage through the ice and disappeared. The American Navy records say the German icebreaker returned a year later (1925), stopping ten days at the capitol city of Iceland before sailing for her homeport of Hamburg, Germany. The ship and crew had spent the better part of a year in the earth's interior, the American intelligence records reveal, with its final destination unknown. It is rumored that the German Navy made a third visit in 1932, but this report could not be confirmed.

(The Russians also attempted to penetrate the interior world in 1956. They sent in a battleship, according to Canadian intelligence sources, but a deliberate warning beam of laser power stopped the Russian trip. Allowed to exit to the surface with superficial damage and a stern reminder to the captain and crew to never return. The next year, in the dead of winter, the Russians sent in a 16,000-man task force of troop-carrying vehicles, heavy artillery, regular tanks and armored cars over solid ice fields and islands through the polar throat into the interior. The invaders came up off a landmass in the extreme north of the interior where they encountered the old Vikings. The Vikings bombarded the task force with lasers, stopping all the Russian motorized equipment, so that the army was powerless to move. By radio they ordered the invaders to turn and head back to the surface. "Should you return," the voice warned in Russian, "it will be a one-way trip." The Russians retreated. A 30,000 man back-up army of reserves waiting in Siberia was not called upon to take the inner world by force.)

In 1939 and ensuing years the Germans continued their exploration of the Inner Earth, and in the autumn of 1943 Germany dispatched an aerial expedition into the hollow earth by way of the South Pole region. The expedition was peaceful, its purpose to inquire if Inner Earth lands were available for colonization by upper world Germans. The upper Germans brought gifts and were well received by those Germanic Saxon cousins who had migrated below in the 1600's. On the same exploration, the upper Germans from the Third Reich encountered what is perhaps the world's most superior race in development -- the Bodlanders, another German offshoot whose cradle of life began in the Antarctic but who had migrated below 30,000 years ago via tunnels from what is now Iran. (Language scholars claim that the Iranian [Persian] language retains a similarity to ancient Germanic writing symbols and the spoken word.)

As the reader is already aware, the visiting Germans from the upper world were invited into the capitol city of Bodland, named Bod, where they were guests at Parliament and were entertained by the King. Officials explained to the upper Germans that their hosts were ancestors of the first distinct race that had migrated to the inner side of the planet's shell. Later interior arrivals included the Vikings, the Atturians (or Atlanteans) and the Eskimos. The Bodlanders claimed that the Japanese had no ancestral relatives inside the earth, but were, in fact, descendants from the sunken continent of Mu, which some records say predated the sinking of Atlantis by as much as 250,000 years. The Bodlander chroniclers below said that four civilizations had already developed and faded away on the upper Earth, the present being the fifth.

In 1943, the visiting Germans were also told, and NASA confirmed in 1979, that there are three large continents below in the interior world and two smaller ones. (See map in appendix.) There are seven named oceans, the largest of which is the North Ocean. The name often applied to the entire interior is New Atlantis.

The German expedition of 1943 also discovered that the largest interior continent is that of Agraharta, covering a continental area three times larger than that of North America, and occupied mainly by a distinct people called Atturians. These groups are the descendants from the sunken continent of Atlantis whose ancestors immigrated into the interior 15,000 to 11,500 B.C., prior to the final sinking of their original homeland when many millions of their ancestors perished. The Atturians claim they are related to many surface white races and that their combined mother race was brought from Venus 33,000 years ago, but that adventure was not the first Venusian attempt to re-colonize Earth. They also claim Venus was originally an Earth colony.

But information on the Inner World procured strictly from German sources seemed unreal to the author, so further corroborating evidence was sought. In 1977 some startling information was obtained from the U.S. State Department. A department source revealed the whereabouts of a man named Haammaan from New Atlantis who had been relocated into the mainstream of American life. He was married to an American girl and raised a family in Massachusetts. If the professor would talk without jeopardizing his American residency, we would have a scoop to rival all scoops. This material, therefore, on Men of Atlantis was prepared chiefly from interviews with this Atlantean contact. Then in 1979, unexpectedly another contact was made with another Inner World man of exceptional brilliance, an outstanding scholar in philosophy and ancient history who, with his wife, is currently on a five-year visa to the U.S.A. where he teaches history at George Washington University and spends his spare time counseling students and non-students about family and social problems.

His anglicized name is H. G. Jerrmuss (properly spelled Jerruum-mouss) and he comes from another continent in the Inner World, Bodland, with a population of roughly 36 million. Interviews with these two men on life in the Inner World will be found in the Appendix A, but the remainder of this chapter will tell briefly of the tragedy that caused the sinking of Atlantis in the upper world and the exodus of the Atlantean survivors to the inside of the Earth.

The following, therefore, is the summarized story of how Atlantis and other upper-world lands disappeared beneath the ocean as explained in the chronicles of their race and studied in the history books used in the schools and universities of Atturas in the interior of the Earth, as told by Professor Haammaan:

The original Atlantis began as a Venusian colony 33,000 years ago in the fertile valleys and plateaus of a continent located in the mid Atlantic. (Venus itself was originally a space colony of Earth from which the inhabitants had fled at an unknown time because of an earthly cataclysm of planetary nature.) Before destruction 11,500 years ago in an atomic war, Atlantis stretched from the vicinity of Africa to what are now the Islands of the Caribbean. It was once a land of great wealth and had developed a society and technology equal to the leading nations of the upper Earth in the 20th century. Their space ships traveled Earth skies and also ventured into outer space where trade routes to other planets were developed.

But the Atlanteans had a mortal enemy. This was a people named the Athenians living in great cities located in the Mediterranean valley and principally the Aegean area. A three hundred year old trade rivalry gradually became insufferable as each nation prepared for war to destroy the other.

The indirect cause of war is listed as trade or economic reasons, and not the need for land acquisition. The prize was trade dominance among inter-stellar planets in the Milky Way beyond our own solar system on which colonies of Atlanteans and Athenians had been established. Several small local wars had already been fought on Earth and abroad, leaving behind passions of hate that festered and grew.

The date of approximately 11,500 years ago is given when the Athenian King ordered a surprise attack on major cities of Atlantis. It began as a controlled land war, and Athenian armies landed on Atlantis and gained strong footholds using devastating ray weaponry against Atlantean armies and objectives.

On the 21st day of the war, the Atlanteans retaliated and broke through Athenian air defenses dropping atomic bombs on the capital city of the Athenians. The city was totally destroyed, whereupon the Athenian military ordered a retaliatory atomic attack on the capital of Atlantis.

All out atomic war by these two enemies took place. For the next nine days a total, unrestrained atomic war prevailed. (The legends of Greece, Scandinavia and India, as well as Bible references tell of this war in varying stories.)

Millions of Atlanteans and Athenians perished in the holocaust and their great industrial and cultured worlds were to be lost forever, the Athenians (Greeks) never to regain their ancient glory, and the Atlanteans to be wiped off the surface of the planet. Remnants of the Atlanteans made their way to Egypt and disappeared underground into caves and existing tunnels throughout Africa. Lost groups of Athenians also climbed the higher elevations of what are today in Italy, Turkey and Caspian Sea areas, to mix with other races. Atlanteans also headed for Brazil and America and became the forerunners of its Mayas and Incas and certain North American Indian tribes.

But during the nine-day atomic war, the elements became so disturbed that the wind and water caused greater damage to the land than the bombs. First came the heat caused by the atomic fission. Radioactive dust filled the upper heavens and blotted out the sun. The atomic heat spiraled up and fanned out on giant hurricane winds, melting immense glaciers covering what was then the North Pole (today Switzerland). New rivers were formed such as the Rhone, Rhine, Seine, Danube and Po, as the melted polar icecaps ran off their fresh water. Britain, which was beforehand joined to Europe, became an island as the connecting land bridge was washed away, while the lowlands of the Baltic and North Seas disappeared under rising waters. The melted ice covered great sections of Europe, eventually filling the Caspian and Black Sea basins. As the tidal waves and winds mounted in the Atlantic, they flooded over the continent of Atlantis, and it, too, sank beneath the waters.

For the Athenians, the end was much the same. As the new rivers poured fresh water into the Mediterranean valley, giant tidal waves of salt water (produced by a wobble in Earth's rotation) breached the high land precipice at the Pillar of Hercules between what is now Spain and Morocco. Accompanied by the bursting of the natural land bridge dam at the western end of the Mediterranean valley, torrential rains fell on the remaining inhabitants during the ensuing days. At that time the entire Mediterranean was a lush valley where the Athenian empire had begun. Over the next 100 years, the water from the Atlantic completely covered the human habitations and monuments of man throughout this Mediterranean oasis. Only the mountaintops stood out such as Malta, Crete, Sicily, Corsica, Sardinia, etc. The new water depths covered what remained of the Athenian cities of Appoloias, Atheanisas, Appalto, Hellinas, Spartillois and Spartias. For many years afterwards, Atlantic waters continued to tumble over the precipice between the Pillars of Hercules until the sea levels were equalized and the Mediterranean valley was to be the original home of the Greek race in legend only.

It took longer for parts of the Mediterranean highlands to be totally engulfed, up to 300 years. Surviving Atlanteans on the western fringe who had gone underground into bomb shelters and tunnels during the attack, surfaced, cleaned up their cities and prepared to relive in them again, but the waters rose yearly and the Atlanteans were forced to cover their cities with three foot thick plastic shells made of a substance we have not yet developed. As in the Houston Astrodome, the Atlanteans covered over their entire city habitations. Those elevated cities were eventually engulfed with water and today lie on the bottom of the ocean, some of them adjacent to the continental U.S.A., as is that unnamed city ten miles in diameter located off San Juan. Communications exist between the eight major cities in the vicinity of the West Indies via a tunnel system. Entrance to the surface is from underwater air locks. Their spacecraft emerge through the ocean to the surface.

A total of 28 underwater cities exist today throughout the world. Haammaan elaborated by stating that what is now the Black Sea, Caspian Sea, and the Gulf of Mexico, plus other ancient inhabited valleys were inundated in that flood. American scientists and other governments know that, Haammaan said.

The most recent movements of the earth's crust took place during the global flood, Haammaan added. New mountain chains were formed and old ones like the Himalayas rose considerably. Sediments were deposited on our American plains and fossil graveyards were left in various places. After the Genesis flood was over (the same account of which is told in the Bible), old lands like Atlantis had disappeared and new ones formed. At first the tidal waves rushed back and forward over most parts of the globe, but eventually the captive waters left on the high plains ran off and drowned costal lands via the newly formed streams and rivers such as North American's Mississippi, Ohio, Missouri and St. Lawrence. Geologists are still uncertain as to what caused the last Earth destruction, but it was actually the Biblical flood brought on by an atomic war.

In his parting remarks, Haammaan said, "But I have come up from below and exposed myself to you and your government particularly to warn you people of the upper world of the immediate danger of a new nuclear war which you all face. A clue is in your Old Testament prophecy, 'As it was in the days of Noah, so shall it be in the last days.' Your civilization in the U.S.A. today stands unprotected from such a war and when it comes it will destroy the people and change the character of the land so that your great coastal cities and low lying areas which the bombs may miss will be submerged under water. It has taken the upper Earth civilization 11,500 years to reach again that same point that was sacrificed under the atom bomb long ago at a time when most of this Earth was truly a Garden of Eden. If you think Earth was cursed previously following the atomic war I referred to, then believe that this next war will be many times worse with your stockpile of thousands of nuclear bombs and their delivery systems."

Haammaan paused again. "Read Plato, dust off your old fables and take another look at Noah, the Athenian, and his ark. If you think I cry wolf, believe me, I don't. If insane Earth leaders refuse to listen, the end of this world is again almost upon us.

"It was worth it to sound the alarm. I could have surfaced in a part of the world where my words might have gone unheard and my lips made mute. Then the world would never have heard my plea."

He finished on a note of hope: "If you surface people can restrain your military ego for a century, then you will discover new frontiers of travel and engineering triumphs through your new space craft the likes of which you have never dreamed. Meanwhile the United States is welcome to come down to Agraharta and Bodland officially, and make contact with the inner world. Of this I am certain."

(For remainder of Haammaan's remarks on life in the inner world -- see the Appendix.)

PART III

Primer for a New Age of Space

Chapter XV

Post-War Military Development of the Anti-Gravity Principle

"Britain and the United States are working together, and working for the same high cause. Bismarck once said that the supreme fact of the 19th century was that Britain and the United States spoke the same language. Let us make sure that the supreme fact of the 20th century is that they tread the same path." Winston Churchill, United States Congress, January 17, 1952

In May of 1945, Churchill wrote his first highly classified letter to the new and unpretentious President of the U.S.A., Harry Truman. Thus began the most important series of documents ever written on the round-wing plane as the determining factor for protection of allied skies in a world where future supremacy in the air would be the goal of succeeding generations. Churchill's first letter read: "The war is over. By our combined efforts we (Great Britain and the U.S.A.) have learned to work together. But, because Russia already has revealed itself to be our future adversary, I urge that we maintain, with the highest priority, all round-wing plane research, development and military deployment . . . with the secrecy necessary to insure the survival of democracy."

Within a month, President Harry Truman answered Churchill in a decisive reply. His letter began: "Dear Winston: Your sentiments express my own thoughts. I totally agree with your political appraisal of Russia." In Truman's answer to Churchill, it was evident that as the head of a nation of free people, he too had resolved to face the Soviet challenge of world domination, using the latest weapon of peace that the U.S.A. had developed.

Churchill wrote his next letter. "Dear Harry: I suggest we get together and that I come to the U.S.A. where we will draft plans to continue the round-wing plane program. Its very existence must remain locked in silence. We should never forget that we have in our possession an invention so vast that we cannot yet comprehend the benefits it will bring to the world. Militarily we must never let the Russians discover the knowledge of how to build a round-wing plane (although I doubt their capabilities) because we do not want a bilateral arms race to develop. I understand there is much continuing research of a scientific nature that should now be started by first choosing the best physicists from among our combined peoples. In the meantime, I think it is wise that we not let up our military vigilance, but consider the whole world to be our new area of reconnaissance."

That the free world survived and prepared to meet the inevitable onslaught of Russian communism was due in large part to the letters of commitment by freedom-loving Churchill and a plain speaking Truman, neither of whom had any personal ambitions to rule the world. Only future historians will be objective enough to venture if the process of democracy was weakened by the ultimate secrecy that their decisions invoked.

Mr. Estes Plateu, an unofficial representative from host planet Venus, added his thoughts on paper. That letter is on file with those of Churchill and Truman in the U.S. Air Force Tombs in Kensington, Maryland. Mr. Plateu wrote in 1945: "My government of Venus, and the solar council suggests, for the present, that you keep a force of 500 round-wing military planes ready for action to repel any attack that might occur from any place on or off the globe. The figure of 500 is not an arbitrary one, but has been calculated by Venusian scientists, based on the present, safe amount of magnetic power that the round-wing fleet would draw off the earth's grid system during any single peak period.

"Furthermore, 500 round-wing planes in the hands of English speaking people for their protection and that of their allies, will be over-adequate to effect any counter military action that might be initiated by Russia, on land or in the air." Mr. Plateu continued, in his letter, "A global passenger and freight fleet of 2,000 round-wing planes could eventually be developed by the year 2000 (commercial aeroplanes in the USA now (1978) number less than 6,000), by initiating a global ground system of magnetic boosters. Such a total complement of round-wing planes would allow a safe margin for power withdrawal from the earth's magnetized force being developed in part by the planet spinning on its axis," the Venusian declared.

Plateu later wrote: "I am not concerned about the eventual depletion of the earth's petro-chemical resources. The round-wing planes (as well as future ships and trains) operating without petro-chemical derivatives will be in service long after the oil reserves are gone." Plateu said all forms of electricity are provided by the earth, no matter how the current is derived. "Tapping this vast electromagnetic energy in different ways will be an inspiration to the next generations of earth scientists," he added.

In the months of 1945, and thereafter, meetings between President Truman and Churchill were carried on outlining priorities for peace-time military use of the round-wing plane. To assure secrecy after wartime development (handled under the American OSS till September 1945), the new operation would begin under the newly formed CIA in the United States and MI 2 in Canada. British Intelligence, the head of which was known to only three government persons, would also carry on the project. The combined air intelligence of the three nations would, of necessity, figure heavily in the cover-up, too.

Great Britain, the U.S. and Canada, with the knowledge of selected persons in their executive branches, and certain legislators and civil servants, thereafter set up secret funds under National Defense Research and Science budgets destined to assure guardianship of the world by the annual continuation of the top secret, round-wing plane program.

Meanwhile Russia withdrew further into her insular world under Stalin to concentrate on rocketry, and the gap between Russian and Western interests became known as the cold war of undeclared hostilities (which continues unabated in the early 80's).

Caldwell had ceaselessly worked through the war in almost every aspect of development and testing the round-wing planes that were turned out at the secret Western complex. However, in many facets of the operation, scientists and physicists of greater academic abilities had superseded Caldwell's genius. Caldwell clung to his positions of control and delayed research of a highly mathematical nature that was difficult to pursue because of his intransigence. Like many inventive geniuses, Caldwell was domineering and at times downright eccentric, and these traits often produced irksome interference which scientific minds assembled at the complex wanted to avoid. The problem was long recognized that research would serve the cause better if testing facilities could be removed from the original base to another site.

In 1945, Los Alamos became the post-war facility for round-wing plane research endeavors. The scientists had identified basic, unsolved problems. For instance, it had to be determined by speed tests how fast the phenomena could fly over 7,000 miles per hour. Also, they knew it was easy to fly such a fast plane off the curvature of the earth, following which a sense of direction was easily lost. Many diffused research problems, related to such unknowns, had to be overcome in order to make the round-wing plane a trim ship.

On authority of the US Chief of the Army Air Force, General Vandenberg, the move to Los Alamos was ordered. A team of five with scientific minds was chosen: A Canadian from the University of Manitoba, an Englishmen from Oxford and three American physicists. The new code name for the round-wing plane development would be a misnomer -- Project Milk Can.

In charge of the new project would be a man of proven capabilities. His name was Col. Chas. B. Wilkerson. He held a PhD in physics and was a doctor of mathematics. Among his unpublished credentials was his ability as a crypto-analyst with the OSS during the war in breaking the German code, which perhaps shortened the hostilities by three years and changed allied sea losses from near defeat to victory.

Col. Wilkerson and his scientific cohorts moved to Los Alamos to complete the next phase of round-wing plane development. Early in the Los Alamos based project, the physicists began the first detailed determination of speed, using Earth's magnetic forces applied to the performance of the new motor. The Los Alamos group was given one 33-foot round-wing plane for test purposes, and with this craft, speed factors were tallied by racing the plane over the prescribed north-south course and dividing the time factor of hours, minutes, and fractions of seconds into lineal miles traveled. The resulting speeds, and acceleration responses between the two centers, formed the basis of the standard training manual being used in round-wing planes today.

The researchers ascertained the round-wing plane flew faster on a north-south axis than east-west, and also noted that the magnetic planes automatically accelerated on successive trips round the world. For instance, in 1946, two trips around the world in an easterly direction were made in twelve hours time, the second trip being the faster. The object was not to establish speed records but check performance. Wilkerson also flew the plane through the interior of the earth and around the outside three times without stopping. It was noted that the earth emitted less magnetic power in the interior than on the surface, as during each pass through the interior the round-wing plane slowed up measurably, for reasons then unknown.

The same year, on a routine speed determination, Col. Wilkerson and his crew got into serious trouble. Before they were aware of a navigational error, it was noted with some alarm that they had flown off the earth's convex curvature and were about 10,000 miles out into the void of space, traveling at an incalculable speed under the greater interplanetary magnetic force between planets.

Suddenly a face appeared on their visual screen and a voice announced: "Gentlemen! You are lost and have strayed from the regions of your planet." The voice continued: "You flew off the curvature of the planet. I witnessed your departure. Your calculations went wrong when you computed magnetic navigation as though you were traveling on a flat plane. I will now place on your video screen the navigational formula to allow you to correct course and return safely to your very point of departure. As you get used to space travel, you will become familiar with this problem. Stellar perspective in space is confusing to a mariner familiar only with journeys in Earth's atmosphere."

On the screen there then appeared a table to correct flight deviation. Col. Wilkerson knew there were many calculations that had to be figured immediately to rectify their navigational error and prevent the same in the future. There was, of course, direction, velocity of the machine, rotational turn of the Earth, Earth's orbital speed, the changes of magnetic influence from the Earth's atmosphere to outer space, interplanetary magnetic perturbations, etc. to consider. As the U.S. ship adjusted course, the crew suddenly saw a slightly dissimilar, but smaller spacecraft, fly past them. Col. Wilkerson knew that their space benefactor was one of the occupants of that unknown craft. Shortly thereafter, the American round-wing plane returned safely to Los Alamos.

From the experience of being off course in space Col. Wilkerson and his physicists developed the navigational tables and directional system in use today among the English speaking round-wing plane pilots whenever they are required to fly either in Earth's atmosphere or outer space.

Besides a new navigational guidance system, there was also added a speedometer that compensated for changes in acceleration due to changing magnetic forces emanating from the Earth's surface.

In 1945, it was decided to conduct experiments in vertical speeds of ascent and descent. The problem was to translate for instant cockpit readout, the reverse fluctuations of magnetism induced at specific points of the electromagnetic perimeter surrounding the centrally located positive magnetic coil. This information was charted and put into an instantaneous visual cockpit read-out altimeter, also in use today.

Determining the round-wing plane's lift capabilities was then tackled. They successfully lifted by suspension a jeep, a Sherman tank and a large steam locomotive. Once attached to four magnetized I-bolts built into the bottom of the round-wing plane, the physicists noted that the small five pound anti-magnetic motor had no greater difficulty lifting the locomotive than the jeep. Weightlessness in the object being lifted was achieved by direct current from the motor passing via the I-bolt lifters on through the chain into the object being lifted. In the experiments mentioned, the locomotive, for instance, became an integral part of the craft, repulsing Earth's magnetism.

The push-pull capability of the experimental round-wing plane was then demonstrated. The locomotive was shoved and pulled down a section of track, and the Sherman tank, with motor dead, was pushed across a field without apparent effort. Later, a set of multiple plows was placed behind a tractor, and a virgin plot was plowed with ease. The scientists calculated the round-wing plane was the most powerful tool or machine in existence and that its peacetime uses were as varied as an engineer could imagine. In the right hands, different applications of the anti-magnetic motor could change the world, so that everything in nature that required changing or improving would be in reach of man.

As the Los Alamos scientists contemplated the awesome power of the round-wing plane during discussion one day in 1952, a thought occurred. The engine and two cars of a 62-car Union Pacific freight train had fallen off the roadbed the previous night into a canyon creek seventy feet below the tracks. The wreckage of cars lay sprawled in the watery bed. The location (still classified) was in a desert area of the Southwest. That day orders went out for the wrecking crews to vacate their work and return to base several miles away. Under cover of darkness, a crew from Los Alamos was flown to the train site. Using heavy navy chains, the round-wing plane effortlessly lifted each railroad piece back on the tracks. Today there are probably railway men in that area who still tell the story of the wrecked train that mysteriously was returned to the tracks one dark night in 1952.

The conclusive test was yet to come. It was a test, which if successful, would have wide implications in the modern world of travel. The Los Alamos team first thought of the idea when they used the round-wing plane in experiments pushing the Sherman tank. At that time, they wondered how reliable or how fickle would be the performance of the small lightweight antimagnetic motor installed in a car in place of the heavy piston driven engine. An English car was chosen and modified. Taken out was the engine, the drive shaft, gears, etc. The little five-pound anti-magnetic motor was placed under the hood in a position allowing its axis to be pointed in any direction for forward or reverse motion. Lift was not required. A generator drew power from the back wheels. Brakes were left intact. It is assumed that a battery bank was used to control the amount of electricity necessary to energize the electro-magnetos.

During that summer of 1948 a two-jeep convoy fore and aft of a little English car was seen by thousands of people as the group traveled cross country to New York, then to Washington, up to Ottawa and finally west across Canada's prairie provinces to the grueling roads over the Rockies into British Columbia. A daily log was kept on the car's performance and speed. The only problem encountered in the gas free automobile was the constant use of the brakes, the shoes of which had to be periodically replaced. Car speed throughout the tour was literally controlled by braking.

To prevent curious onlookers swarming over the car, a sign saying "experimental automobile" had to be printed on each side, and the hood kept locked. Once, while crossing the Saskatchewan prairies, the lead jeep broke down. Moving up front, the little experimental car hitched an iron chain to the jeep and effortlessly towed it into Regina for repairs.

A tired, but contented, group finally reached the tunnel entrance to the Western Pacific complex. Only a single electric railroad went through the mountain tunnel. Mounting the rails, the car took its power from the overhead hot line and went through the tunnel. Caldwell was incredulous when told how the small car had towed the jeep several miles. "I'm not surprised," said Caldwell, "but let's see its pulling power demonstrated on that railway flat car loaded with heavy machinery." At that challenge, the 3,000-pound automobile squatted on the rails in front of the many tons of railway car and equipment. The little car moved ahead, the chain became taut. Had it been a tug of war, the railway flat car would have lost. The rail car simply took off and followed the auto as though it were a walking dog on a leash. Caldwell yelled, "That's enough! I'm a believer."

After many months of experimentation, Charles Wilkerson was convinced that modern man had never plotted the positions of the true north-south magnetic lines of force. That these force fields existed without particular resolution, all people were vaguely aware. Certainly Wilkerson knew that the longitudinal, as well as the latitudinal, lines drawn on maps were only to describe navigational positions and no more. He also felt that the Earth was not covered by a magnetic field like an invisible blanket, but rather that the magnetic force was built up from pole to pole along constant, defined parallel concentrations or perhaps interval bands. Col. Wilkerson reasoned that if that were the case, and he knew the distance between these lines of magnetic force, a much more powerful and responsive anti-magnetic motor could be built into the round-wing planes making commonplace future travel in any direction without adjustment. He had recognized that Earth itself was a gigantic magnetic generator that could propel properly harnessed objects such as the round-wing plane in any direction at phenomenal speeds, even 30,000 miles per hour. The planes magnetic fluctuations must first be tuned onto the Earth's generating bands.

At Cornell University, he came upon an old manuscript showing drawings on the wall of a secret room in the Pyramid of Giza.
Those drawings strongly suggested to Wilkerson that his "lines of
force" theory was correct. Flying to Egypt, he went to the University of Cairo where he was shown further evidence that such a
room existed in the great pyramid. A professor and photographer
accompanied Wilkerson to the great pyramid. Through a secret
passage near the top of the ancient wonder they came upon a door.
On opening the door, the group found themselves in a completely
round room about seven feet high. It was a perfect reproduction of
the globe left by ancients for succeeding generations. Charles B.
Wilkerson had been the first contemporary man to be drawn to that
hidden room and deduce its meaning. As he looked at the relief
map of the Earth, he distinctly saw north-south lines shown at
exact intervals between each other. The three stood in awe without
speaking as they beheld the pictorial message handed down from
several thousand years before. Wilkerson realized then that his was
not the first advanced civilization. At least one other race of knowledgeable people had existed long before. Some one, or group,
recognizing that their ancient world was declining had decided
to leave a record of truth for men of the distant future who might
rebuild the world from records of the ancient past.

The surrounding walls of the room were photographed in detail.
Wilkerson took home the photos. In the next months he had solved
the most difficult enigma of his life. It was his greatest triumph.
When finished, he had plotted a new earth grid system of true
longitudinal lines running exactly 32 miles apart at the equator and
angling off into the throat of the earth at the 85th parallel. Emerging inside the earth's mantle to the interior, each pair of magnetic
longitudinal lines from the surface came together to form only one
magnetic line running through the interior to the South Pole. Later
on, it was discovered that the directions of ocean currents were
also affected by those same magnetic lines of force.

Defining the true magnetic lines answered a host of perplexing
questions that had bothered round-wing plane pilots for years.
Wilkerson had identified earth's magnetically generated bands

or highways where they were strongest, where they disappeared, where they reappeared again. The immensity of his precise discovery was self evident for a number of electromagnetic applications, but particularly as it applied to future round-wing plane travel. When the subject tests were completed at the Los Alamos site, it was decided that replacement of the existing anti-magnetic motors was paramount in the Anglo-American round-wing fleet. When motor conversion was completed, the round-wing plane fleet could fly in any direction either straight or obliquely, geared to a self-correcting flight pattern. General William Donovan, OSS Chief, had been far sighted when, in 1945, he said to the head of the U.S. Army Air Force, "he was sending the greatest mathematical mind to help perfect the round-wing plane for future use."

Mr. Plateu, the resident Venusian who had helped earthmen more than any other outer terrestrial, had said in the early 40's: "We must let you perfect the round-wing plane yourself. We have guided you towards proper beginnings. Among you are intelligent minds who will appear from time to time to show you how to solve the problems of future travel in space." Col. Charles B. Wilkerson, later promoted to Lt. General in the US Army, and also knighted, was one of those earth people who came along at the right time.

In 1978, there were twelve centers in North America, two of which are in Canada, conducting research on the round-wing plane and other facets of the anti-magnetic propulsion system. The original efforts of the Project Milk Can researchers had added significantly to the operational improvement and guidance of the Caldwell round-wing planes that swept the skies so majestically in the final days of World War II. The new fleet of Anglo-American round-wing planes could hurl themselves faster than any other like or un-like conveyance on the face of the earth. The earth scientists knew that they were still not as sophisticated as the outer space craft from the sister planet Venus.

Sir Charles Wilkerson retired from the round-wing plane research program in 1962. Some time in the future biographers and historians will be allowed to evaluate the contributions that he and his Los Alamos cohorts made.

Only one major problem now remained to be overcome. The round-wing planes could fly faster and create more friction than their outer skins of stainless steel and duralumin could safely withstand. Furthermore, to encounter dust particles and pebble sized meteorites in space traveling at perhaps 200,000 miles per hour would be disastrous as they bombarded the ship's outer skin. There were no existing materials developed on Earth impervious enough to withstand space particles. (During tornadoes, it is on record that straws have been driven into telephone poles.) The stainless steel, duralumin skins might get an Earth craft to another planet, but while on the journey it might become so pitted as to make impossible the return voyage home.

The outer space people had watched the Anglo-Americans for almost 30 years. In 1975 they apparently had decided that the formula for the last remaining technological improvement should be given to the U.S. and its English-speaking relatives.

Thus, late in the evening of February 18, 1975, an unidentified outer terrestrial landed in Washington and, shortly thereafter, appeared before President Gerald Ford. After his salutation, his first words were, "We are of the opinion there should be no further delay in lending direct help to the United States of America to complete her outer space program." When the being dematerialized, he left a disk on the President's desk. Nicknamed the talking book, the disk spelled out the formula for making the rare, light, unbreakable metal needed to cover the outside surface of the round-wing plane.

Within 32 days after the disk was given, America had successfully turned out its first batch of the new metal. Five top chemists and metallurgists worked on distilling and firing of the flux at Wright Patterson Field. After being certain of success, Stanley Tool and Die Works of New Britton, Connecticut, was called in to complete the development of the material into structural components. A steel company rolling mill turns out the sheets before they are sent to the fabricators. The new metal is electrically non-conductive against lightning and lasers. It resists heat and cold and once formed cannot be filed, shaped or drilled after one year. The metal does not build up friction heat and protects from radiation.

Spacemen will now be able to journey far into space and back without cumbersome protective suits. The use of this metal has so modernized the American space industry that nearly all the components of space travel, from the ship's outer skin to astronaut's clothing, are now being refashioned.

On October 30, 1976, there appeared over Washington, and other North American cities, a hovering squadron of the latest model round-wing planes, on the underside of which there was stenciled the insignia of the United States Air Force.

The appearance of these wondrous machines was a silent salute to thousands of North American workers, who, not knowing the faith placed in them by the leaders of their nations, and those of another celestial body (Venus), produced a spacecraft that henceforth would take its place amongst the ageless vehicles that already shuttle between the planets of the universe.

Somewhere on the west coast of North America a man named Jonathon E. Caldwell, alias Major Crawford, who developed America's round-wing plane in 1936, was surely pleased, regardless of the fact that he must live and die incognito.

Chapter XVI

Germans Build Life below in Hollow Earth: New Sovereign Nation Evolves

Accelerated colonization of the inner world by departing World War II Germans enabled them to build their primary settlements below at least a generation sooner than normal. There was one major reason and that was attributed to the speed and load carrying capabilities of the new round-wing planes.

For the bewildered arrivals, it was despairing in the 40's and still tough in the 50's. Getting a foothold below had caused family separations, hardships, loneliness and, of course, austerity. Both men and women suffered some adverse aspects of the escape from upper-world reality.

In the last months of World War II, Kurt Von Schusnick, a German-speaking, Swiss born war ace, took many hundreds of handpicked Germans to rendezvous in South America for ultimate delivery to the New German hideout. Each night from Von Runstedt's western front headquarters near Ulm, in the Bavarian Alps, specially chosen officers and civilians arrived to emigrate in a round-wing plane piloted by Von Schusnick. By war's end, this same man had transported several thousand key Germans via South American staging points to their new homes inside the earth. Following hostilities, Kurt Von Schusnick in his round-wing plane continued to ferry key Germans from Switzerland who arrived there both legally and illegally. (On a post-war raid on a Soviet prisoner-of-war camp in occupied Poland on October 26, 1946, three German round-wing-plane crews, led by Van Schusnick, killed the Russian guards with lasers and rescued over 100 key German prisoners.)

A few of the Germans taken from a Bavarian chalet before Germany's surrender were: Felix Von Rattenwell, aide de camp to Von Runstedt; Franz Von Heigle, Assistant Minister of Foreign Affairs; Baron John De Landsbert, (Major General), descendent of Charlemagne; Charles Wurzack, liaison SS officer at Von Runstedt's headquarters and a Nazi party member; and Eric Blwuberg of Swedish extraction, a civilian technical engineer in a German round-wing-plane plant, formerly with Zeppelin works.

On December 10, 1944, an American colonel had just been brought through the chalet checkpoints, blindfolded and under guard. The guards were alerted surrounding the headquarters of Von Runstedt, 140 miles northeast of Zurich, Switzerland, deep inside Germany. His mission was to find Von Runstedt, the Commander of German Western Armies, and also the Commander of all German Armies since the real Hitler had vacated in October of the same year.

The 26-year-old American, who went by the intelligence code name of Hal-ford Williams, was known by Germans only under his nickname of the "Fox." Col. Williams had just arrived from London, England by way of plane, sealed railway car, jeep, and finally on foot over the last mile into the closely guarded German fastness. Escorted into the presence of Von Runstedt, the American officer apologized for his un-pressed officer's dress attire due to what he termed 'unfavorable' travel conditions. From the young American's belt hung a golden sword. After properly saluting the senior officer, he removed from the lining of his coat a letter from General George S. Patton to Von Runstedt, a letter approved by all the allied leaders except President Roosevelt. The letter stated the Germans should expect an immediate change of western allied intentions during the next weeks of the war and that Von Runstedt should arrange to meet Patton as soon as possible in Berne, Switzerland with his most able staff officers to discuss a total allied change of strategy favorable to recent German peace overtures. Von Runstedt read the letter, removed his monocle, thanked the young American colonel, and offered him breakfast, bath and bed till 4:00 P.M. the same day. By then the German commander's reply would be ready for the Allies. Then the General dismissed the guard and aide and got up and closed the door to the office in order to interrogate the courier.

"Stand at ease Colonel," began the German officer politely. Then he painstakingly studied the Yank. The General returned to his desk, removed his monocle and finally spoke directly to the emissary.

"You are most certainly not English. This is the first privilege I have had of meeting you, Colonel Halford Williams." The German lingered on the colonel's name. "Halford Williams is your code name, I presume." The German general tapped quietly on his desk as though contemplating the pieces of a jigsaw puzzle. Then he looked up and said: "We Germans all call you the American Fox because your rescue missions are legendary inside Hitler's occupied lands from Norway to the borders of Russia. They say you are invincible -- that you can't be killed. It is also reliably reported that you have been dropped or appeared suddenly inside Germany dozens of times, perhaps 40 or 50 times in the last two years alone."

The German's eyes lighted with admiration as he studied the waist of the American colonel standing before him. "All the stories say the same thing: that the Fox always carries a golden sword to direct his five or six-man band. Imagine, such a ridiculous medieval symbol of authority! Of course you don't need your sword on a mission like this where only diplomacy is necessary, do you Colonel?" The General's tone was not sarcastic but quizzical.

The American colonel still stood silent. Then the interrogation continued. "Can you hear me Colonel?" "Yes sir!" the younger man replied. The General said, "Hitler's reward for delivery of the Fox, preferably alive, is over $100,000 in gold. Perhaps I should tear up this letter and collect the reward."

Colonel Fox smiled faintly. Von Runstedt went on: "I know deep within me that you are the Fox. Eisenhower would not send anyone but his bravest and most trusted for this mission -- because he had to be certain the message reached me. But even allowing yourself to be blindfolded, under guard, I don't think your destiny is to die -- yet -- although I must consider why I should not turn you over to the despicable S.S. who already knows of your presence. Please reply, Colonel."

As though unmoved by the penetrating analysis, the American agent answered, "Even if I were the one whom you call the Fox, I should not worry. Among the Allies, General, your name too is legendary. You have been tagged as a gentleman of honor -- an enemy to be respected. Even if your Fuehrer ordered it, you would not keep a bonafide courier as a negotiable instrument of blackmail."

The General nodded almost imperceptibly. "May I suggest that you now go directly to the breakfast room? But if you value your nine lives I suggest you not leave the main floor of this building. And do not venture onto the grounds or visit the waterfall!"

As the American colonel sat in the officers' mess eating a breakfast of Bavarian rolls, jam, sausage and tea, he never suspected that just beyond his gaze, in a clearing below the cascading waterfall, sat on three legs a 30-foot round-wing saucer-like craft, one of five just completed that would carry the elite German remnants of World War II to a new land in another world.

During Williams' meal a number of German Army and Air Force officers passed in and out of the room, not unusual in a staff headquarters, he thought. But one face he noted carefully he was to see twice again. This was a Wermacht Air Force idol that had shot down 33 allied planes, Kurt Von Schusnick. He was a top ace whom the English, up to Churchill, respected for his audacity and combat ability. Another visitor was a favorite of Hitler's, the tall, piercing-eyed Otto Skorzeny, who demanded exodus by round-wing transportation for himself and key Nazis. Later Williams heard that Von Runstedt had turned him down categorically.

As darkness fell later that day the American colonel was escorted blindfolded back to Switzerland.

Eight days later the Wolfgang Bar in Berne, Switzerland, was the scene of a strange meeting as the same American, Colonel Williams, witnessed the ever so correctly dressed Von Runstedt sweep into the bar with two staff members including the air ace whose face he had seen in Von Runstedt's mess. Minutes later the bar door swung open again and General George S. Patton stomped in, dressed in helmet, crumpled field dress and high boots. Patton led his group over to the table whereupon the Germans stood up, exchanged formal greetings, and the ensemble sat down and ordered drinks. Von Runstedt asked for scotch, and Patton, bourbon.

Setting down their glasses after a quick toast by one of the American staff officers, General Patton rose, ordered another round and while still on his feet, gulped his bourbon down in one swallow. He looked directly at Von Runstedt and exclaimed, "Hell, General! What are we fighting each other for when the worst bastard in the world is that S.O.B. Stalin?" Those opening remarks set the tone for the meeting, the rest of which is still classified.

But the military plans agreed upon at that secret rendezvous between the leading allied and German Officers were to be held in abeyance -- forever.

Two weeks later a disappointed Von Runstedt, back at his headquarters, told his officers present that the plan proposed by Patton at Berne had been vetoed by President Roosevelt over even Churchill's and Eisenhower's objections. Von Runstedt said there was now no hope to end the war except by surrender of the German armies. "There is not much time left before the end," he said. "We shall hold out only long enough to collect all those on the staff list for transfer to the new land. Soon it will be every man for himself. Whatever you do, arrange to give safe harbor to your families while there is still time. It is hoped that someday they will join you in your new home."

Then, turning to Kurt Von Schusnick, later made a general, the Commander introduced him and said, "This brave young Air Force officer is in total charge of the new method of evacuation on a craft which is called a 'round-wing plane.' Many flights in the future days have been ordered to ferry special Germans to the new land. That is why some of you are here."

Von Schusnick then told the group that more top ranking Germans would be arriving daily at the headquarters and the nearby village for evacuation. The round-wing plane would transport at least 20 bodies packed in like cordwood and each man would carry only minimum personal belongings. Von Schusnick said that within the next month, he would make at least two trips daily with a full load of VIP's to Argentina, the staging area for the new land. Turning to Von Runstedt he remarked so everyone could hear, "My duty eventually is to take the respected General Von Runstedt down under when defense here can no longer be maintained."

Unexpectedly, Von Runstedt replied, "Thank you -- no! I would rather stay behind and become a guest of the English in their prisons. Better to do that than serve that Bavarian Corporal and his Nazi followers, and train his Nazi army in the Promised Land for the next war."

In the ensuing weeks, Kurt Von Schusnick took thousands of hand-picked Germans, no doubt including prominent Nazis in disguise, out of the country.

Regardless of those Germans who got on the list for emigration to the Inner World of the New Reich, the decision as to who would be permitted to reside below rested exclusively in the hands of the Bodlanders who screened incoming Germans at the tunnel entrance in Brazil and also at an undisclosed point of departure for the Inner World somewhere in Argentina. Several million Germans from Nazi Germany were rejected over a thirty-year period by the Bods as being unsuitable for citizenship in the Inner World of New Germany. Many of those refused entry were Nazis who, unable to return to East Germany under Soviet Communism or for fear of imprisonment in the Federated Republic of West Germany because of war crimes, took refuge principally in Brazil where the wartime German apparatus continued to flourish unchecked.

Meanwhile, Kurt's brother, Eric Von Schusnick, was deploying another round-wing plane in the removal from Germany of special documents, plans, medical supplies, valuables and essentials needed below. Although much of the timber needed for the New German world went through the tunnel or chute in Brazil, certain items needed quickly were flown at once through the South Pole opening to the new land. The round-wing planes were simple in construction, had few moving parts and required little maintenance. Their load bearing weight factor was determined only by volume.

In one of the operations, Eric von Schusnick made repeated trips from inside the Earth's South Pole to the surface in the Antarctic where the round-wing plane picked up tons of ice, suspended it below, and deposited it in a fresh water reservoir for the inhabitants of a new settlement. Such was the diversity of the new round-wing plane that the Venusians had helped the Germans to build. In retrospect, Germans interviewed in 1978 admit that the colossal power and multi-use of their limited number of round-wing planes, augmented by limited aerial transportation from Bodland round-wingers, not only made possible the birth of their new nation but speeded up its development by forty years.

American Immigration now realizes that the Germans moved many post-war dependents into their new world by means of visas with temporary stays in the U.S.A., the Caribbean Islands, or Brazil. Regardless of routing, the tide of German men and women continued to take their post-war ways to the new land. Germans within Germany proper kept the secret and no dispatches or serious leaks occurred. As the settlements below were expanded, additional technical help was sought in the Fatherland, and these colonists, like the German mercenaries of 1572, followed the same routing. But, by 1948 they passed through the mantle to the interior in a leisurely 24 hours rather than the three generations it had taken their German soldier ancestors and relatives.

The chute or elevator or train trip, which it was called, was no longer tedious or difficult. By 1953 it had transported up to two million Germans below and brought up to the outer surface hundreds of thousands.

In 1958, Kurt von Schusnick was struck down by a heart attack due to the burden of work performed in the years 1944 to 1948 in the round-wing-plane services of New Germany. This man who had earned the highest German decorations, and whose name appeared on Churchill's list as an enemy not to be dishonored, died in his prime at 38 years of age -- never to see the New Germany below fully bloom with the apple, the pear and the grape, the seeds of which he and others had carried down to be transplanted.

The same year, Eric, who also lived in New Berlin, took Kurt's family, including the youngest son, David, into his home and prepared to support them in keeping with a pact he and his brother had made together years before.

All official New Berlin records began in the year 1945 at which time pouring of the bottom floor of the ten-acre capitol building was begun. Today the entire government complex is housed in this one atomic-bomb-proof building whose walls are six feet thick. The ministries within this state house include Chief of State Office (Hitler II), Treasury Office, Secretary of Defense for Air Force, Navy and Army, Department of Prisons, Department of Transportation, etc.

The State House is in the center hub or oval of New Berlin. The streets are the spokes radiating from the State House and the avenues are never ending circles located at intervals in the city. The land is flat with no rivers intersecting it.

Today New Germany has 18 million people, approximately eight million who were born below. One and one-half million people live in New Berlin. There are 40 million descendants of the old Germans from the 1572 expedition, making approximately 60 million late arrival Germans inside the hollow earth, plus, of course, the early Bod arrivals of 30,000 years before who numbered only 36 million in 1980. The city of New Berlin now has state colleges and hospitals, and the entire metropolis is served by a monorail system with German-made cars, buses being the other means of public transportation. Although the first housing was wooden and prefabricated set up by the Bodlanders, many of the new residential buildings now being erected are of cement, brick and plastic siding and roofing, as there still remains a lumber shortage on the arid German occupied continent below.

The main church is Lutheran although there are several other denominations. A reformed Catholic Church was established after 1945 when Hitler I decreed it should contain no idols except the figures of Christ on the Cross. The first ministers and priests were brought down from above. Marriage rites today may be either secular or civil but any constituted member of parliament may also perform the ceremony.

As above in 1945, Hitler was proclaimed Chief of State (functioning as Prime Minister and President) over the German Reichstag consisting of a lower and upper house.

Three candidates form a slate for each office within the Party System, and those running for office must have served at least one four-year term and be a graduate of either a college or a trade school.

Qualifications for candidates to the upper house are as follows: church membership, party membership, at least 30 years of age, professional or worker, and preferably a veteran and at least three terms in the lower house.

The lower house is elected by popular vote and members must serve three terms or six years to become eligible to run for the upper house.

The State charges a straight ten percent of a person's gross income for taxes and has not nationalized any industry. Churches are not allowed to hold property other than the land and edifice of worship. Neither are churches allowed to accumulate liquid wealth. They are separate entirely from the state.

The school system is 12 years duration. No dropouts are allowed. Aptitude tests and job preferences during the last four years determine the student's vocation. Upon graduation, each male must serve four years in one branch of the New German Defense Military. The student can specify a preference for Army, Air Force, or Sea Force. Those with leadership qualities are sent to Officer's Training Schools. Upon completing the four years military service, the young German, who may now be about 22 years of age, is sent to a university either below or above. Diplomas from trade schools are considered as important as university degrees in the life of New Germany.

Hitler's own son, Adolph, at age 12 was sent to Switzerland to complete his academic learning where he attended the private school, St. Albans, in the northeast under the name Adolf Wolfgang, a common Austrian surname. While there, he was carefully guarded, and he also had a telephone by his bed to enable him to speak to his parents daily. He graduated in 1956. Although Adolph had decreed that his son assume the Feuhrer's role on the old one's retirement, he had said that Adolph II's future leadership of the new nation should be judged solely on ability.

War ace General Kurt Von Schusnick's son, David, chose to enter the Air Force after his four year compulsory military training as an officer cadet at which time he also qualified for the air service.

Flight training required of David Van Schusnick was that he first flies conventional aircraft and graduate to the round-wing plane. German pilots are armed with individual hand-held ray guns.

The Germans refused to discuss the ship's weaponry except to say that silent laser beams and other ray guns are used in place of conventional firepower. The Germans had also developed a laser shield on their ground ray guns and other laser counter measures had been perfected on the airborne craft.

David Schusnick received his wings upon graduation from the New German Air Force flying program on April 18, 1972. They were pinned on him by Air Marshall D. C. Kitchiner.

On April 20, his uncle, Eric Von Schusnick, and his mother called

David aside. The uncle began, "You have earned your wings. Now it is time to talk about your career." Thus began the talks of where the godson of Eric Von Schusnick would study and what vocation he would follow. Young Schusnick was urged to attend a university in Germany or Switzerland and there to study the vocation of law which he had chosen. The young man replied that he wished to go to an American university, preferably Harvard.

Over strong objections, David convinced his uncle and mother to send him to Harvard. He came up to the surface via railroad and flew to Bonne to meet his relatives, and later, after a vacation, he went to New York. In September 1972, David Schusnick enrolled at Harvard University as a West German national under the name David Schmidt, giving a Swiss address, the home of his uncle Johannus of Zurich.

According to a State Department source, he majored in international law and took general business law, graduating in 1976 in ceremonies attended by his uncle Johannus and other American relatives including his deceased uncle Elmer's wife, June.

When he returned to New Berlin below, David Schusnick reviewed his American college experience with his uncle Eric. Among other things, they discussed the German ethnic element in the U.S. population.

David Schusnick reminded his godfather, "Germans have no trouble becoming Americans or Canadians or British. In fact 50 percent of the stock in English-speaking North America is probably of German origin or had some German in it, and of course, we're taught that the English are of Germanic origin. I felt at home in the U.S.A."

David ended the conversation by saying, "Someday when the Russian question is settled, I want to live and practice law in Florida. But for the present, uncle, I want to go back into the flying service." (At the time of the final interview with the Von Schusnicks in 1977, there were still 30,000 German soldiers held by Russians in Siberia's prison camps, which could account for much of the

German hatred for the Soviets.)

As David Schusnick immersed himself back into the New Germany life below. New Germany continued to develop much like that above in West Germany.

New Berlin had two daily newspapers telling what went on in the upper world, but one day in November 1974 large headlines featured a different story. Bannered streamers on November 12, 1974 in the "New Berlin Daily News" (circulation 450,000), editor Max Speigel (formerly New York Times who left that newspaper in 1941), read as follows:

"THE FUEHRER IS DEAD." The paraphrased subtitle told how Hitler, founder of National Socialism, passed away in a foreign land, failing to reach Germany where he wanted to end his days." New Berlin's second daily, "The New German Enquirer" also ran the story in large banner headlines.

In respect for the former fuehrer's death, all flags were flown at half-mast the following 30 days by order of that German government. West Germany government flags were lowered on the day of the funeral and for ten days in Spain. In New Germany it was an official day of mourning. The son and heir of Hitler, Adolf Hitler II, had been in power for three months when his father's death occurred in Zaragoza, Spain. As Hitler neared death on October 25, a German round-wing plane took young Adolf Hitler and other close relatives and friends to the bedside of the fuehrer.

In the absence of Adolf Hitler Jr., the adopted son ruled as Chief of State. The present name of the son adopted by Hitler and Eva Braune is Dr. Hans Tirsther, Deputy Chief of the New Reich. When Hitler's motorcade was passing through Strasbourg in 1944 on its way to France and Spain for ultimate evacuation to the new German retreat, young Hans, then a 12-year-old admirer of Hitler had thrown a bunch of flowers into the fuehrer's car. When bodyguards apprehended the boy, Hitler rescued him and asked his name. The boy told Hitler his mother and father had been killed in a bombing raid. He looked at Hitler and is reported to have said: "You are my great father now, sir." Moved by his remarks, Hitler took the boy aboard his cavalcade and eventually adopted him legally. (Hitler's son was interviewed by the authors at a certain location in the western hemisphere in 1977.)

Hitler had made his farewell speech on August 7, 1974 from his residence (begun by his ardent admirers in New Berlin in 1943). Following his parting words, he turned over the reins of New Germany to his son Adolf II and boarded a German round-wing plane. A squadron of three companion craft escorted him as they set course for Spain. In the old castle La-Aljaferia, Zaragoza, at 5 A.M. on the cold, wet morning of October 25, 1974 Adolf Hitler, founder of Germany's Third Reich died at age 85. He had outlived all his avowed enemies, Roosevelt, Stalin, and Churchill. Practically his last words were, "We would have won the war except for those damned Americans! Today they lead the upper world, but I hold no hate for them whatsoever, except that traitor, Roosevelt. But on my deathbed I prophesy that the Americans will now have to take care of the Russians before the Russians take care of them and the rest of the world."

The late fuehrer died with his close relatives and friends beside him including his friend Generalissimo Franco. The funeral was attended by most of the West Berlin cabinet including President Helmut Schmidt. Present also were the West German Ambassador to Spain; Professor Dr. Francisco Javier Conde; the Archbishop of Cologne, Cardinal Joseph Hoffner, who conducted the last rites of the Catholic Church; and by Franco's request, Cardinal Marcelo Gonzales, who sang mass assisted by Monseigno, a leading Catholic cardinal of the Vatican who told the authors of the following Hitlerian reply to the Pope. "Excommunicate me and I'll persecute and kill all offensive Catholics and other Christians within Germany, and I'll destroy the Vatican itself." At that time with Nazi ambitions in ascendancy, the papal order to excommunicate Hitler was never carried out in the face of such a ruthless threat.

General Franco placed the town of Zaragoza under martial law during the week of Hitler's death.

Genesis for the Space Race

The solidarity of National Socialism in the New Reich had been established during the Hitler years beginning in 1945. In 1974, by vote of the Lower and Upper Houses of Parliament over the signature approval of the new Chief of State, Adolf Hitler II, the Parliament recommitted themselves and the 18,000,000 New Germans then living in the hollow earth to the continuance of National Socialism as a sovereign state. They would no longer be under the watchful eyes of the Bodlander government, since the 30-year treaty was about to end.

Six other Kingdoms of 40,000,000 old Germans ruled by monarchies also existed beside the New Germans on a nearby continent in the southern hemisphere. Adjoining and connected to the New German lands via road and rail was the ancient Bodland whose overseers had channeled the New German beginnings throughout all facets of society from limited military advice to education, transportation and capital construction of factories and relocated industries. In the northern hemisphere on the Vikingland continent there dwelt a pocket of Scandinavians descended also from Germanic tribes. The Viking influx to the inner world had taken place 2000 years before with the last group arriving 900 to 1000 A.D. Like the 20th century new German influx, the last wave of ancient Viking sea rovers had sailed into the inner world as marauding conquerors and had to be tamed into a pastoral people by earlier Scandinavian and Bodlander arrivals.

On the outside of Planet Earth, West and East Germany remained divided politically by diverse conquering ideologies, but nevertheless, Germans of the same ethnic beginnings occupied much of Europe including Alsace Lorraine, the Saar, now part of France, and numerous other German areas in Eastern Europe.

But in a political scene, a united Germany was still as illusive as it was in the 12th century when 367 Germanic Duchies, Dukedoms, Kingdoms, etc., stretched from Holland to Italy and Russia. Neither the Kaiser nor Hitler had been able to amalgamate the separated German pockets in Europe. However, an undercurrent of German sentiment calling for unity was still bullish in Western Europe and outright bellicose in German foreign policy and ideology engendered since 1945, particularly in the Brazilian Germans relocated in South America. Also, the upper-world Germans and the New Germans in the interior continued to espouse the belief that Russia was the offensive nation whose power must be broken before the German Empire could be restored in Europe.

A knowledgeable Bod spokesman on a five-year U.S.A. visa said this about another possible Upper World conflict. "We (the Bods) understand the German reasoning for their hatred of Russia." This learned man who speaks seven languages stated "Soviet Communism is an evil force -- but it will eventually destroy itself from within without involving outside interference.

Our intelligence below and our prophets contend that internal insurrection within Russia will triumph by the year 2000. Therefore, the solution to the Soviet problem will take care of itself without the renegade Germans starting another war that could become a spreading holocaust."

Asked what the Bods would do in case of such an Upper World War, the Bod spokesman replied: "We would not get involved. If those Upper World Germans in South America persist in destroying themselves, we (the Bodlanders) will not take part." But this Germanic scholar said he had faith that if such a war were to begin, their New German neighbors would have been re-educated enough to remain neutral.

The alignment of the three contenders for superiority in any forthcoming world conflict currently presents a paradox of ideologies. There is the vociferous Soviet system of Asia with its denial of God and rejection of man's spirit by which he would try to lift himself to higher spiritual levels of consciousness. Opposed to Soviet dialectic materialism is the modern day Nazi movement, strong, but submerged in all German societies -- an ideology founded by Hitler and his SS nucleus in the 20's on the basis of racial superiority ~ might makes right. Against these two systems that murdered countless millions of their enemies in order to stay in power is the giant America of Christian inception. While still keeping its personal freedoms relatively intact, America has allowed its moral strength to be eroded in government, business and institutions so that the question of its national virtue is now being debated publicly. In the ensuing years, one asks whether America, which now leads the upper free world, will have difficulty in firming its economic, political and spiritual philosophies in sufficient time to gird itself against its two adversaries of evil and madness. Within the American sector it will take a national leader of Gideon's stature to rise up and awaken the nation into renewing the faith handed down by the founding fathers.

In 1978, New Germany recalled Eric Von Schusnick as the second secretary to its US embassy of the Federated Republic of West Germany. Von Schusnick was accused of treason for revealing New German Nazi intelligence concerning possibilities for renewed surface war. The brave German did not deny the accusations, stating that in talking to us his objective was to prevent war. He was tried and condemned to death. The United States and Great Britain interceded on his behalf. Today he is serving a lifetime sentence without parole in a New German prison.

By the early 1970's German/American/British anger over World War II differences had begun to soften. Young David Schusnick became part of that amelioration.

Thus, in 1977, the first timid venture of an inter-world friendship occurred between New Germany and certain surface nations under the most un-political circumstances. It was perhaps the beginning of a new era of understanding between New Germany and some upper surface nations. The carefully planned program began on Sunday, July 31, 1977 when New Berlin in the earth's interior and Cape Kennedy, U.S.A. on the exterior shared in common a spectacular event. Winged emissaries from New Berlin inside the hollow earth began the marathon to the surface.

On that morning, Captain David Schusnick was given a special letter to President Jimmy Carter of the U.S.A. from the New German head of state. Captain Schusnick and two other round-wing crewmembers boarded a non-military German round-wing plane and took off. Crewmembers were 2nd Lieutenant Karl Ludendorf, grandson of Count Von Ludendorf; Inspector General of the Imperial German Army in World War I. Grandson Karl had dropped the prefix "Von." Felix B. Armondstein, 1st Lieutenant, was the other crewmember.

The trip to Kennedy Space Center could have been made in less than two hours, but the crew was given permission by the New German Air Force (Wermacht) to take their time and schedule their arrival over Cape Kennedy exactly 12 hours later at noon that Sunday. The instructions were to carry out certain activities and stops beforehand but once over American air space to fly directly to their expected point of arrival.

As the German round-wing craft began descending over the Cape to an altitude of 1,000 feet, Captain Schusnick addressed the tower and waited for recognition response. At this point, the craft appeared to waiting ground spectators as a luminous ball of fire as it suddenly shot down to less than 28 feet above the east end of the remote Kennedy runway. The Americans had witnessed this ball of light speed toward them. When at a specially marked spot on the tarmac the light went out, and from within the glow there emerged the outlines of a flying saucer. The three legs dropped to the cement, and suddenly the thing stood alone like a round bug.

A door on the craft's under section opened, and dropping to the ground it formed a stairway on which the crewmen stepped down for formalities. Their uniforms were black, the trousers lined with silver side vents tucked in high black boots. German type caps showed the insignia of the Air Corps of New Germany.

Captain David Schusnick, officer in command of the German craft, was introduced to representatives of the American Air Force including; General David Jones, then Chief of Staff, U.S. Air Force; General Harold Brown, Chairman, Joint Chiefs of Staff; and Security Advisor Zbigniew Brzezinski. A US Air Force photographer for the author's associate made an official photo of the German plane and its occupants, but the picture (as well as the notes) were confiscated by the U.S. Air Force and never returned.

Waiting in line to receive the young commander and his crew was the newly appointed (April 20, 1977) Second Secretary of the German Embassy in Washington, the old ace of World War II, the Godfather of David, and Eric Von Schusnick. After formalities, at the request of General Jones, Schusnick was asked what he and his crew would like most to do. Almost in unison, the young Germans from the Inner Earth spoke up "Ride an American motor bike." As 100 selected Americans gathered in the hanger and freely inspected the German machine inside and out, the U.S. Air Force Band played German music. Meanwhile, the police blocked off the ocean road to Melbourne while those curious who were privileged to be near saw three young men and a police escort enjoy the power of Harley Davidsons in the Atlantic breezes. (Before the craft departed, a similar bike was placed aboard.)

Viewers of the interior of the German ship were told how the controls worked. In addition to the computerized navigational system, sensitive touch buttons for feet and knee-pressures were also used to control the electro-guidance system. A left foot button turned the ship counter clockwise; a right foot button turned it clockwise; a center foot button was for ascent and descent. Left knee pressure on the electro magnetic button was for reverse and right knee pressure was for forward. Finger keys duplicated the foot maneuvers. The foot and knee buttons were used in case of combat, so that the hands are free to operate the electronic laser weapons.

The German round-wing itinerary was to have included a stop over at Ottawa, but Prime Minister Pierre Trudeau rebuffed the German request according to Canadian authorities while the German craft hovered over Canada's capital.

On July 17, the same German craft arrived at an RAF military station southwest of London, England. Although it was not a scheduled stop, a formal reception was hurriedly prepared by the British, whereupon David and his crewmen were taken to Buckingham Palace in a royal limousine where Queen Elizabeth cancelled previous engagements to graciously receive the visitors.

The young New Germans, born inside the earth's interior, whose parental roots had sprung from their fatherland above, had emerged openly to be accepted with enthusiasm by Americans and the British.

From London, the German craft was flown to Rome where the Italians paid honors. While at Rome His Holiness, Pope Paul VI, asked if the German craft could visit the Vatican. "Certainly," said David, and that night Captain Schusnick gingerly sat his craft down in a Vatican garden enclosure. After an audience with the Pope and a friendly chat with the Secretariat of the Vatican, the Germans' craft departed late the next day for Berne, Switzerland. Swiss police guarded the craft while David and his crew went into the city to visit his relatives and his father's birthplace.

Like American heroes being welcomed with a ticker tape parade down New York's Fifth Avenue, the young German ambassadors-at-large arrived back in New Berlin. They had forged a new but fragile link of friendship with old surface enemies. Perhaps only such a new generation could have so succeeded.

Chapter XVII

Intrusion of Alien Beings into World Societies and Interviews with Leading Extra terrestrials

A U.S. State Department spokesman, whose name and position is classified, estimates that in 1980 over 50,000 outer terrestrials of interstellar and intergalactic origins are living on planet Earth. Within United States borders there are at least 5,000 registered aliens of which the public is unaware.

Approximately 200 new aliens arrive in the U.S. annually and are given permits or visas to remain up to ten years, subject to renewal. The arrival of beings from other planets to America is not pre-arranged by this government nor is their admission on a quota basis. When a space ship carrying such unannounced alien arrivals approaches Earth's atmosphere, the Interplanetary Police Net usually picks up their signals of intention to land. Such being the case, Earth monitoring stations are notified and generally a government reception delegation is there to meet the alien craft. (A hostile spacecraft does not abide by the interplanetary rules of recognition and hence gives no signal.)

When a friendly landing occurs, whether on a military base or at a commercial field, the State Department is immediately notified. Then, upon an acceptable interview by State Department representatives, aliens are given typical Earth clothing and shoes. Their wardrobe, which is always a space suit and boots, (both exceedingly light in weight) is usually boxed and stored at an airport locker.

Friendly aliens are usually English speaking. (Major Earth languages are taught at an interplanetary language school on Venus, compulsory attendance for immigrants.) They are advised that in case of civilian misdemeanor or traffic infraction, they must immediately get in touch with the State Department or ask arresting officers to do so.

The outer space immigrants comprise about 40 percent females with the arrivals being both male and female singles plus family units with or without children.

First task under the guidance of the State Department is to rush the aliens by round-wing plane to the Washington area and thence to Walter Reed Hospital where they are quarantined. A medical team including an outer-terrestrial doctor familiar with interplanetary diseases and types of people conducts very thorough physicals with the recorded medical data punched in code onto a 3 x 5 inch card, which also shows the alien's thumb print.

By what authority, or for what reason, the aliens leave their planet for an earthly sojourn is unknown. Generally the reason for their coming to this planet is listed as "I have come to Earth to help" (and they indicate a special trade or professional category.) The arriving aliens occasionally are revealed to have four lungs and perhaps two hearts, plus other anomalies. A supernatural ability that certain aliens possess is the ability to change their form or appearance at will to resemble Earth racial characteristics. This change is usually made after they come in contact with Earthlings shortly after deplaning. In addition, they usually can exhibit superhuman strength as in the case of a registered alien girl who simply lifted a car off two men in a Washington, D. C. accident, while a group of bystanders watched helplessly. Some aliens have four eyes, strangely colored skin, unusually shaped ears, and other oddly shaped appendices. These are all changed to conform to earth appearances. What is obvious is that their minds and sensory feelings are identical to Earthlings, regardless of body structure.

Education and job qualifications of the arriving aliens are always extraordinary by Earth standards. The newcomers usually end up in a profession and are outstanding in physics, medical research, et cetera. Such cases have helped Earth industries develop plastics, chemical steel industries (hardened steel), fuels and other scientific breakthroughs.

For a time after arrival they are observed taking their nutrition by means of a variety of colored pills and water, distilled water preferred. However, they are soon able to eat small amounts of foods that are typical of the menus in their host country. Once they have passed their physical and the quarantine is ended, the aliens are able to move out unobtrusively and vanish into society. (Quarantine is 90 days.)

However, each year they must report their whereabouts to the State Department, which no doubt notifies Immigration.

The United Nations also admits newly arrived aliens and sends them to host countries willing to accept them. In a recent case, Russia accepted six new Earth arrivals, but instead of relocating them in requested job categories, the Soviets placed the aliens in isolation under 24 hour observation. Later the aliens simply vanished, showing up again at the United Nations in New York for re-posting to another country.

Not all aliens may stay, even overnight. A craft of six-legged men with green skin, eyes, hair and teeth, who could not change their appearances, arrived at a Western U.S. military air station in July, 1977 from a planet catalogued by NASA as Eeti. The friendly men called themselves Baahs and said they had been on an expedition for seven Earth years, visiting various planets in the Milky Way. The captain of the Eeti ship was able to make it known they had first touched down in Russia but had been fired on. They decided to try one more Earth landing and by chance, chose the western U.S. airdrome. On alighting, they followed the jeep across the tarmac at 45 miles per hour, traveling like centipedes. They could laugh, joke and smile, and indicated the position of their planet on an interstellar map. They said their planet was more advanced socially and technologically than Earth. They were asked to leave and did so promptly.

Sources, which do not want to be identified, say there are aliens already integrated into the Russian political and scientific societies. But, unlike their American, Canadian or French counterparts, none of the aliens inside Russia are known to Soviet immigration or police. They could be called sleepers and would reveal their true identities only in case of an international war. An unimpeachable source said he was aware of an interstellar bar in Paris which French gendarmes claim is frequented by registered aliens.

Eighteen known aliens live in the Tampa Bay area of Florida, and perhaps double that number make the Los Angeles area their temporary home. In all, three interviews were conducted with registered Venusian aliens in Florida.

The friendly invasion of these outer terrestrials is mainly from Venus, Pluto and Mars. Some come from other parts of our entire solar system, and they have a purpose. Their objectives supposedly are to mingle into earth's mainstream and report activities to their solar ambassador so that planet Earth may be guided away from the self destruction course on which it is presently veering. If there is a more sinister reason, no one in authority has revealed it to the authors.

One alien coordinates and determines the direction of Extra terrestrials on this planet. He is the chief representative to Earth for this solar system's governing body. He is in constant touch with all governments, and his presence is known by the United Nations. As head of the global network of information, he is in daily communications with the Interplanetary Police Net and the Solar Council on Venus.

The name of this warm, friendly non-human is Mr. Estes Plateu. He has been the confidant and friend of presidents, kings and statesmen for centuries, but Mr. Plateu not only sat for an artist's drawing of himself (he is not photographable), he also agreed to be interviewed as would any well-known earth celebrity.

To begin, this "illusive phantom" from Planet Venus, as he is referred to around Washington, says he was born in1228 just a few years after the signing of England's Magna Carta. He began shaping the destiny of America as far back as George Washington's time and has been posted permanently in the American capitol since 1943 from which he disappears for months at a time, probably to return to his home planet on furlough. Although his body resides in a particular office, on most occasions when he is seen, even by Presidents, he is a three dimensional projection of his true self.

Mr. Plateu claims his home planet to be Venus, but he says Earth was the original habitat of his ancestors who fled just prior to a global catastrophe. Nevertheless, this interloping ambassador, who first arrived without credentials, stated he is the official representative of his planet where four billion people live within and on the surface of the planet united under one government. Since the Earth's discovery of nuclear energy and its peacetime applications, as well as the negating of the gravity force by a universally understood form of electro-magnetic energy, Mr. Plateu says that in the next two decades Earth science and technology will be unbelievably advanced and in the service of human progress. But, just as earth is about to achieve its goal of a Utopian civilization, it may be set back thousands of years again by another nuclear holocaust, the ambassador forecast. Mr. Plateu described Earth as a leading planet in science and learning as recently demonstrated, whereas there are many planets with more primitive civilizations.

The question of how to prevent earth from destroying itself is a favorite subject of the Venusian ambassador. As he sat in his office in a high building overlooking the Potomac, Mr. Plateu gazed out at the river for several moments, and then turned around.

His pale, blue eyes changed from a trance-like expression to a piercing stare that somehow reflected no arrogance. An oval face with high forehead and long ears gave him a distinguished, philosophical appearance. His hair is still black and no wrinkles show on his face. Here was a being who had talked with all the deceased leaders responsible for involving their nations in World War II, as well as all the American Presidents, including George Washington and Abraham Lincoln, but excluding Presidents Coolidge and Harding who refused to hear him out.

Mr. Plateu was first appointed official ambassador to Earth by the present King of Venus on approval by that planet's parliament (but his accreditation has not yet been approved by the U.S. Congress). He officially arrived in 1943 during the last term of President Roosevelt after a preliminary visit to the same President in 1936. The family of Plateus has long been trained and involved in Earth duties, Mr. Plateu's eldest brother having been advisor to Napoleon when he urged him not to fight the battle of Waterloo.

Mr. Plateu reminisced that his father was on Earth at the time of Christ -- and knew him.

This being, who came from Venus, claims that except for higher spiritual qualities among a segment of their people, Venusians are identical to white Earthlings who wantonly destroyed their civilization 11,500 years ago in an atomic war, bringing about the sinking of the lands in Atlantis and Athenia. (Haammaan, of the Inner World's Agraharta, also makes this claim.) Mr. Plateu says that planet Earth is the only one of twelve (not nine) planets within this solar system not belonging to our solar federation of inhabited spheres. (The ambassador recently advised the United States of another inhabited planet located in this solar system and unknown to earth astronomers. Its name is Anarus. It is roughly the same size as Earth or Venus and was discovered according to directions given by the Venusian via electronic telescopic camera at the Washington, D. C. observatory. The new addition is approximately 125,000,000 miles from Earth.) Earth is scheduled to become a full member of the Federation of Planets in this solar system when and if it is united under one world. Only then can the earth representative sit on the councils of the Interplanetary Government, headquartered in Venus, capitol planet in the solar system.

Venusians are not openly connected to every government on earth. But Mr. Plateu considers himself to be the first representative from Venus to Earth who must answer to his King and Parliament and to the Supreme Emperor of the Solar Federation as to what progress

Earth is making towards a united world order. His reports to home base and his watchfulness on Earth happenings are critical at this time because of the nuclear precipice on which the nations of the world are poised. Venusian and other solar agents, living incognito in those countries from which they continuously report, keep track of the major nations' war aggravations and intentions, sending the information in code to Washington-based Plateu, who transmits the gathered intelligence constantly to Interplanetary Police Net and to the solar headquarters in Venus for action. Mr. Plateu declined to mention what action would be taken, if any, in case of a nuclear outbreak on earth.

The Ambassador chose America as his past and present headquarters because he says America, consisting of a free assembly of diversified races, holds the greatest hope for leading this planet to overall lasting peace and prosperity. Mr. Plateu's abiding fears are: (1) that Earth is lagging in universal brotherhood, mainly because of Russia's hindrance, and (2) that armament makers are preventing international unity by keeping the various nations veritable armed camps. According to Plateu, the global arms race is engineered through efforts of international forces loyal to no nation. These hidden power structures influence all governments and their military, including those of Soviet Russia and the U.S.A.

Mr. Plateu believes that if a world plebiscite of all people were allowed, it would outlaw war at once and all the instruments and armaments of war. The last war on Venus was fought 3,000 years ago, he declared. Prior to this war, Venus had been a highly evolved civilization, the planet's greatness going back countless millennia. Before the war erupted, international bitterness had burst into violence among certain of the 16 nations of the Solar Federation. One nation had been the most quarrelsome and they instigated the first punitive action. An unnecessary nuclear confrontation broke out. Destruction was colossal. The land was devastated. Major cities were leveled and millions upon millions perished.

Far sighted men had saved and protected in deep underground caves, tunnels, and pyramids vast libraries of learning, chemical formulae, and industrial designs. When the survivors came together in truce, the first thing done was to renounce war forever. A new city in a new land became the capital of one nation instead of the former 16 warring members. Like the bird of Phoenix rising from the ashes of the past, Venus was reborn. Today, said Mr. Plateu, Earth nations are where Venus was just before that global war of self-destruction. The Venusian historian concluded by saying that "while mankind understands the precepts of peace, it is ironic that the self-idolatry of the Earth nations won't let them practice peaceful co-existence."

Venus is entirely free of diseases that kill the people of Earth, including senility that Plateu referred to as a curable disease of aging. By Earth measurements, those living on Venus are considered young at 100 years of age, and are still in their prime up to 300 years old. From three to six hundred years, Venusians are considered middle aged, and they are venerated as senior citizens from one to two thousand years old. Death on Venus is self-willed.

Earth's probes of Venus show outside temperatures over 900 degrees Fahrenheit under thick clouds of sulfuric acid that rains on the surface and pressures 100 times those of Earth. Plateu suggested that the United Nations appoint a delegation to be taken to Venus to learn the facts. The departing Venusian craft carrying the delegation would leave from any spot so designated by the United Nations before a number of witnesses. Mr. Plateu said that several prominent Earthlings have already spent time on his planet including a well-known Catholic churchman who was there as a 'guest' of that government for three months.

Venus is described as being geologically almost identical to Earth in atmospheric content including the interior. Constant temperatures there are 60 to 70 degrees Fahrenheit. Even plant life is similar. Their trees are like Earth's pine, oak, cypress, mahogany, et cetera. All crops grow more quickly there because of a cleaner air environment.

Venusian family formation is the same as Earth with marriage sanctified. A mother on Venus (where birth control is in effect) has the same great responsibilities as an Earth mother in bringing up a child the way it should grow, says Plateu (himself a father of three sons).

The moral laws of all planets are the same as those on Earth, and they spell out conscious recognition of right and wrong acts in criminal, social and civil obligations. Moral laws are similar to the Ten Commandments handed down from God through Moses.

In earth's three dimensional world, the visitor said, it is difficult for spiritual qualities to develop in a modern earth person as all values seem to be related to that three dimensional finite life in which earth people have subdued spiritual values. Earthlings must recognize that there is an eternal law of cause-and-effect that has a recognizable relationship to karma, or as said by Christ: "You reap what you sow." This law is not only individual; it is family, national and planetary. This truth also concerns one's thoughts. The alien explained: "The difference between conscious behavioral norms and the subconscious spiritual nature of civilized earthlings is made indistinguishable by modern education that is taught in schools and universities. Right and wrong actions of a person, regardless of what one is taught, are answerable to a higher power. A Supreme God has made it so."

On the first interview with Mr. Plateu, he was asked bluntly how Venus expected to help Earth through his ambassadorship. He replied succinctly: "Number one priority is to prevent the use of nuclear missiles. Next, to have Earth nations develop into one world government where war is outlawed. Finally, it would follow that other planets in this solar system who are also watching the outcome would share their technology and science with Earth so that it could take its place among other inhabited planets."

Some direct questions and answers follow concerning Plateu's political, religious and philosophical ideas:

Question: Mr. Plateu, secret White House records say that your permanent stay in America began on February 1, 1943, or there-abouts, when you visited President Roosevelt. On that occasion you laid out plans for a one-world government along the lines of the present United Nations. What exactly did you suggest to President Roosevelt as to how this planet could be governed peacefully by one ruler under the guidance of the solar council?

Answer: When I spoke to President Roosevelt that evening in 1943, he was reminded, by me, that I had visited him also in 1936 to enlist the friendship of America. I had indeed visited him in 1936 because we could see World War II approaching.

I explained that our people had been visiting earth for many centuries and had also met most of Roosevelt's predecessors in office. It was also explained that I represented the interplanetary government of this inhabited Universe, of which Earth was the only non-member. Therefore, the purpose of my 1943 visit was to invite Earth into our solar confederation of planets, according to my explicit instructions from home.

At first it was incomprehensible for President Roosevelt to accept the fact I could materialize at will and also that other planets in this solar system were inhabited generally only in their interiors -- earth and Venus being two of the exceptions, i.e., surface dwellers as well as interior people. Following a discussion centered on Earth problems, your President was told that other planets in the Universe had been monitoring Earth's emergence from primitive societies for centuries. But the possibility of nuclear war had changed outside surveillance to one of immediate concern that involved bringing planet Earth into the Interplanetary Federation. I cautioned Mr. Roosevelt that ultimately we would desire total participation of all world governments under one chosen head if earth was to take its place among the interplanetary governments to which I referred. Knowing quite well Mr. Roosevelt's ambition to head such a world government, I emphasized to him that such a world leader would be acceptable only if all personal, selfish ambitions for power were subdued.

It was explained to Roosevelt that all the potential world leaders of major nations had been evaluated, and that he had been regarded as an emerging Caesar. I gave no good words for Stalin, and I stated that a cloud hung over Hitler and Germany for the present time. The President was told that the other planets were aware that America led the world in prosperity and industrial output, and that its leadership and respect among all nations would remain undisputed for many years to come.

The President, gaining confidence, asked me to outline my plan for a united world government under a single head. I told him that he was somewhat familiar with the plan already, having learned much of its format from former President Woodrow Wilson. The legislative leaders had rejected Wilson's proposal for a League of Nations. Roosevelt had picked up the germ of a United Nations idea on his Atlantic Ocean crossing with Wilson following the Paris Peace Conference of 1918. Frankly, his political personality changed after that crossing, and he became a dedicated enthusiast of one world government and an advocate of international order among nations.

Quite clearly, Roosevelt had not forgotten Woodrow Wilson's dream of one-world. He was determined to resolve the future peace of mankind, and to use this concept as a cornerstone in any agreement before committing United States forces to World War II.

Roosevelt had already drafted a forerunner of the League idea, and it became public knowledge in August 1941 following his meeting on the high seas with Churchill off Newfoundland. The document was called the Atlantic Charter. The eight clauses concerned mainly the hope of a better post-war world, free of war. The Charter had been Roosevelt's idea. Prime Minister Churchill, whose country was already at war and chafing at the bit to defeat the Nazis and their allies, had signed the document in the face of Roosevelt's ace in the hole, Lend Lease, or American Aid to a needy and struggling Britain that was fighting alone.

Significantly, Roosevelt had won Churchill over to all clauses, without any remonstrance, except for those clauses that opted for restoration of sovereign rights to countries that Churchill considered would return the world back to its former position of quarreling nations.

Plateu continued: "I could sense the future record of the post-war United Nations, and I reminded Roosevelt that the concept would fail unless the member countries of a united world order were to totally yield their individual sovereignties to the President of such an order. I stated that the other member planets had already placed each of their sovereign nations under one such ruler.

This then became the heart of the idea that I addressed to Roosevelt: one ruler of the entire world with that ruler voting in proxy on all controversies of nationalism, law, religion, etc. Would such a Utopia be feasible? That was the idea I left with President Roosevelt."

Before Mr. Plateu was asked the question of a one-world government, the authors had researched the White House records and verified the findings, locating various references on the dream of President Roosevelt to become leader of a new collective body of nations following World War II.

As the Venusian was about to leave the White House that evening in 1943, the President's actions are described as follows:

President Roosevelt wheeled his chair to the door to allow the visitor to leave in a conventional way, but the stranger simply dematerialized while in the room. The President of the United States, never to be the same again, was once more alone. The record of that traumatic experience has remained virtually unknown by the general public.

Finally the President returned to his desk. Not entirely certain of the reality of the experience of which he had just been part and the actuality of the conversation, he hurriedly made notes of the visitor's remarks: "...from ancient times before it existed, the United States was destined to become a nation and a leader of the world. This unborn nation had to acquire a new land away from the national and racial conflicts of Europe. The original inhabitants of the continent (the so-called Indians) were permitted to be pushed aside and make room to allow America to become a reality."

Other scribbling he transferred to typing was simply called THEIR PLAN FOR THE WORLD. Attributed to the man who called himself a space emissary were the following notes that are paraphrased here but are in the same context that President Roosevelt recalled the conversation. The notes began: "All the divergent politics, cultures, and religions of the earth would become 'one world'.

"All armies would be mustered out of existence, their soldiers dismissed and their armour broken up and melted down, as in Tennyson's poem 'when men shall beat their swords into plough shares.' A small international police force would act as a judiciary body in the case of national disputes, and direct police action would be taken when and if the adherents to a dispute took bilateral punitive action among themselves.

"Monies from the war chests would be diverted to education, various capital improvements (some of which were named), medical research, etc. Unemployment would be banished by new work projects and new inventions (he talked about the peaceful uses of the atom). College admissions would be by merit only. Tests for non-college-caliber students would direct them into areas where their special skills would be fully utilized.

"Plateu's plan touched all facets of society. Juvenile delinquency was to be educated out of existence, making reform schools and prisons obsolete. Assuming that human nature was still criminally inclined, special schools were proposed where the 'social abnormalities' found in offenders would be corrected in less than a half year at the maximum. In the case of direct criminal action, the offender would be sent to a correctional hospital where the ingrown deviation would be eradicated before the offender returned to society. Incurables would be sent by authorities to isolated regions where they would live normal lives apart from society."

That synopsis of Roosevelt's recollections was the nucleus of the Utopia for earth that the spaceman had conveyed. The proposed Utopia did not propose a cure or a change of men's hearts, but it indicated a disciplined use of education and force.

On that night of the 1943 presidential visit, Plateu had stayed approximately one hour and forty-five minutes. In that brief span, he had appeared from an unknown dimension in space and time, and had revealed a profound understanding of the inner drive and character of the Earthling, Franklin Delano Roosevelt, both as a human and also as a leader. The visitor had plumbed the deep reservoir of Roosevelt's psyche, which Roosevelt, the man, may never have fathomed himself.

Looking out the window before returning to his desk to make notes, Roosevelt was glad the mystic ordeal was over and that everything in nature again seemed real, as he knew it.

However, to this 32nd President of the U.S.A., the visitor would return again and again.

In the ensuing alien visits President Roosevelt would remember one graphic statement of his intentions. "Our numbers in your country will increase. Do not be alarmed. This is not an ominous threat. If we are received well, our future presence may be a blessing that the U.S. and the whole world can share."

Mr. Plateu admits that in this decade the present United Nations, from which a future world leader would be expected to arise, is not working for the good of mankind or as an instrument of peace. The reason given by the Venusian is the deviousness of many of the representative nations in the U.N. that vote on issues according to their own power block considerations and not for the good of the world in general. He added that the present U.N. in its political alignment is a vehicle of mistrust among the representative countries rather than a base of mutual trust.

President Woodrow Wilson of the U.S.A., who was tutored on the idea of a league of nations by Plateu, is described by the Venusian as "that world statesman who arrived ahead of his time." During their meeting, Plateu told President Wilson that it would take another war (World War II) for Earth people to realize that peace should again be attempted on an international basis – but that a third world war would erupt before war itself would be outlawed and a united world order instituted. When asked, Mr. Plateu refused to comment with precision on the certainty of another world war in this century or the time lapse thereafter heralding the beginning of a peaceful planet united under one world government. Mr. Plateu was asked whether his remarks at this juncture were prophecy or assumption. He replied, "I see the future over the horizon but I can't change it; it is destined to be. The next war will be between the forces of good and evil or God and Anti-God. Good will triumph and lasting peace will come to this planet. When war is no more, the symbol of the ruling Christ will eventually replace hate in the hearts of men, and peace will reign forever. Out of the ruins of the next war the remnants of mankind will form the nucleus of a new world."

Question: Mr. Plateu, may we ask you what part religion as presently practiced on earth will play in this new age that has come upon us? Earlier you said a global government would be ideal to stop nations from warring and that we should use our human and natural resources for peaceful purposes. How could organized religion help in this utopian dream?

Answer: I have not been involved directly in the religious visitations of our Extra terrestrials to your church leaders. Such visits have been taking place since 1944. But I am well aware that church leaders have been visited by us on a regular basis with one message -- peace. We have been preaching peace to Earth's leading clerics and believe that church and state should work more closely to that end.

In the last year of Pope Paul VI's reign, he had drawn up an encyclical letter stating that people should expect Christ to return to Earth as a conquering Lord to establish permanent peace. Such an epistle was not well received by many Catholic Cardinals. The last Christian Pope, John Paul I, also went on record that Christ's return is anticipated.

Before John Paul I became Pope, the authors had submitted several questions about his spiritual beliefs which he answered. He said that the Catholic Church must be reborn doctrinally and that latter-day-revealed truth might become a divisive factor among Catholics, even splitting the church because of its historic doctrinal errors.

Pope John Paul I believed that all Christians should remember that the apostolic fundamentals were still unchanged -- Christ's virgin birth, His atonement for mankind separated from God, defeat over death and bodily resurrection -- along with His promised return to Earth as Lord and ruler.

The late Pope also acknowledged that Christ's love and teachings were meaningless in this permissive society if ethical and moral standards continued to be ignored.

Our final interview with Mr. Estes Plateu, Ambassador from Venus, was extensive, but only this brief account is reproduced here.

One of the face-to-face talks took place Sunday, March 19, 1977, in a small vacation lodge located in the woods of West Virginia about 60 miles from Winchester. (Other telephone conversations were held as late as December 1978).

No journalist had previously interviewed Mr. Plateu. His office is guarded around the clock by two government agencies including Air Force Intelligence. This imposed guardianship prevents the Ambassador from moving freely about. Often, therefore, when he must be at another location where he does not want his Earth guards to observe him, he leaves his body by projection (which he says he can teach others to do) and visits those principals to whom he secretly wants to confide or deliver a message.

American intelligence sources apply no ulterior motives to Plateu's frequent, unannounced materializations before Presidents and senior government officials and even sitting committees. But they say his astral interruptions are sometimes meddlesome. Churchill ordered Plateu out of his office and when he wouldn't depart, Churchill struck out at him, but met only air. Churchill then asked Edgerton Sykes, the famous English psychic for an exorcism and Sykes supplied the means. The next time Plateu visited Churchill without invitation, the Prime Minister, following Sykes' advice, held up a two-barred Druid cross that legend says came originally from Venus. The cross was pure gold except for the lower, shorter cross bar that was silver. As Churchill held the cross before the projection of Mr. Plateu, the Englishman said, "Depart from me, thou intruder!" In deference to the holy artifact, the Venusian took his leave without further conversation. King Haakkuuss, the Third, of Bodland also encountered Plateu in astral projection when the Venusian appeared in the Bodland royal palace. King Haakkuuss, himself adept in astral projection which he seldom uses, told Plateu never to return except in flesh and blood, using the traditional forms of inquiry to get an audience with him. Then King Haakkuuss went into that etheric dimension practiced by Plateu and escorted the visitor back to his space ship where his body had remained.

In an historical sense, according to Mr. Plateu, he had observed the development of our world, continuously, and in greater depth than perhaps any other living being today. From the time of Christ, and particularly since the Middle Ages to the present, he knows of great events of political and religious importance that occurred on Earth. Perhaps this book will be the forerunner of ensuing revelations as to what influence interstellar beings have exerted on world leaders since human Earth time began, and it might also inspire others to come forward and shed further light on outer terrestrial purposes toward Earthlings.

As the final interview with Mr. Plateu ended, we asked if he would give a parting word to mankind.

"Yes," he replied. "I could frame my remarks around one word. That word is listen!"

"Listen, Earth nations! Unite peacefully before sudden nuclear war makes it too late to listen!"

The genius of this stranger of non-Earthling origin cannot be probed in this introductory chapter on his involved sojourn on this planet. When the government of America and sources within the

United Nations are undivided as to the announcement of the Ambassador's presence or that of his successor, complete information as to why the Venusians are monitoring the affairs of Earth may be made known. Then Earthlings may understand how the other orbital civilizations in our solar system are attempting to shape our destiny, here and perhaps in the hereafter, for good or evil.

Chapter XVIII

A Day to Remember on Planet Earth

The following urgent and secret message was delivered in October 1977, by the Russian Air Attaché in Washington through diplomatic channels to the Commanding General of the U.S. Air Force.

Subject: Alien base

Place: Siberia, above Arctic Circle

Date: October 23, 1977

The narrative is paraphrased as follows but changed to third person context with actual names and places omitted.

Official Soviet awareness of a secret, extra terrestrial base was first confirmed on October 1977, when an Eskimo appeared at a military outpost.

The lone Siberian Eskimo had watched the yellow lights for many nights as they hovered near a high rocky bluff several miles distance from his camp. The lights didn't belong there, and they bothered him. Finally he set out on foot to investigate the curiosity.

It was almost a month later when the Eskimo decided to tell authorities what he had seen. He headed for a Russian outpost north of the Arctic Circle and reported to the commandant unusual aerial lights that issued from and disappeared into the side of a rocky bluff near his camp. And he also reported something that frightened him and his friends more than the silent aircraft. It was the unheard of appearance of huge, eight feet high, gray furred creatures that walked on two legs and left three-toed huge footprints in the snow.

The alert Russian commander surmised extra terrestrial activity in the area and called for help. Acting on the outpost evaluation of the Eskimo's report, 3,500 arctic troops were moved quickly into the area by rail, parachute and tracked vehicles. Within a week, a field station was set up, and the Arctic troops equipped with artillery and automatic weapons surrounded the rocky bluff that the Eskimo had pinpointed. The Eskimo scout who accompanied the troops then pointed to a particular area in the side of the rocky bluff. Artillery zeroed in on the target area and began shelling. What was thought to be a rock and clay hillside fell inwards exposing a 40-foot square opening leading into a black interior.

Troops moved in on signal and the artillery landed another salvo inside the exposed cavern.

Suddenly, the interior lit up and amidst small arms and shellfire, three scallop-like craft issued from the opening and went straight upward. Troops rushed the cave and poured inside. The hollow was empty aside from a workbench and special tools, and other significant evidence of the recent alien occupation was sparse. However, Geiger counters picked up strong indications of radioactivity.

As the alien space ships sped away they showed their parting contempt for the earthlings who had ousted them from their cavern. What Russian science termed a black ray was beamed down on the ground troops and the temporary buildings. In a moment of time up to 1,000 superbly trained troops were dead and their bivouacs destroyed. The Russian commander called his base for relief troops.

As the alien ships disappeared, other Russian forces closed the net of a larger perimeter surrounding the cave. Advance troops began reporting huge, furry, green-eyed monsters stalking them from the shadows. One front line soldier was grabbed by a snarling creature and hurled 20 feet. The soldier, his weapon still in his hands, recovered and pumped bullets into the creature, advancing for the kill. While the bullets bounced off the creature's hide, a second soldier, knife in hand, rushed the three-toed Yeti. The soldier thrust the blade into the creature's side and it broke away screaming in a trail of blood that led into a nearby cave. Troops followed the groans into the interior, but the body was never found.

Using animal nets, the Arctic troops captured 20 live Yetis. These were taken to a former exile concentration camp and each placed in separate human stockades. One of the Yetis was over nine feet tall. That night the unexpected happened. Guards reported that one moment the creatures were securely in the cages and the next moment they all had vanished. What remained was a sulphurous odor. Next morning the guards responsible for watching the stockade were shot.

But before the first day's battle was over, the Russians sent out an international warning. From Moscow over the hot line to Washington a priority message was sent: "Formation of three hostile UFO's on southeasterly course headed for vicinity of Alaska. Complete text follows."

As the Russian signal was received, American and Canadian radar stations began tracking the alien ships. Eventually the bogeys were seen moving across the United States into the vicinity of a National Forest preserve surrounding Brooksville and Ocala, Florida, where they were lost.

In 48 hours after the Russian attack on the unknown alien ship, the Russian Air Attaché delivered a comprehensive account of the episode to a liaison officer at the State Department for delivery to Secretary of State Cyrus Vance. Ultimately the Russian account reached the Commanding General of the U.S. Air Force.

Meanwhile, the search for the alien ships took an unexpected turn, as the Ocala area in Florida became host to some strange visitors.

Ocala, Florida is a town of about 35,000 population located near

Route 1-75 on the edge of the National Forest. Strangers are generally noticed and there was no exception when an old Chevrolet with a Marion County license plate pulled up to a gas station in late October for a fill up. In the car were four passengers. The driver got out and paid for the gas in cash. As the attendant made change, he noticed that the driver, without the aid of sunglasses, stared intensely into the direct sunlight for several seconds and then remarked, "Isn't that sun beautiful?" The attendant sized up the thin stranger. About six feet tall; long, yellow hair; cold blue eyes; pointed features and sharp fingernails, each coming to a point somewhat like a claw. The attendant then watched the stranger go to the car's gas tank and pour in liquid from a small bottle. The liquid smelled different from that of the petro-chemical additives with which the attendant was familiar. He also noted that the men addressed each other in quick snarl-like sounds.

When the old Chevrolet moved off the attendant phoned the local sheriff who logged the following note: "Informant insists he just had a bunch of funny doers, funny lookers and funny talkers down here."

Acting on other similar phone calls over the next week, the Ocala sheriff called McDill Air Force Base in Tampa from which three trained observers were sent out to watch the area. Around the Ocala and Brooksville area a sudden increase was reported of a different strain of Yeti activity -- not the five-toed creatures familiar in the area, but three-toed ones. A sheriff's posse located the creatures northwest of Brooksville. If the Russian episode were to be repeated here in Florida, the three-toed Yetis would be clues to the whereabouts of the alien space ships.

After the posse report had been filed, the Brooksville area became the immediate focal point for a series of army maneuvers into the National Forest. Field commander in charge of the operation was Marine Major General Peter K. Miller.

Tactical response for all U.S. national emergencies is under the jurisdiction of Readiness Command, who had called for army maneuvers to begin at once on orders of the president. Again, it was a local incident that resulted in a more intensified search being ordered. The incident that follows was nearly tragic.

A reconnaissance team of soldiers in the Brooksville area had followed a trail off a secondary road into a treed area. Up ahead, they suddenly heard a girl's scream -- then the neighing of a frightened horse. Speeding up their jeep, they emerged in a clearing where they saw a young girl on horseback being brought down by three grayish-brown, eight-foot creatures uttering vicious snarls as they grabbed at the balking horse and captive rider.

The jeep halted and the soldiers fired at the creatures. All three fell. Quickly the men ran over to the girl who had gone from hysterics into shock. They calmed the frightened horse and called for medics and an ambulance.

At nearby Gainesville Medical Center the unidentified girl was treated for the nightmarish ordeal and, several days later, was released. The horse took longer to recover; it too had been sent to Gainesville for observation.

The U.S. Air Force was now actively aware that the appearances of the "monsters" in the Brooksville area were coincident with a 90% probable UFO presence. Readiness Command headquarters had been moved into the National Forest and a quiet soldierly penetration proceeded to scour the extensive caves for which the area was well known.

Besides shooting the three creatures that had attacked the horse and its female rider, the soldiers (armed with special ammunition) came upon and killed more Yetis in self-defense, capturing two.

From reports of the patrols coming into the field headquarters of Readiness Command it was concluded that they now were about to uncover the alien hideout in that part of the forest. Continuous contact was maintained with Readiness Command, who in turn kept the Joint Chiefs of Staff informed.

Army patrols probed further into the cavern area. In the second week of November, they came upon a site that instruments indicated was a cavernous interior with radioactive readings on the surface. Perfectly camouflaged as it was, the soldiers were sure it was the lair of the aliens.

Readiness Command was prepared for such a situation. On the night of November 23, 1977, a space ship from Interplanetary Police Net landed at McDill Air Base and left an occupant -- a Venusian. Washington had requested that an expert be sent whose experience could aid in identifying the alien spacecraft that perhaps operated from a hidden base located in the National Forest, 23 miles northwest of Brooksville.

The Venusian language expert was ready when on the same night another spacecraft, identified only as North American, also landed at McDill. There was hyper expectation among the various chains of command at McDill and in the National Forest Preserve as the military men waited for a potentially explosive development.

In the nearby town of Ocala tense foreign visitors were arriving. At the Holiday Inn a Venusian language expert waited. He was from Plateu's unofficial Washington Embassy and had been brought here because he had mastered the Nagirth language, in the event a Nagirth alien was captured. At another Ocala motel two Soviet Air Attaches from the Russian Embassy waited with a standby American jeep and driver.

At Andrews Air Force Base in Maryland, Plateu's private magnetic powered spacecraft stood in readiness to transport their chief to the Ocala area. A private airstrip in the vicinity of Brooksville had been taken over for that and any other eventuality.

And during the night of November 23 or on the morning of the 24th, President Carter was told to expect a call if alien contact were made.

Dawn of November 24, 1977 gradually broke over the National Forest site where Readiness Command pinpointed the alien hideout. American soldiers who were quietly dug in around the area looked up at first light to see a new visitor in the sky. It was a saucer-like craft hovering silently and unmoving at 3,000 feet above the supposed entrance to a cave. The haze lifted and the sun broke out. The birds began to stir.

The radio exchange of Readiness Command (which draws emergency personnel from the combined services), McDill Air Field, the Pentagon and the Secretary of Defense had been operating jointly during the last 72 hours. Especially anxious were the Joint Chiefs of Staff whose departments had endeavored for several days to identify the source of the interloping alien craft which had fled Siberia for another of their prepared bases in Florida.

Eyewitness ground accounts and aerial sightings had now substantiated the origin of the aliens in the forest hideout. In brief, collective evidence indicated they were from planet Nagirth. Nagirth is described by NASA and two observatory officials as being a "wandering planet" which was under intensified observation by various world astronomers during the mid 1970's.

Successive Apollo moon missions in the 1960's continued to observe Nagirth while it was on the far side of the sun. A new type of laser photograph operated from the moon made determinations as to the planet's structure and content. Follow up tracking devices on a moon observation site established in 1974-75 by Canada and the U.S.A. clearly showed Nagirth's projected orbit. Acting on this scientific evidence, the United States and Canada, with the direct advice and aid of Venus, began to harness their scientific brains and technology to meet the challenge when it came.

The planet is two and a half times the size of earth; it turns on its axis every 26 days; is hollow but its specific gravity, notwithstanding its larger size, is at least 2.5 times weaker than that of planet earth.

To understand the nature of our own planet's normal magnetic field as it relates to Nagirth, Dr. H. Babcock, retired director of Mount Wilson and Mount Palomar Observatories, was contacted for an explanation of Earth's magnetic characteristics.

Of course it is Earth's strong magnetic field that keeps the planet in a steady orbit. Dr. Babcock says "the strongest point of Earth's magnetic force field is located at the equator, around the planet's bulge, where the magnetic force pull extends up 114 miles. At the poles, the pull is only 14 miles. The Earth's true magnetic South Pole is positively charged, and from it a strong magnetic line goes out to the Sun, returning to Earth through the true north negatively charged Pole. The principle is identical to the method by which automobile batteries and the like produce a current of electricity."

The above description refers to Earth under normal astral conditions that have resulted in our relatively unchanging seasons of spring, summer, autumn and winter for countless eons. For without the sun there would be no seasons and no life. Earth would simply be a giant iceberg. Furthermore, it is Earth's atmosphere that completes the cycle by turning the sun's magnetic rays into heat.

Then came Nagirth into Earth's orbit about 20 years ago for the eighth recorded time in the last million years. The random planet immediately began interfering with the Earth and Sun force field. The magnetic line running between Earth and Sun became broken at times by Nagirth's intrusion with predictable interference.

Huge Nagirth's weak negative force pull therefore has drawn it into smaller Earth's strong magnetic force field with Nagirth thus attaching itself to the pull of the strong Earth. Scientists refer to the condition as "dipping into Earth's orbit," moving from a reflective interference to a deeper penetration, (about 3 days in every 30) causing at those critical times a partial eclipse of the Sun, and other disturbances.

According to an unidentified physicist at Goddard Center, their instruments, charting the flow of natural electric waves through Earth's north and south magnetic lines since the arrival of Nagirth, indicate a terrific power drain as if power was being drained from the entire Earth. Just as a power station takes electric current from the Earth via the station's turbines, Nagirth seems to be constantly drawing power from the Sun/Earth force field. It has been noted that extra heavy power is drained from Earth during a severe snow storm or hurricane, these weather disturbances being created either intentionally by the inhabitants of Nagirth or unintentionally by its mere presence.

Regardless of the explanation, summers over the last several years gradually became hotter and winters increasingly colder, and by the mid-70s the scientific world knew for certain what would be the outcome of Nagirth's intrusion. In America, the first pronounced adverse changes in winter occurred in Buffalo, New York during 1977 and also in Cincinnati, Ohio. Other areas are expected to be similarly affected. Throughout the continent by the mid 70's (as in northern Europe), unseasonable weather patterns also changed measurably by creating abnormal rain falls and subsequent flooding as well as hurricanes and tornadoes. The seasons in the entire northern temperate world climates were undergoing change.

The world of science says Nagirth has interrupted Earth's weather seven times already in the last million years. This wandering planet last appeared over Europe in 1456, in a brief by-pass orbit, and was called "Haley's Comet" and described as having a tail 60 [?, editor] miles long. The "comet" was excommunicated by Pope Calixtus the Third and according to Roman history co-incidentally disappeared, leaving a terrified populace in its wake.

But in this century, the Nagirth menace has become more serious in its blockade of the Sun/Earth force field. America's sister nation Canada has an orbiting Space Probe called COSP watching Nagirth. The Japanese and Russia's Academy of Sciences in 1980 are working closely with the U.S.A. Goddard Center and its Canadian counterpart to watch Nagirth 24 hours daily and exchange information hourly.

Thus, as power crazed egomaniacs create religious and political strife throughout the world, the real issue in the coming 80's has become the deflection of an inhabited alien planet named Nagirth (also called Naggarith).

How are we harnessing our scientific brainpower to prevent a lumbering giant of a weak planet from destroying much of Earth by the mere presence of its shadow or eclipse of the Sun? Primarily, the U.S. has a telescopic eye in the sky named OSO, (Orbiting Solar Observatory), relaying electronic messages to the Goddard Center. In addition, there are other special-function satellites monitoring Nagirth, the major one of which is Skylab, put up into orbit in 1965. (It was conceived by the late Robert Goddard after a discussion with Jonathon E. Caldwell in 1958.) There is also a combined Canadian/American manned planetarium and data center located on the moon since 1974 studying Nagirth closely.

But of greatest interest to this book is a telescopic eye which is a 40 inch electronic telescopic mirror suspended from a double bag space balloon 15 miles in the stratosphere. Because of the position above Earth-clouds and atmospheric impurities, this 40-inch telescope has the power of the 200-inch one at Mount Palomar. The 24-foot-long, suspended telescope continuously travels with the sun, circling the earth every 24 hours. The intricate scope is operated by remote control from Goddard Center where viewing screens are monitored continuously. Also, thousands of radio signals are beamed down to eight receiver stations set up around the globe, with these computerized readouts discussed and forwarded to the Goddard Center for action.

The big telescopes in California, including the 200-inch Hale telescope at Mount Palomar and the 100-inch mirror on top of Mount Wilson, (both built under the direction of Dr. George Ellery Hale, astrophysicist who first mapped the Milky Way in the 20's) operate in conjunction with Goddard. Dr. Babcock used the Hale telescope at Mt. Palomar six hours each day to study Nagirth as it approached Earth. It was this cataloguing of the intruder that first brought the phenomenon to world attention. Mount Palomar has its own electric space probe that takes X-ray photos of Nagirth and transmits the finished pictures onto the Hale telescope and into data collecting computers.

The Mount Palomar telescope has detected life on the blue planet Nagirth, as have Russian telescopic sightings. While Earth, viewed from outer space, is pale blue with a mixture of pinks, Nagirth is a dark blue with no change in color. The color density makes it difficult to view well except thru the 200-inch Hale telescope at Mount Palomar that yields amazingly close-up pictures and slight color variations, even within the dark blue.

Either a man-made or natural force turned a manned rocket fired from Cape Kennedy back when it neared the blue planet. This made astronomers believe that a civilization on or in Nagirth is closely monitoring Earth by telescope as well as by manned probes. Unconfirmed reports say that an American spacecraft has flown around Nagirth and verified its Earth-watching activity.

To prove that Nagirth is occupied by highly intelligent beings, a strange space ship 90 feet in diameter was seen hovering over Mount Palomar in 1976. It had sent a telepathic message down saying, "We mean no harm." The big scope watched the ship and even observed a face and form peering out of a porthole, when suddenly it took off at incalculable speed. A few days later, Mount Palomar astronomers believe they saw the same ship in the Nagirth environs.

With the alien blue planet causing climatic interference, scientists at Princeton, Harvard and other centers connected with the research, state unofficially, that unless earth prevents further interference and dislodges Nagirth from the earth's magnetic field, another full ice age lasting from 20 to 100 years is in store for the northern hemisphere. In North America, that would stretch down to about the 35th parallel where the northern state line of North Carolina meets Virginia. Meanwhile, winters will become increasingly severe--with greater amounts of snowfall in those areas above the future ice line. Already Arctic waters have been frozen over for the last four summers. They have been ice-free in July and August since data was first recorded. Extreme temperature changes have occurred in the northwest Pacific, the spawning place of some major North American weather patterns. Associated with these changes, cold Arctic air masses are pushing the east-to-west jet stream further south, allowing cold air to be shoved further southwards into hitherto temperate areas. At the same time, Pacific air riding the jet stream is being transported to the Great Lake areas, carrying with it heavy precipitation from two Pacific hotspots. Modifying waters of the Great Lakes are causing winter precipitation in the form of snow to nearby, particularly southerly, communities. Valleys and watersheds each year will continue to move this freezing air further southward. After the buildup of unprecedented winter snows, heavy spring thaws will occur, and summer weather patterns will also be altered. Below the present Snow Belt, a rainy weather pattern will prevail for several years.

Historically, Nagirth has already come into the Venus orbit in this century causing much alarm to the citizens of that planet. Techniques that the Venusians developed, along with help from Pluto, succeeded in creating a reverse magnetic force that shoved the blue planet out of the Venus orbital attraction. Nagirth, because of its low center of gravity, has been roaming around the Milky Way for untold eons, unable to attach itself to any particular constellation to remain permanently, as did earth's moon in times past.

A special government "Committee for future planning" is now developing plans to protect, and even cover with plastic domes, those cities to be most severely affected. Rail lines will also be covered. The Russians already have made plans to cover Leningrad and Moscow. Although the northern weather patterns will become more severe, a gigantic scientific effort is already in progress to reverse the new freeze trend. A technique has been developed by American research, with the aid of advisors from Venus and Pluto, to prevent Nagirth from getting closer. Authorities are confident of success.

Three methods to move the planet Nagirth from further endangering Earth's solar orbits are now being used. They proved effective when Venus experienced a Nagirth intrusion. These projects are located at Earth's polar regions, a similar one is functioning on the moon and the third method will involve 12 antigravity orbital reactors sent sunward to the proximity of Nagirth to stop it from creating an eclipse between earth and the sun. Four of these antigravity orbital reactors are already in space. The function of all three methods, whether space orbital reactors or static stations on the moon and earth, is to create in specific areas powerful reverse magnetic forces to repulse Nagirth. Keep in mind that Earth's own rotation and orbit must remain unaffected.

General Electric International (Geo Physics Division of California) is building the stations with help from Stanford University scientists.

Harvard and Princeton Universities and Carleton, a Canadian one, are working with the Baffin Island anti-gravity station and another site located on the tip of southern Argentina.

As work proceeds in building the new installations to repel Nagirth, the existing Arctic glacial regions are being watched and sampled down to bedrock by Dr. George C. Martin and his meteorology department. Ice insulation (industrial soot) is being dropped in wide areas of the north to retard further buildup of ice.

Officially, no one in a "responsible" position will admit (or, to be explicit, is allowed to admit) that Nagirth exists or is a threat to Earth's temperate zone climate. Such a commentator is Richard E. Hallgreen, Director of National Weather Services, who in the December 2, 1979 issue of the Family Weekly insert section of the St. Petersburg Times was asked the question

"What is the reason for our last two bitterly cold winters?" Hallgreen's reply, as it appeared in that newspaper was: "Two consecutive cold winters are not an indication that we are on the threshold of a modern ice age -- only that the weather is variable. Then the Director of the National Weather Service added, "An Ice age is brought about by a gradual cooling over a period of thousands of years."

That is double talk, with no mention of the real cause -- Nagirth.

But is there a survival reality that ordinary people should be told? And at what time or period should word be released of an unforeseen planetary change? All the science and technology of modern man is now being harnessed to prevent that change. Dr. Babcock had this to say about the world's future weather concerns. "It's only a matter of time before everyone knows the problems and how we are attempting to keep the status quo of our present climate relatively unchanged. But the mysteries of the universe are so great that what happens to Earth must be part of God's master plan for a better world. The Supreme Creator is still in control, even if it seems a planetary accident has taken place."

How many inhabitants live on Nagirth is unknown. We know little about them except they are desperate beings whose planet (because of its weak gravity force) has been at the captive mercy of one solar system after another for perhaps millions of years. Its people, therefore, may be cunning as they endeavor to locate in scattered hideouts throughout earth. To date no one is sure what they are trying to do on earth, i.e., whether some Nagirthians are trying to establish advance colonies on earth, with or without their own planet's approval, or whether the cavern outposts already discovered were intended to be spy pockets in case of a coming war.

At daybreak of November 24, 1977, the combined military emergency forces of the United States of America stood waiting on the ground and in the air for the entrenched aliens from a hostile planet to show themselves. The sun rose higher and it was 10 o'clock when the landscape below the American saucer craft began to change also. A section of brush and grass on the side of the hill disappeared. In its place was a yawning square black void. From the abyss a bright light took the place of darkness. Not a ground soldier stirred.

Suddenly, an object floated horizontally from the cave; and, clothed in a bright yellow ball, it shot up at a right angle. It was only a matter of seconds till the object stopped abruptly at 3,000 feet.

As it hovered in mid air, an invisible plastic-like blister on one side of its leading edge slowly turned and scanned the first object hovering silently about 400 feet away. The first object was unchallenging like a toad.

Perhaps for a minute the alien ship from Nagirth surveyed its first encounter with a saucer-like craft from its unwelcoming host planet Earth. As they sat immobile, a dozen Earth nations waited fearfully for the outcome. On this moment there rested the fate of this planet in the words that had haunted the military since 1936. "If a hostile alien force ever lands, intent on conquering earth and subduing its people -- how could we protect ourselves?" Only 40 years had been given to the Anglo/American inventive genius of its military before the day of reckoning had arrived.

In the alien ship the same beings that had walked the streets of sleepy Ocala calculated the airborne threat nearby. Like two giant bugs, the ships seemed to stare unblinking at each other.

They would not see it from the ground. But the same black ray that had obliterated the Russian soldiers and their equipment three weeks before was to come into use again. Were it to have been seen, it would have been a pencil-thin flash as the ray found its mark on the American craft. Suddenly the ray shot out. There was a pause. Then another burst of destruction was discharged -- a force that could cut a hole through a battleship or tank. Finally, the alien ship delivered another flash of laser light. The American craft seemed to tilt ever so slightly, as a million volts of concentrated energy and heat struck her. Then, without warning, from an indistinguishable spot on the American ship, a red ray silently spat like a viper's tongue. The alien ship wobbled and began slowly to skip and tumble. As it spiraled down, the American object moved beside the alien craft as if to kill, but still in self defense.

A holding beam held the alien craft aloft and slowed its descent to the ground. The alerted ground troops watched as capturer and captive moved off towards a nearby airfield. As the two craft left the scene, two more alien vehicles shot up from the cave. Without stopping to survey the aerial disaster, they disappeared to the southeast. A few minutes later a Puerto Rican tracking station reported their flight towards the continent of Africa.

Even before the alien craft had been air shuttled to the nearby landing area, President Carter was notified. His first words are said to have been: "Thank God! From now on we know we have an equal chance to protect ourselves from any enemy invasion of the U.S.A. whether from Earth or beyond."

The alien craft fell on the airfield with a bang that residents heard for miles around. Sheriffs and deputy sheriffs cordoned off all roads into the area of the confrontation. As the alien craft, still intact, slammed into the earth that November 24th, a lowboy swung out of McDill Air Force Base at Tampa and headed north. On the way back to the base, onlookers thought the tarpaulin-covered contraption seen sticking out over the low-boy may have been a high-ranking officer's sail boat being towed south at taxpayers expense.

At McDill, the machine was dismantled that same night. Inside were three charred bodies.

The next morning, across the world to Russia, Germany, England, Canada, France, Italy, plus several African countries, a message went out from America that a hostile extra terrestrial ship from another planet had been confronted and destroyed over American territory. By mid morning, the U.S. Air Force was preparing detailed information on the alien craft and the word was spread among earth nations.

Deep in the center of the earth, New Germany received the news, as did the other old races in the interior. And in earth skies and on the ground, multi-national crews belonging to hundreds of magnetic spacecraft gave a silent cheer on behalf of the Ocala confrontation.

In Hellitoogg, the capital city of earth's sister planet Venus, over forty million miles away, a high-ranking statesman departed in person for a new structure in the heart of the city. Above the doorway as he entered, he read the name in English and Venusian, "United Nations Embassy Planet Earth." On the roof there flew two flags, the United Nations of Earth and the United States of America. Inside the premises staffed by 20 Americans, the Venusian statesman was ushered into the office of the Earth's resident Ambassador.

His first words were, "Mr. Ambassador, I have been sent by our head of state to tell of the news flashing throughout the solar empire. Your country, on behalf of its world, has destroyed an invader from an alien planet."

The anonymous American stood up and thanked the bearer of the news.

Chapter XIX

Strangers in Our Skies

Who are the strangers in our skies? From where do they all come? What is their purpose in spying on Earth? And finally, are they hostile?

The truth is there were over 7,000 sightings of strange craft of unknown origin intercepted and plotted by Earth radar installations in 1978. Frankly, like the U.S. Air Force, the authors who reviewed many sightings must humbly admit that they too are none the wiser as to the purpose of alien surveillance. But perhaps some readers of this book may lend their knowledge in solving the problem. The U.S. Air Force, for one, as well as its Russian and German and French counterparts, is open to suggestion.

To understand the reason for the nose-to-nose confrontations of alien spacecraft from distant galaxies, it should be explained that the U.S. Security Council and its Canadian and British counterparts have the following policy: "Confront the strange craft. Try to communicate. Make radar shape identification and take high-speed photos. Do not take hostile action unless fired upon." The Soviet injunction to its bases is "fire on the alien violators over Russian air space." As to which is correct is not our concern, but of immediate interest is the manner in which the North American Defense responds to the intruders.

Although there are many unknown sightings, the U.S. Air Force usually acts when alerted by radar systems or when public reports are consistent, or if the alien craft shows signs of creating fear or panic in the area over which it is dallying or studying Earth. The order to intercept is issued from Washington and generally involves one or two American round-wing planes that first try to establish communication with the alien ship. Of course, there exists a master plan for total action if the alien ship becomes hostile, but this master plan, for obvious reasons, is unknown to the public.

Several recent sighting reports, that involve confrontation with specific alien ships and the intelligence of the beings or creatures or whatever flies them, have been declassified. The method used by the U.S. Air Force to distinguish the origin and nature of the craft will be discussed briefly to acquaint the reader with NORAD's attempt to comprehend the reasons for beings scanning Earth from beyond.

Before describing the alien encounters, it is important to note that none of the confrontations were from craft based in this solar system that is only four billion miles across. Our local interplanetary likenesses always announce their presence and request permission by pre-arranged signal before coming into Earth skies. Furthermore, U.S. Air Intelligence has eliminated the possibility that the alien craft are from elsewhere on Earth's surface, its interior, or from the 26 known subterranean cities scattered on the floor of the world's seas. Therefore, it could be assumed that the alien presences are from star systems four to five light years away, such as Prima Centauri, 4.3 light years distant. They could also originate from double star systems like Alpha or Capella -- or even Polaris, the North Star composed of three suns. But at present their origin is only a guess.

The reason for revealing these strange alien presences arriving in space craft, which may be more sophisticated than those of this Earth's star system, is to say loudly that we must begin to realize that Earth is not alone in the Universe. It is but a speck among a collection of a dozen grains of sand surrounded by a system of 100 billion or so Suns called the Milky Way. Earth's solar group is said by astronomers to be near the twelve o'clock position in the elongated Milky Way, about one third in from the outer edge. (Diameter is 300,000 light years.) All of the stars that Earth people are able to scan with the naked eye are near this twelve o'clock position. Beyond our Milky Way, astronomers estimate, there may be a billion other similar systems. How many of those worlds are inhabited? That old question has now become fashionable again! And from where do the aliens come who likely left their home planet years ago to observe beings like us who dwell in this remote area of the galaxy.

In sequestered locations across Britain, the U.S.A., Canada, West Germany, Russia and Argentina great scientific minds are trying desperately to decipher the new riddle of where the strangers originate and how to induce them to declare themselves. Aside from additional scientific questions being asked, there are varied questions of more interest to the average layman. Do the strangers have an inherent or learned psychic ability to probe our minds? Do they recognize our fears, our conflicts? Do they think we are different mentally than they? How do they regard us on their mind scale? Or, did we bring them here by our warlike history that now finds us on the brink of nuclear oblivion?

Whatever the reasons, the sky strangers know instinctively that we are different than they. Otherwise, why do the violators of our skies stare down our chimneys, watch our teeming masses, and no doubt monitor the endless trash on our TV's that they probably judge to be a facsimile of our true lifestyle. And, is it also possible that they are tuned in to the moral decadence that, not only our public movies and literature portray, but our inmost thoughts also send into the ether? The beings could also have a higher purpose than is apparent, connected with unknown coming events of a world-wide nature. All who know the facts of outer space surveillance are perplexed but agree on one thing: The arrivals are carefully monitoring this entire solar system. There are those in officialdom and the military who think it timely to share the fact of the unknown presences with the public. No threats or menaces from the alien ships have been recorded other than those we have described. Here, then, are some typical alien arrivals in our skies that a U.S. military source has secretly provided.

A sighting on October 8, 1978 over Key West, Florida by Navy personnel has been referred to as the largest egg ever seen. It was estimated to be 300 feet long by 150 feet in diameter at its widest part. Contact was eventually made with the aliens in the craft. They did not cluck like a chicken; they conversed in whistling sounds. Like other unknowns, the egg craft flew as low as 2,000 feet, and was indifferent to human curiosity. Much of its surveillance took place over the Caribbean islands where its smaller scout craft were often engaged in watching fishermen, particularly shrimp catchers. Of the approximately 30 small scout eggs released, each appeared to be operated by a singular being. One such occupant sighted in the yard of a Key West resident was said to have long, slender dangling hands and an egg-shaped, hairless head with two eyes and ears, plus a nose and a mouth. Later, a Venusian language expert permitted to land on the mother ship south of Cuba and interview the chief officer confirmed these features. The Venusian reported the strangers verbally communicated in different whistle scales. A tour of their ship was refused, but the beings explained (1) that their anatomy was different than that found in this solar system, (2) that they were unarmed, (3) they were engaged in mapping the universe and (4) they were from a distant galaxy in the Milky Way over four years away as measured by Earth time and not the speed of light. However, they would not reveal their optimum speed of travel. The egg craft has been seen on four other planets of this solar system, where, as over the U.S.A., no punitive action was taken by the planet being observed and mapped.

January 8, 1979 a 100-feet by 25-feet cigar-shaped object, bluish-silver in color, was seen traveling slowly over Atlanta observing the city. Sightings of the same ship over Macon, Georgia were later called "ghosts in the sky" by a Macon newspaper. An attempt was made by a U.S. round-wing plane to establish radio contact over Atlanta. No replies were heard, but the Earth craft kindly asked the alien ship to vacate the air space over Atlanta and to acknowledge the request by wobbling as it left. The alien ship did exactly as instructed and departed. Cigar ship sightings are numerous all over the globe whether over the jungles of Brazil or scattered cities of Asia. They, too, are being seen on other planets within this solar system. These ships exhibit a polite indifference towards our inter-planetary round-wing planes, but show no hostile intentions when approached. They appear to have an additional energy propulsion system besides that of anti-magnetic, because they were seen emitting exhaust gasses from the stern end. There is global and some interplanetary concern about the boldness of the numerous cigar shaped craft. The Solar Council sitting on Venus is evaluating the reports.

February 12, 1979 a silver-colored pencil-shaped craft estimated to be 1,000 feet long and 100 feet wide was studied by several witnesses travelling at high speed over the Atlantic and hovering over Bermuda. Miniature scout pencils were observed emerging from the flat end of the craft. Cockpit controls were in the blunt nose of the pencil. The craft was intercepted by a round-wing-plane, but the Earth craft was unable to make contact with the mother ship or scouts.

The list of unknown sightings grew in 1978 at an amazing rate. Of the 7,000 seen by witnesses in a 365-day period, the silhouettes and sizes described were varied. They were usually large in size, indicating that they were heavily manned. In addition to the shapes mentioned, observed and catalogued were: eight hundred feet long wedges, bottle shapes, flying tubes, footballs as long as a football field, spherical, and cylindrical. Hardly a shape was not reported except perhaps the square. And even the square was part of the shapes the Air Force knows to be flying cities, two of which took off perpendicularly when sighted in remote areas of the world, one over a southern desert area in the U.S.A. A large city, several miles in height and moving at great speed, was radar tracked above Canada's northern DEW line.

The U.S. Air Force has excellent pictures of some of these intruders. For instance, on September 3, 1978, a fighter squadron arriving at McDill from Eglin AFB in Florida, photographed a huge spherical object 90 feet across that joined the squadron about 300 miles west of Tampa over the Gulf of Mexico. Faces were seen at the windows of the alien craft suggesting a large observer corps. One of the U.S. radio operators received what he said was a telepathic message saying, "We are here in peace -- we mean no harm."

Genesis for the Space Race

Over Minneapolis on July 25, 1978 another radio controller received a telepathic message when a formation of strange lights alarmed many viewers. The message beamed into his brain was: "We are friendly. Our appearance is so unlike yours that your people would be frightened if you saw us."

In compiling its directory of sightings, the U.S. Air Force team sent to sighting areas has issued a series of questions regarding size and form, location, height, maneuvers, etc. that witnesses are asked to answer. A headquarters intelligence group then evaluates the various statements. Similarities of color, size, speed, etc. of the object form the basis of the finished reports such as described in the cases above. Sometimes there is little useable information, as in the February 4, 1979 sightings over Minneapolis. From 100 feet away the object appeared as pure light with no form or size visible. But radar showed it had definite shape. On being accosted by a round-wing plane, the light departed straight up, and its speed was so fast it could not be clocked.

An intense light form that hid the shape of its nucleus also appeared over Los Angeles on January 29, 1979. The object in the light was not distinguishable by human eyesight or binoculars, but the jagged edges of the light spun constantly. It was described as similar optically to a spinning spoke-wheel, which, as the wheel turns faster its spokes become invisible. NASA began evaluating the Air Force pictures and radar patterns.

Earth nations are baffled by the strange sightings. So are other planets. There are no official answers, but there are some possible explanations. For instance, unless there is a form of energy unknown yet to Earth science, all interplanetary craft likely use an anti-magnetic form of energy to carry them through the cosmos to their destinations, even to distant star systems. Such a craft originating in the Sirius constellation would use its own sun(s) to catapult or repel it into space, and when past the halfway mark towards our sun system, the Sirius craft would use the magnetic forces of our sun to draw it toward this system. If the alien craft were continuing on to another more-distant destination after observing earth, it would use Earth as a magnetic way station to provide the required velocity through our solar system. It would have to make a half circle around Earth, or, if it came down near terra firma it would require one and a half orbits around our planet to repel itself towards Mars, Venus, Pluto, or Saturn, whichever was in proper conjunction. It would use those planets as it did Earth to achieve extra momentum.

Although the strangers undoubtedly are space travelers using this method to arrive here, it is unlikely they are coming by accident. The sightings are too numerous. The patterns of alien observation are too similar to suggest random curiosity. Major air force intelligences of the world concur that most of the occupants are too dissimilar to land and be seen among us, but their true intentions remain mysterious -- except for one area of agreement. They are carefully studying Earth people and their civilizations in a totally un-hostile way.

Perhaps there is no present explanation why strangers from unknown dimensions are in our skies. The revelation may come later. The reality of their presence and the magnitude of the cosmos itself may yet be too illusive for us to fully comprehend in terms of science.

Eventually, it may be realized that part of the linkage between time and space is spiritual -- and that a host of beings from other worlds under generally benevolent direction are determining how unruly Earth masses will bridge the gap into a new millennium.

Chapter XX

A New Age Dawning

"My friends," President Roosevelt grimly told his cabinet in 1936, "We are being visited by beings from other inhabited planets in our solar system. They are a thousand years ahead of us in mastery of air and outer space. We don't have a thousand years to catch up! Perhaps we have only a generation -- or maybe two."

Forty years ago, on the day of that utterance, the President's words were ominous. To the planners of a nation's destiny, the President had issued a challenge. Its pursuit seemed folly. They could only gasp at the specter of a national or even world emergency let alone trying to comprehend the enigmas of space. They almost feared to speculate whether the academic and industrial might of America could safeguard, in their lifetime, life, as they knew it in 1936. They dared not to philosophize on the spiritual or ideological changes that a new order of relationship with other planets might bring.

For years the U.S. government has been aware that other beings similar to humans existed in our own solar system. We also know now that they never intended to launch an invasion of America so fearfully envisaged by Roosevelt. The aliens had arrived in peace, and they had come to help.

Now, as the new decade arrives, again an alarm has been sounded. This time it has grown to global proportions. Earth nations are hurriedly trying to unravel the reasons for a new wave of uninvited visitors, this time from the far side of Uranus and Neptune.

These visitors come from beyond the frontiers of the universe that our space technology can decipher. Deep in the minds of all who know is a hopeful question: Will this new throng of strange Earth-scanners also remain peaceful? Meanwhile, where do we go from this point in the modern history of mankind? The answer is that, we must trust our science to carry on in the inevitable search to remove Earth from a million years of isolation. As science advances, so must knowledge of the spirit and purposes of man. Otherwise, Earth, as we know it, will cease to be.

As for the United States, she can look at the achievements begun two generations ago and be assured that the dream of creating a counter force of round-wing plane protection for Earth has been reached. It is what President Roosevelt and his cabinet first hoped for. The air forces of the United States, in conjunction with their compatriots in Britain, Canada, Australia and New Zealand are patrolling Earth skies 24 hours a day. As once the British navy guarded the world's seas, the United States now is guardian of the skies. The sea-lanes of the world have now become the pathways in the skies where round-wing planes move noiselessly and fearlessly day and night. With their newfound wings, this breed of aviators could race the rising sun from any given point on the Earth and circle the globe 24 times or more before the sun rose again. Optimum speed of one such craft was confirmed, in a 1965 radar-clocked, U.S. navy sighting over the Caribbean. The object was said to be American, and the identification has not been denied by naval and air sources. That round-wing plane in particular showed on the radar screen of an American destroyer to have moved 350 miles, from a stationary position, in only 0.7 seconds. That means that it accelerated to 40,000 miles per hour instantly. So fast did it disappear off the radarscope, radar technicians verified, that the object looked like the trail of a radioactive particle in a cloud chamber.

The weaponry of the new aerial phenomena is entirely laser oriented, whether light or magnetic-induced. Rather than leveling a city and destroying its population, the city's entire electric capabilities such as generating plants, motors, cars, etc., could be disrupted or totally immobilized by this conical blanketing force. Its destructive power also is awesome. Cities the size of Havana, San Francisco, or Moscow could be wiped out in minutes by one round-wing plane, and existing ground defenses could not prevent the destruction.

It was military defense in the air that became the nation's first responsibility, as laid down by the planners of American destiny in 1936. It was not until the year 1977 that an Air Force spokesman would confidently address civilians and say, "America's military requirements to protect our country were the first priority in development of the round-wing plane. It can be assumed the nation's planners have already placed that aerial shield over our land, for if not, the military could not pass on its knowledge for civilians to build commercial round-wing planes in the next decade." The spokesman did not boast.

The United States Air Force historical book number 12, in its repository in Kensington Tombs (Archives), documents the invulnerability of such a U.S. Air Force round-wing plane during an unauthorized trip over Moscow as far back as the early 50's. The pilot was Colonel Edward B. Wright, graduate of the U.S. Air Force Academy, and great-grandson of Orville Wright. On return into Earth's atmosphere from orbit over Asia, young Wright decided to test the anti-aircraft defenses of Moscow following a report that a New German round-wing plane piloted by Kurt Van Ludwig had already done so years earlier. Col. Wright dropped down over the Kremlin and trimmed his craft at 6,000 feet, low enough for trained Russian observers to see the U.S. flags painted on the undersurface. Half the U.S. crew manned stations while the remainder played cribbage. Colonel Wright counted 25 direct hits from a variety of shells and missiles fired by accurate Russian gunnery. The Russian shells exploded or bounced off the American craft as Colonel Wright unhurriedly took the ship up to 100,000 feet and continued passage for home. (The round-wing plane used on the flight is now obsolete and out of service.) The commanding officer, at the return base, berated the Colonel and exclaimed: "I hope you have good pictures of Moscow gun positions to show for your joy ride." Indeed, the crew brought back excellent photos. The story of Col. Wright's escapade over Moscow went around. The episode became as intriguing to tell in Air Force circles as had the ancestral Wright brothers' flight at Kitty Hawk, generations before.

Such was the audacity of the new breed of airmen riding Earth's skies in a new type of aircraft. Such spectacular performance caused young pilots occasionally to forget that the whole world was not their back yard; the cold war was not a game.

Becoming a member of the exclusive new group of round-wing crews is no easy task. Indoctrination begins at the U.S. Air Force Officers' Training Academy in Colorado. Top volunteer graduates of this school then are enrolled into the round-wing plane training school at Eglin Air Force Base in Florida, where all basic round-wing instruction is first given in dummy ships [simulators, editor].

After actual flight training is completed at the end of two years, the young U.S. airman graduates as a 2nd Lieutenant with rank insignia of a gold bar in a circle. (He may wear this insignia only on a round-wing base.) Britain and Canada also send their future round-wing pilots to the U.S. for training. A few also are admitted from Australia and New Zealand.

The round-wing training centers are part of the Strategic Air Command; hence, in 1978, the Superintendent Officer Commanding the Eglin Round-wing Training Program was an unnamed Canadian General. The command rotates among the participating English speaking nations. McDill Air Force Base was the training center where further flight instruction included interplanetary missions with experienced crews. On arriving at McDill, the student was expected to take the controls immediately. All training flights departed and returned to this base in Tampa, Florida during the hours of darkness. North American universities provided related courses for the Reserve Round-Wing Plane Service.

So ends our brief references to the Earth-based training of U.S. round-wing pilots.

The Anglo-American military fleet of planes numbers about 500 craft. The New German fleet is significantly smaller with superb laser weaponry. It is the magnetic generating capacity of the earth that decides the maximum number of round-wing planes that can be operational at one time. The New German quota of round-wing planes would be dictated by several factors; among these being the number that the Bodlanders in the earth's interior decide the Germans could operate. New Germans were part of the multinational guardianship of the interior-based nations' defense.

The primary factor dictating the permissible number of round-wing planes is the earth's magnetism. The interior earth generates much less magnetic force than is produced on the surface. American scientists believe the interior surface could generate power for only half as many round-wing planes as are used above. What upper-Earth duties the New German round-wing planes perform is unknown, but it is understood that they and the Anglo-American pilots abide by a tolerance that precludes hostility. World War II enmity is dead.

Much of the wartime belligerence between New Germany, the U.S. and her allies gradually disappeared in the post-war period. The June 1977 goodwill flight of David Schusnick and his round-wing plane crew to Cape Kennedy broke some remaining barriers of military mistrust, although there are many Germans, and Americans of expert opinion, who have not altered their caution of each other's perspectives.

It was not until October 1977, when the U.S. Air Force, by request of the Security Council, dropped its lingering mistrust of New Germany and sent a return flight of an American round-wing plane to New Berlin in the interior of the Earth.

Edward D. Wright (now General) was chosen by the U.S. Air Force to captain the latest American round-wing plane on a return courtesy visit to New Germany. The goodwill journey was a success, and to this day the New Berliners (the older veterans of World War II) refer to the visit of General Wright and his American crew as German/American Friendship Day.

The story of the flight was headlined in all the German dailies of Earth's interior. The commanding general of the New German Air Force personally met the American crew. The entire complement, except the Flight Officer, left the American craft for most of the day. After several hours of sightseeing in New Berlin and being honored by the populace, the crew was wined and dined in the Capitol Building, where they also met the President of New Germany, Adolf Hitler II.

An American squadron of ten planes has been invited back to New Germany for a goodwill visit. The General Aviation Sub-Committee, subject to approval of the U.S. Congress, had sanctioned such a flight for a time after January 1979. A few high-ranking Americans are expected to accompany the mission. New Germany had requested an ambassadorial exchange with the United States as far back as 1976; and, as a result of General Wright's mission, Congress was expected to decide on the request in 1980.

In the upper atmosphere and space surrounding Earth, both the Anglo-Americans and New Germans have a limited but expanding role in the Interplanetary Police Net, whose duties are to police this solar system, to be on the lookout particularly for hostile intergalactic spacecraft. By virtue of their combined police relationship in the Interplanetary Police Net, enmity must be passé for cooperation in this body, and hence a new climate of friendliness is the vogue among the pilots.

The American/Russian problems of dual adversary relationships have been kept quiet. The two (yes, two) Russian killer satellites were shot down over Canada, early in 1978, dispatched by the Canadian Air Force using a round-wing plane. That followed Russian remote-controlled satellites downing three American unarmed satellites that were monitoring the troublesome planet Nagirth. It was coming closer to Earth environs each year. The Americans, on behalf of the free world, had placed 12 such monitor satellites in the upper atmosphere, and the Russians had knocked out three before retaliatory action was taken.

Who or what has the ultimate authority to say the round-wing plane can or cannot be used in a future war? The answer, of course, is enigmatic. A considerable amount of the technological advice in construction of the round-wing planes for the Anglo-American and the New German forces was provided by beings from other planets within our solar system -- on condition that the new planes not be used as a strike force against any other Earth nation (or intergalactic invader) unless first attacked. It is presumed the Americans and New Germans are committed to that unwritten agreement. If so, the main role of the round-wing planes as a world military or police force would be one of deterrence. In case of attack on North America, retaliation would be instantaneous. It is also understood Anglo-American allies would come under the umbrella of protection.

Round-wing planes manufactured on Earth may not be as sophisticated as certain advanced types flown by the other solar planets. The U.S. Air Force must, therefore, accept help from the Interplanetary Police Net. The U.S. still may require ten or more years to catch up to the technology of Venus, its big brother helper. New German and American laser technology is a top priority in their scientific worlds.

It will be difficult for the average reader to comprehend, with any serious intention, the story of other inhabited planets relatively like our own. It is a big mental leap to accept such declarations that this book attempts to explain. Yet, the facts cannot be ignored a day longer if the Earth is to protect itself and take its place among other planets. Aside from the outer terrestrials who are most qualified to talk about themselves, NASA and the U.S. Air Force are best able to establish the truth.

The U.S. legation to Venus was formed and made operational with the executive approval of the Jimmy Carter administration. Key members of the legislative branches sanctioned it.

Thus, unknown to the world, the U.S.A. has been vigilantly patrolling global skies since the mid-1940s, making training sorties nightly into outer space since the mid-50s, and will be establishing regular exploratory lanes to nearby celestial planets in the next decades.

U.S. legation exchange with other planets in our solar system is already occurring, and certain of the solar planets already carry on careful diplomatic dialogue with the U.S.A. On the 7th floor of the U.S. Diplomatic Training School in Washington, there are some offices with strange sounding names. One is the Inner Earth Delegation, and one floor above this delegation is a suite of offices referred to as Outer Space Delegation. In the latter suites are the Venusian, Martian, and Plutonian legations. Only coded badges acceptable to electronic eyes, plus a Marine guard checkpoint, gets visitors into these premises. The diplomatic solar cousins of Earthlings and their female staffs walk the streets of Washington unnoticed by hurrying throngs. The Venusians are the least notice-able because they are identical to the white races of Earth. They claim a common ancestry and say that our mother race was blue in color. The Martians are big people, the men usually about 6'6", with piercing eyes. The Plutonians have a skin color that at times has a greenish tinge with tones of brown rather than white. Their walk sometimes appears to be uncertain or jerky. Each planet represented has a five-man delegation. There is constant consulta-tion between the space delegates and the U.S. because of problems that affect all the solar planets. The subjects range from defense to health and education.

Leaving the outer space legations, let us look for a moment at the Inner Earth exchanges: The United States has a ten man diplomatic legation, headed by a retired Air Force officer, located in the nation of Atturia (New Atlantis). In return, the Atturians have a delega-tion located on the 7th floor of Washington's Diplomatic Training School. The Bodlanders ask why the United States has not request-ed an exchange of consular officers or bona fide observers.

The New Germans, from below, house their five-man delegation in the same premises as the Federal Republic of West Germany. Their chief is referred to as the Second Secretary in charge of the Inner Earth Delegation. Former head of the Inner Earth, New Ger-man delegation, Eric Von Schusnick was recalled early in 1978 for talking to the authors. This heroic man did more to cement Ger-man-American relations than those who condemned him, claims a member of the U.S. State Department.

Genesis for the Space Race

The U.S. also has had a delegation in New Berlin since 1977.

For almost 20 years there have been civilian and cadet exchanges between the countries of the Inner Earth and the U.S.A. Cadets from West Point (army), Annapolis (navy), and the Air Force Academy at Denver have been sent below via the round-wing planes on a regular exchange basis. (They have been strictly directed to maintain silence about this at the cost of court martial.) Tour visitors from below, who visit the U.S., usually must wear thick, smoked glasses to shield their eyes from the upper sun. Otherwise, they go about unnoticed.

Constant visits by unknown aliens to the National Science Foundation and NASA have been verified, and there is a strong possibility that American scientists are already working on Venus and that varied scientific papers are no doubt being exchanged.

On June 7 to 12, 1975, leading scientists from Venus, Mars and Pluto were invited lecturers at a symposium for sharing interplanetary, scientific information. It was held at the National Science Foundation in Washington, D.C. Earth counterparts were from Yale, Northwestern and Harvard.

One of the varied subjects discussed extensively was the method used by other planets to safely tunnel into the earth's subterranean surface for future inner city and intercontinental thoroughfares. Earth scientists were told how such tunneling could be completed by lasers at the rate of a mile per day and how anti-magnetic trains and cars now run within such subterranean tunnels in other planets.

To millions of earthlings, revelations on the spiritual life and beliefs of the inhabitants would be more appreciated than revelations of their third-dimensional, finite pursuits. There is divided opinion among contacts with Venusians as to the future role and purpose of the aliens in plotting the world's course in the remainder of this century. Those who are familiar with Venusian beliefs and can enlighten ordinary, bewildered people on the subject of outer-terrestrial religion should express their views. Those of the Christian worlds who are challenged by the alien presence are agitated by the failure of the U.S. government to allow the outer-terrestrial visitors to speak their beliefs. The real purpose of these beings has been critically debated ever since a group of Protestant ministers met with them at an Orlando, Florida motel in 1977. The Christians base their hope on a typical bible verse: "There is no other name (except Jesus Christ) under Heaven whereby we might be saved." They ask whether this admonition applies only to Earthlings and not to Venusians and other planetary beings. Who knows? A Christian minister at the conference also accused the reluctant Venusian prelates of deliberately ignoring ancient biblical prophecies in the Old and New Testaments regarding the relevancy of those prophecies to a restored Israel in the 1980's. Christians contend Israel will be the focal point of all coming world events in the remainder of this century. The Venusian's reply to these bible prophecies centered on a returning Messiah. It has not been aired yet.

If upper Earth nations had problems of interpreting other world religions, this did not hinder the continuance of technological advances in the interior world. For instance, the diehard remnants of the German Third Reich who settled in Earth's interior onward from 1944 soon learned that their Utopia was not attainable without superhuman sacrifices. With sacrifice being the first ingredient required to build a new nation, the subliminal longing to dwell in peace overcame the New Germans emotions that earlier had kindled recent passions leading to World War II. As they became preoccupied in building a new sovereign nation, they channeled their formidable inventive ingenuity into peacetime pursuits.

For those displaced Germans it was a matter of survival that they should employ the round-wing plane both militaristically and commercially from the first day the planes were flown. The first 120-foot craft carried in its bowels livestock, tractors, railway cars, trucks, bulldozers, machinery and passengers wherever they could be squeezed in. Much of their original heavy equipment came from the U.S.A., where, as already noted, it was illicitly loaded on their round-wing planes and flown out in darkness. One such trip loaded four new caterpillar road machines near New Orleans in 1946.

In 1978, a German round-wing plane company called "Airtruk

Limited" operated two 120-foot craft that haul freight, and a third 90-foot craft of 42 seating capacity was used exclusively for tri-weekly passenger service. Also carried on the passenger flight is mail and consumer express between West Germany and the interior.

New Germany imports 1,000 West German rail tank cars of refined oil per year via the round-wing planes and expects to increase these shipments to 10,000 carloads within a decade. (Of course, the Bodlanders, Atlanteans [Atturians], and the old Vikings have been using the magnetic plane for multitudinal uses for untold ages.)

Three planes comprise the total commercial equipment, these having been retired from New Germany's military inventory because of obsolescence.

In the upper world, the young, unchallenged American Eagle had been flying the far-flung areas of the globe in her new round-wing fleet since 1945. The early models had been dramatically improved in performance. There remained little resemblance to the first Caldwell craft of the pre-forties. As the lofty Eagle sailed over the battlefields of Korea or the jungles of Vietnam, or as she skimmed the rooftops of Moscow, Havana, or Hanoi, she had never shown her talons. They were there, and still are. The laser and microwave weaponry had been proven, from which there evolved a confidence of invincibility expressed by top military leaders of the nation, and by crews who ride the winds, night and day, in the new planes.

Because of military priorities and, because the round-wing plane was not required for commercial needs, the U.S.A. did not consider it necessary to plan for transition to commercial and passenger use until the early 1970's. By then, the military felt that all the latest ultra-developments had been incorporated into their version of the round-wing plane. In typical American fashion, they acted decisively.

Flight priority again will be the military. In 1980-81, a scheduled military round-wing passenger service will be inaugurated between British Columbia and Ottawa, Canada, and Washington; D.

C., U.S.A. Washington will also connect with London, England. Depots in Ottawa, Washington, and London have been or are near completion. Travel time from Washington take-off to Ottawa landing will not exceed 13 minutes. The Washington-London route of 3,674 miles will be a leisurely 45 minutes. These routes have already been tested.

Changeover from the military to commercial requirements began in the mid-60s. A team, composed mostly of experienced engineers, was withdrawn from the aerospace complex in British Columbia to delineate proposals for the transition.

On recommendation of the transition committee, representatives of the American/Canadian aerospace industry were advised in 1974 of the round-wing plane capabilities. The first group was invited to the mother factory where they toured the plant and later witnessed demonstrations and startling performances of the astonishing new plane, including a three-decker plane developed in the 1950s. Then the group was given insights into the building of the planes from drawing boards to testing of the finished machines. A thousand questions were answered.

The following year a second top-level group from Boeing and Fairchild was brought into the original complex for on-the-job training. Others from industry followed later. Only the design and basic aerodynamic principles were taught these key industrialists. Information on the electro-magnetic motor was withheld since it is intended that the commercial craft, during the next decade, will use only the very successful jet motors perfected in the early military versions. The aircraft manufacturers will not be allowed to use most of the military navigational system designed for anti-magnetic motors in outer space. They will build instead their own systems into the commercial craft with help from the first North American facilities.

In September of 1977, leading representatives from major American airlines were called to Washington to be informed of the unexpected revolution in airline transportation. Thirty spokesmen were invited and met secretly on the Presidential yacht at anchor on the Potomac. They were shown pictures and films, and listened to discussions on the world's most advanced plane. Executives of the airline industry were then told that the round-wing plane could be in restricted use on domestic flights over North America before the end of 1990, and that complete changeover should be possible by the year 2000.

In the near, foreseeable future, the fixed-wing planes in use on passenger lines will become obsolete. Advantages of the commercial round-wing planes, even with jet motors, will be evident to travelers: (1) A short take off and landing strip. (2) They will fly over five times the speed of sound. (3) Sonic booms will not be created. (4) More people, luggage, and bulkier payloads will be carried in planes perhaps up to 200 feet in diameter.

Eventually, when commercial research is complete and the anti-magnetic motors are allowed to be installed to replace the jets, no place on Earth will be more than an hour or two hours away. For a typical one-day travel jet set excursion, one could take off from Tampa, Florida after breakfast and step down in Singapore or Sydney for lunch, returning home for dinner by way of Honolulu and Los Angeles. Old-fashioned travelers may prefer to make the same aerial journey with an overnight stop. Regardless, the serious businessman or woman will need only an hour between New York and San Francisco. It is assumed center-city takeoffs and landings will be feasible.

Nostradamus was right when, in 1566, he foretold: "After a great human exhaustion, a greater makes ready. The great motor renovates the centuries."

When NASA's space platform is completed and functional in late 1990 and begins orbiting 240 miles above earthly impediments of clouds, gravity, and air friction, it will give Earthmen a clear look skyward – a look into the activities of our solar system and revelations far beyond.

Takeoffs and landings from this space platform vantage point will allow the magnetic powered craft of the U.S. and her allies to become interplanetary vehicles of commerce well before the next century.

The new round-wing planes have not made the space program obsolete. The manned space platforms to be launched aloft by NASA will mean that all American space probes, whether manned or by drone satellites, will be launched without the problems of air friction and earth gravity. Booster rocketry will become obsolete.

In 1977 two so-called unidentified flying objects passed each other in the blackness of space. One was traveling from Earth to the hollow planet, Venus, where almost four billion inhabitants live on both surfaces. The other so-called unidentified flying object had left Venus and was Earth bound. As the two almost identical craft passed within 100,000 miles of each other, recognition signals went out to each. From the craft, Venus bound, there went the signal: "U.S. Air Force training craft -- Venus Bound."

And from the craft headed for Earth, a message replied, "Peace! Signal received -- New Germany Air Force training craft out of Venus -- bound for home, destination Earth."

The space ships from planet earth had made history. The crews of each whose fathers were from two former Earth-warring nations had passed each other 20 million miles out in space with peaceful and friendly greetings. The captain of the American ship pondered, "How good it was to know that out in this lonely, trackless void another earthling ship from Home Sweet Home had passed by and called hello."

In the middle ages, earth was regarded as the center of the universe. When Dr. E. Hubble's 100-inch telescope was first used in 1925, man's observation of the heavens knew no bounds as he spied perhaps billions of galaxies beside our own.

Now, only a half-century later, as Earth-beings gaze heavenwards on starry nights they can be sure that the first Earthmen have walked on three and perhaps twelve new worlds that a century before poets only dreamed about.

Not many simple Earth people were aware of it, but in little more than a generation, mankind -- with help -- had conquered near space -- at least the space within our own solar system.

Epilogue

"The United States is actually and potentially the most powerful State on the globe. She has much, I believe, to give the world;
indeed to her hands is chiefly entrusted the shaping of the future."
- John Buchan, 1940

Prime Minister Churchill and President Truman had, in the mid
40's, determined the firm course that the United States and her
Anglo allies would forge in the last half of the 20th century. Subsequent U.S. Presidents and Prime Ministers of Britain and Canada,
with secret concurrence of their governments, continued to develop
the anti-gravity principle into a variety of military-logistics and
civilian-industrial uses not yet revealed.

The military apparatus surrounding the round-wing plane had spun
off into wider civilian facets after the war. By 1950, that civilian
service conglomeration had expanded into various government
departments while disconnected scientific projects were crammed
into the ever, expanding National Science Foundation. Overall
decision-making was cumbersome.

For cogent reasons, President Eisenhower continued to regard
the secret round-wing conglomerate as the nation's first response
against Soviet power, should war break out. So, with typical military planning, Eisenhower decided to consolidate the round-wing
diversities under one government agency. A group of men was
brought together, unaccountable to open forums, to exercise ultimate control of all round-wing functions.

With blessings from key Congressmen and Senators, President
Eisenhower picked twelve responsible government leaders answerable only to him. The year was 1954. The new Presidential Com-

mittee was named "54-12."

In setting up the Committee, President Eisenhower openly reasoned: "Diplomatically, we can't stop the spread of Soviet Communism. If the cold war becomes hot we must prepare to win."

Thus, from 1954 on, all final decisions relating to round-wing plane production, research, or security (whether military or civilian) would henceforth be made by this select group of advisors. Later on, the public mistakenly would come to regard the U.S. Air Force and C.I.A. as the repositories of the so-called hidden UFO evidence.

The 54-12 Committee continued to monitor American round-wing development through successive Presidents since Eisenhower. The committee developed strategy intended to maintain the nation's air supremacy into the 70's, through the 80's, and beyond 2000 – if possible. So extensive was their watchfulness that secret civilian research for anti-gravity applications would only be authorized by them. They had orders to increase peacetime applications for use before this century ends. The Canadians would house their related endeavors in the National Research Council, Ottawa, and integrate their round-wing scientific development with Washington and London.

By 1979 these international bureaus, working in unison, would forge closer links of cooperation with each other than had ever existed since Englishmen spread their language and common law around the world.

Various models of the round-wing planes, as described in this book, dominated global skies until the 1960's. Then the first planes were phased out. All of those are now obsolete, with representative types destined for future display in museum exhibits.

Entirely new models, with sophisticated electronic gear and weaponry, replaced the original formations and unbelievably altered their performance and military effectiveness. Because of necessity, the first round-wing squadrons were basically Earth aircraft. The latest fleets are all interstellar and intergalactic, able to venture into the far reaches of space on a complete life support system that can keep the crews alive for many weeks. The machines are also sea-worthy and water submersible, allowing them to dive into the ocean depths to avoid detection or do tactical surveillance of an enemy shoreline from the ocean's bottom.

The third generation of Anglo/Canadian/Americans operates the latest craft. The original neophytes of the new age of flight, now retired grandfathers, are daydreaming of yesterday's glories.

One of those grandfathers is 80-year-old Jonathon Caldwell. In 1978, he was living somewhere in the Baja area of Mexico, confined to an estate that is guarded like a feudal castle by patrols and a dozen attack dogs. Caldwell's wife, Olive, moved graciously with him through the retirement years, and the old disease that once threatened to cut off her life has not returned. The illness was completely purged by the power of Christ through the healing agent, Father John.

The last photos seen of the older Jonathon and Olive Caldwell were taken in 1959 and are part of the historical collection filed for safekeeping in the Air Force underground Tombs at Kensington, Maryland. Snapshots of the families of their son and daughter show happy children in various poses. Where the Caldwell son lives today, what names he has chosen, and his vocation is unknown. The daughter, whose married name is also unknown, is said to live in California. The grandchildren of the senior Caldwells would now be in their 20's and may perhaps be married.

An attempt by Russian-paid agents to kidnap Jonathon Caldwell was made in the late 60's. Guards killed three of the kidnap forces and the remainder were tried and imprisoned. After that event, there were subsequent attempts to kill him. Caldwell's name and residence were changed again.

Caldwell retired as a Lieutenant General in 1967 but was recalled three times. Before giving up the office of Supreme Commander of the Aerospace Center, great honors were bestowed on him. He was flown to England where he was knighted by King George VI and also awarded the Victoria Cross. An admiring General, Charles de Gaulle of France, presented him with the French Legion of Honor. (France was under German subjection when the grand round-wing alliance was formed and hence was not included in the secret; although, de Gaulle later sat in the allied Councils and was privy to round-wing secrets, which, by oath, he never divulged. After the war, allied intelligence was wary of communist infiltrations into the French government and military.) Canada also bestowed upon Caldwell its Victoria Cross. From his home country, a singular Congressional medal was struck and presented to the living hero by General Dwight D. Eisenhower.

Although Sir Jonathon E. Caldwell reluctantly laid down the mantle of his pioneer round-wing plane powers, he never dropped his love of the new dimensions in space travel. From planes he switched his drive to people. For years he has pressured Congress, through the Aviation Committee and the Executive Branch, to recognize and augment a distinct Round-wing Plane Corps answerable to its own commanding officer. Such a new military service would become General Caldwell's last attempted program, and an informed U.S. Air Force spokesman believes Caldwell will live to see this establishment become reality. For security reasons alone a separate Round-wing Service would be advantageous to the U.S.A. and its allies.

If Caldwell was forced to hide his identity and live his life unpraised and unloved by his countrymen, so were many others. Sir Charles Wilkerson, who led much of the post-war round-wing research, also walks about incommunicado. All who meet him are pre-screened by intelligence agents. He must carry a weapon at all times and retain the companionship of an attack dog. When at home his dwelling is doubly protected.

As scientific minds were mustered out of the round-wing wartime detachment, men like Sir Charles Hadden of England were glad to get back into peacetime society. Interceding in high places, Sir Charles was flown back to England by round-wing plane in 1945 and dropped by parachute near his hometown. Landing safely, he bundled his chute and hitched a ride into town -- and home again.

That year, Englishman, Hadden and Canadian, Stewart S. McLane of Ottawa were called to Buckingham Palace where each was knighted by the British king and awarded the Victoria Cross at a special service. (The British granted only 26 VC's during World War II.) As the Palace Band played, the three unsung heroes of science inspected the bandsmen and the Guard. Upon leaving, they shook hands with each other and said farewells. They were instructed never to mention their experiences; and, should they meet again by accident, they were to blot from their memories their years spent together and pass without speaking. Sir Charles Hadden resumed teaching physics at Oxford but has since retired. Stewart McLane returned to Ottawa.

So today a body of senior, silent men walk the streets of a hundred towns, or sit in the councils of industry or the professions, their true war-time experiences a blank to all who might inquire.

The "age of space" is a new order. No longer is our home a small globe inhabited by a few ethnic varieties of Homo sapiens. In the new revelation the globe is hollow. In this interior are other and perhaps the most ancient of the two worlds. Into this inner world the New Germans have ventured and built an armada of round-wing planes as a defense force to be used unilaterally or in conjunction with other Inner World nations in case of attack. The author has learned that the New Germans have not developed their forces for vengeful purposes to be used in the Upper World. They are neighbors of the two oldest nations on earth whose objective it is to prevent war and defuse the global ambitions of the war prone. Confidential sources also reveal that the South American German exiles also have the round-wing plane and have a nuclear strike capability as well.

Another civilization also exists under this planet's seas that certain scientific sectors are aware of, even if denied by them. Added to the ocean dwellers are billions more creatures inside the Earth's mantle that apparently have never surfaced from their aloof abodes to police or contact the wayfarers above.

On the Earth's surface, more than ten nations are capable of waging nuclear war; with the two giants able to launch a holocaust that would make the outer heavens a hundred light years away register the big bang.

Overhead in Earth skies there is still the unsolved alien spacecraft phenomena of strange objects that come and go at will. Not to be forgotten, too, lingering close to Earth's trajectory is that huge, lumbering, inhabited planet, Nagirth, two-and-a-half times the size of Earth, whose ultimate destiny may be collision into the sun.

Who knows what unfriendly worlds beyond our own solar system have picked up Earth radio signals and are among those aliens watching or about to arrive -- even tomorrow?

So the sobering question must be asked. Are the inhabitants of this planet on the verge of a change in our world order, brought on by remote planetary forces about to enforce dictatorial rule on mankind to prevent one of our nuclear clubs starting total war in an Earth shattering finale?

The constant warfare of this planet may be only the visible phase of a far-reaching alignment of unseen opposing forces, whether they exist as three-dimensional or spiritual. These opposing forces, whatever the reader wishes to call them, may already be poised to use mankind in a confrontation that will decide the future of the world. To readers of the daily press, the Earthly or political nature exemplified by these forces may simply be Communism versus Democracy; to the philosophers it may be good versus evil, and to the religionists, Satan against God.

In trying to resolve the riddle, any thoughtful person must wonder: Somewhere upon a higher plane of existence, is there a hidden power struggle of such magnitude that we cannot comprehend its purpose? Are these forces now lining up their hosts for a climactic battle where mankind will be only a pawn, and Earth the prize -- or Earth the pawn and mankind the prize? Or, is this planet simply a square in a gigantic chessboard of insidious interstellar rivalry?

Perhaps to be determined, will be not just the outcome of this small planet, but of its entire solar system, and possibly the universe.

Time moves on. It waits for no man -- or nation. Each is time's captive. There are hosts of questions about the future of mankind in the new age that the authors were unable to reconcile. It soon became evident, therefore, in view of the gaps in our collected data that the incomplete story must be told even if it were more provocative than scholarly.

With this book's release and its subject matter thrown open to critics and scholars, many new attempts will be made to learn and understand the significance of its pages. Primarily, the nation -- no, the world -- must collectively resolve its most pressing problems and face the future together. The English speaking people and all their war-time allies have closed the gap of World War II belligerence toward their enemies, and all these nations now collectively understand the new solar concept of trust and cooperation.

Divorced from politics, it will then be up to the world astronomers, for instance, to address themselves to the problem of how to tell the peoples of the world that we are not alone. Our entire solar system may be occupied by beings that closely resemble Earthlings who think they dwell in isolated majesty on this planet.

How to tell the world about outer-terrestrial visitors? Quite soon it will be the responsibility of all the federal governments of the world to regain the confidence of the public. Describe to them the arrival on earth of intelligent beings from distant galaxies, beings whose evolution even surpasses ours. These governments should also release new stellar maps, as well as complete information available on the subterranean and inner Earth.

In the immediate future it will be up to the Cartiers, the Drakes, the Columbus's returning from new worlds to tell fellow Earthlings of the wondrous things they have discovered in space. When this has been accomplished, and the beginning of a Utopia gained, it may be up to the philosophers to recommend what to do on Earth with that ancient vice, or virtue, called leisure. To be all things, to all men, the scientists of the nations must cross borders and unify their purposes in the interest of a new world free from war with advantage to all.

However, possibly the greatest challenge that the authors were unable to explore was simply this: How will the non-occult religions of the world respond to the new image that man is not alone? Will they continue to have faith that the God of the universe is ultimately in control, working out the destiny of man through man? When the incarnate Christ returns, as He promised, by what means do the faithful Christians think He will rescue His hopeful believers and establish His much prayed-for Golden Age – an age of harmony and righteousness prevailing on Earth?

The central theme of this book has been the arrival of free energy, spacecraft, and its subsequent development by certain nations in the 20th century world.

Thanks to the anti-gravity principle of that magnetic-powered craft, a better world lies ahead embodying the boldest of engineering feats imaginable.

Ahead, there also lies, the broad road for invasion into space, either militarily or peacefully.

Now that man has begun to reach for the stars, where may we ask is that wise and benevolent human leader or cosmic Messiah who will dispel mutual fear from the hearts of men? Will this King of Kings arrive in time to guide us into peace on earth before this planet is reduced to ashes again?

FINIS

Appendix

Social, Political, Economic and Religious Life in Inner Earth

The spoken and written language of the Inner World Atturians in their capitol city of Shambala, from which Professor Haammaan emigrated to the U.S. via an Icelandic passport, is the original Sanskrit. Their flag is orange with black letters beneath a coat of arms under which is the legend, "Peace with Honor," meaning to end a war without surrender.

Their Sanskrit alphabet contains 38 letters, many of which are in double form such as AA, CC, 00, etc. These double letters are used only in proper nouns such as persons, cities, Aarpo, Baacco, Winnaabbaago, Saapraanoo, Jaapanno, Cannaggo. In word construction two words are often joined and pronounced as one. In punctuation, one question mark upside down is placed before an interrogative sentence and a normal, upright question mark then follows the sentence.

The country, of over 300 million people, is served by color television. Newspapers are smaller than ours and contain little advertising because of the shortage of pulpwood.

The home city of Professor Haammaan is the capitol city of Atturia, Shamballa, located on the continent of Agraharta, comprising a population of several million. The city (as is the nation) is served by air transport with other metropolitan centers (i.e. magnetic powered craft which have been in their possession since their forefathers came from Venus). Connecting ground transportation is via railroads that ride on cushions of air instead of rails. (The Japanese are currently experimenting with this method.) Most ground traffic is by means of four-wheel cars and buses, both of which principally use electric energy as their motivational source. Electric outlets are located at roadside intervals of 25 miles from which a three-minute charge of renewed power is drawn at no cost. Cars have a driving range of 100 miles. Radio waves sent from the remitting source to each energy depot supply the electric power, the remitting sources being solar, hydroelectric, and nuclear fusion. Free-energy magnetic vehicles are also used.

Professor Haammaan was asked to describe briefly their immigration system followed by their monetary policy. Regarding immigration, he explained visas between countries in the Inner World were not needed, and international travel was unrestricted. Each nation was very isolationist in its outlook and did not depend on a United Nations body of politics as practiced above the surface. When a foreign traveler visits another nation, the person simply signs a card upon entry saying they agree to abide by the laws of the land being visited. As all coin and paper currency are redeemable by gold according to international monetary standards, travelers therefore may exchange their own money for currency of the host country. Elaborating on money, Haammaan added:

"Like you say above, 'Love for money is the root of all evil.' Therefore, we don't permit hoarding of money. It is to be spent for immediate wants and needs. To prevent hoarding, our paper money is recalled annually and newly numbered serials are issued. Hoarding gets the greedy person 30 years in prison, but savings are not frowned upon when kept in a bank. We also use coins for exchange, their contents of gold or silver being 70 per cent and that of the alloy 30 per cent.

"The reason for the harsh anti-hoarding law is that if money is kept in circulation (which our banks do with peoples' savings at low interest rates) then capital projects in private, corporate, and government sectors provide full employment. One of the problems here above is that so much of the wealth accumulated over the years or centuries by certain groups is kept out of circulation and hidden away in private banks or vaults. In such cases, that money withheld (usually gold) is a form of power that is harmful, and it is often used as a power base to influence sectors of the overall society. I'm sure you are aware of many examples of this hoarding abuse by such powerful control groups.

"Our central government treasury owns all our gold to back up the coin of the realm, which is the established policy of each nation below. Much of our own gold reserves were brought down from old Atlantis.

"Our numerical system is what you call Roman numerals and the Algebraic system -- neither name being historically correct. Our system of numbering is more related to your British and U.S. methods. We don't use the decimal system and I predict it will be discarded up here within 100 years. Some of our units of measure are as follows: 1 quatal = 1 mile *** 1 qquttall = 1 inch *** 1 quntall = 1 foot *** 1 vartall = 32 inches (equivalent to the British yard of 36 inches) *** 16 quntalls = 1 chain. The average road width below in Atturias is 3 chains and an alley is 1 chain wide. (Haammaan said their Inner World is 23,000 quatals in circumference and it is 7 ½ thousand quatals from Pole to Pole.)"

The calendar used throughout the Inner World is based on a year of 360 days, each month having 30 days. The people call the five days remaining at the end of the year "year's end days" during which all non-essential work stops. Babies born on these days are born officially on January 1st following. For thousands of years the above calendar time has been followed below.

Do you have any specific ideas about employment?

"Depending on technical skills or academic abilities, graduates of grade school or college have already been pre-tested (as in Bodland) to determine their careers. We have no retirement laws but limited or part-time employment is the norm throughout the Inner

World in later years. It is up to the man or woman. Certain job categories are considered to be more suitable for women who are not encouraged to compete for certain masculine jobs and vice versa.

"Our medical research has overcome most diseases, including all types of cancer and arthritis by pre-detection or post detection. The people still get injured through a variety of accidents. Emergency methods to mend bones and replace skin are among the advanced medical practices. For instance, a synthetic skin used on grafts or plastic surgery resulting from severe wounds or burns is simply cut from a roll of substance in much the same manner plastic paper wrap or tin foil is removed for domestic use in the U.S.

"Placed over the burned or diseased area, under sterile conditions, along with a special healing gel, the synthetic graft immediately takes to the skin area to be rebuilt. Its use makes plastic surgery much easier and faster.

"Amputations are extremely rare since crushed limbs are immediately rebuilt with synthetic bone that quickly is accepted by the natural bone being repaired. Hearts, lungs, eyes, ears and other body parts are replaced routinely as are decayed teeth. (Damage to nerve fibers was not discussed.)

"Free total medical care is provided to all age groups."

The Atlanteans have overcome most of the illnesses common to surface people, and their life span is apparently over a thousand years, with premature death an exceptional occurrence.

The first two-hour interview with Haammaan was held secretly at an airport in Maryland. Crime was dealt with briefly, and answers were sought as to how their society treats those offenders who violate the age-old system of laws derived to protect members of society.

The gist of the discussion is as follows: a criminal is considered a social disgrace only if he does not respond to treatment, but all crimes are treated as a form of mental illness. A first offender automatically is sent to a state psychiatric hospital. Most respond to initial treatment, the nature of which was not disclosed in the interview. The hospital board has the authority to declare a person a habitual criminal on the third offense.

In such a case, treatment is stopped and the offender considered a criminal. All clothing is removed and the naked prisoner is put to hard work in a public chain gang, made to sleep on a board at night and given only meager sustenance. Six months maximum of this type of sentence usually changes the person and returns him to society again, as an accepted, normal citizen.

If the prisoner does not respond to this penalty treatment, he is committed, by three doctors and a judge, to a remote island where, like an animal, he is worked naked at manual labor during the day, and forced into a lonely cage at night. This routine is followed with full understanding by the public of all its indignities to the human psyche. Public knowledge of this irrevocable punishment is a deterrent to crime.

Branded as "discarded citizens", those sent to the island prison are declared legally dead on arrival and relatives are so notified. All attempts to rehabilitate are ended. Upon death, the body is cremated and the ashes not returned to relatives, but tossed into the sea without burial services.

There are three major crimes, convictions of which automatically label the convicted felon a "discarded citizen" for shipment to the last-stop island. Those crimes are rape, kidnapping and murder. Guns are outlawed.

In Atturias, the death penalty is also in force and may be given at the request of the judge or the prisoner himself, if rehabilitation treatment has failed. In such a case the felon is given a glass of liquid from a tree called the Poison Root that induces a painless death within an hour.

Even in perfect environments certain people are criminally prone and cannot be conditioned to the norm required by a civil code of laws. This fact is true both in societies above and below. In Atturias their confinements for offenders are located in rehabilitation centers and hospitals rather than in prisons. There are few youthful offenders in the interior world, perhaps because the responsibility for a youthful crime rests with the parents who are judged on a guilt basis along with the youth convicted. Obviously, the basic unit of learning and training in their society is the home, even before church or school. If early school tests indicate a criminal tendency in a child, he is removed from classes and placed in a hospital for correctional therapy at an early age.

Our news media below (as in Bodland) does not carry stories of crime, let alone headline them. Nor, do we have long drawn out judicial exercises. An apprehended murderer generally is tried the second week with the death sentence carried out the following week.

Youth gangs are not tolerated and common assaults and muggings, so widespread above, don't exist below. All male youth in Atturias and Bodland must serve two years without pay in one of the defense forces where behavior disciplines are further emphasized.

There is no syndicate crime problem below.

Haammaan continued: "Your police above are still an effective force, but they are much maligned in their duties. Your society seems more concerned with protecting offenders than the rights of the offended. When your system of protection and justice is overhauled, your crime statistics will fall. The legal system is a bulwark, devised to protect all members of your society in the upper world -- as elsewhere. But that system in the lower courts has been detoured from the code that was so carefully built to safeguard all sections of society. There are too many legal loopholes for perpetual offenders against your society in the western world. There are also a growing number of lawyers who are perpetuating the breakdown of the legal code. The law societies themselves must institute the remedies."

Generally speaking, life sustenance within the planet is comparable to that above. Their staple food product in the warmer climates is rice, which was also brought above by the people that we know as the Chinese. Main crops of wheat and barley are grown in the northern locales. Other vegetables are string beans, soybeans, okra, eggplant, cabbages, turnips, carrots, etc. The Atturians are mainly vegetarians, but consume much fish with a variety of artificial flavors such as chicken, beef, pork, etc.

Milk is also their staple nutritional drink. They do not know of the turkey, but, on the other hand, have a large, native bird they call the Duck-quail, highly rated by some for its edibility.

Two building blocks made below would be of interest to surface people. One is a concrete block virtually unbreakable. A powdered plastic, sand, and water are heat-treated like terra cotta, and the product is used extensively in both their residential and commercial construction.

Another substance known as glass-tile consists of finely ground silicone or glass mixed with clay, placed in various molds and heated to a high temperature. The finished glazed tile is used for floors, outside facades on buildings (where we use marble facing) road building blocks, etc. Their Atturian highways are constructed with lateral grooves running across them. Automobile tire treads are grooved to produce a meshing, cog wheel, effect, thus holding the car in position assuring the driver control against brake skidding, or hydroplaning on a wet pavement.

A second final one-hour interview was held with Mr. Haammaan on Sunday, November 20, 1977. Accompanied by a reliable witness from the State Department, we checked into a Holiday Inn at Mt. Vernon, New York and talked in the conference room. The six-foot, three-inch Atlantean had the build of a football player but his hands were slender, more like those of a pianist. Quizzical blue eyes responded to changes in mood. His hair was fair and cut medium short. He looked like a modern Scandinavian.

Time, being of the essence, and certain prepared questions needing to be answered, the dialogue was begun. Haammaan's manner was

Genesis for the Space Race

less reserved than at the first meeting, and after coffee and tea had been ordered each sat in an easy chair and the talks began.

Question: How old are you? Answer: "I am officially 57 years old according to records on file here, but truthfully I am some hundreds of years of age. Average age on my continent of Agraharta is about 800 years."

(Haammaan's claim has not been reconciled with that of the Inner World Bodlanders. Dr. Jerrmus of Bodland's capital city, Bod, is 58 years old and he states that his father died at 135 years, but longevity of 200 years is common in Bodland. Some Bodlanders may reach 300 years, but those passing 200 are elite senior citizens.)

Haammaan's conversation is resumed. Question: Why should you Atturians live so much longer lives than we on the surface? Answer: "Harmful ultra violet and other sun rays are the chief cause of death to those on the surface. You recall we have an artificial sun (600 miles in diameter) that lights up our interior world. That sun takes its energy via crystal receivers from the outside sun and stores it, but the harmful rays are not retransmitted. The second cause of premature death to your people above is your diet, in my opinion. The majority of us Atturians are not flesh eaters as are most of you above, although we eat fowl and fish in preference to red meats. However, let me state categorically that you and I are biologically identical."

Question: You mean our sunrays shorten life?

Answer: They certainly do. Deterioration, sun-caused, starts at approximately 20 years in your lives, even where no disease is noticed. The harmful rays even affect your fruit and vegetables. The effects are passed on to you when you eat them. The meat products you consume are made more harmful by sunrays.

Question: Is longevity below the result of spiritual or psychological advances? Your people have apparently been free from war, economic worries, and other tensions for 11,000 years?

Answer: No, that's a wrong assumption. Our original long life spans below have been maintained and increased over the centuries partly because we perfected our eating and drinking habits. It is mainly because of the filtering of harmful solar rays by our man-made sun. Hence, today we have overcome premature old age and the major diseases that inflict you people on the surface.

Question: Tell us more, especially about the fruit and vegetable juices.

Answer: Combinations of certain natural vegetable and fruit juices, or their extracts, are used below for many medical cures. We call the system of producing these formulas, "Natural Hygiene." We didn't develop these cures all at once, but their precise compounds are the results of thousands of years of research. We, below, are careful with our diet; although, we provide succulent and gourmet menus as do you above.

Question: You say that even with improved diet you are occasionally subject to the same diseases as above? Enumerate some diseases that are prevalent here, for which you have cures below.

Answer: Cancer is one of your worst destroyers of life. We compound a precise mixture of vegetable juices which, when taken at the rate of a half pint per hour over a 30 day period, destroys all cancer cells, replacing them with new healthy normal cells. (Haammaan then explained that he was not a medical man and that his remarks were those of a layman, but the evidence that he offered could be substantiated in tests held in any medical research facility.) Doctors below were first successful in curing particular cancers by means of a drug called "UGROME" Later the drug was eliminated from the formulas. Straight vegetable and fruit extracts were used exclusively with such ingredients as carrots and tomatoes.

Question: You say our upper sunrays kill certain fruit or vegetable cells that contain added life support elements. How can we on the upper earth raise these products and keep their natural cells intact at the time of their ripening?

Answer: Grow them in greenhouses with glass that keeps out harmful rays. Your people already know what glass or plastic formula is required to shut out the sun's harmful rays in the spectrum.

Question: Please name other cures you have below that those above badly need.

Answer: Abscesses, skin cancers and boils. A jelly used by us clears them up in 24 hours. The jelly can also be taken internally in a capsule form. You are already aware of our artificial skin made from a sterile compound of vegetable juices and adhesives. The skin comes in rolls like your band-aids and is placed over large first and third degree burn areas. Body moisture is thus retained over a burn area. The body begins immediately to form new skin beneath. When healing is complete, the artificial skin is peeled off. No scars are seen.

Our dentists below also implant new teeth buds in the cavities of teeth that must be removed due to decay or infection. In the case of cavity filling, dentists below give their patients internal medicine made of natural ingredients that result in a tooth cavity being healed.

Question: Do you have the problem of drug addiction and alcoholism?

Answer: Neither are manufactured or sold in Atturias or Bodland or Vikingland. Drug addiction is considered a serious offense and if it became prevalent as above in your society, its use would not be tolerated. However, we have cures for the major types of addiction found here above. Take your marijuana! We have a weed below that tastes the same as marijuana when smoked. An addict who smokes one such cigarette finds his craving for marijuana satisfied and he, or she, breaks the drug habit without any side effects. We have similar cures for all your other drug problems. The acceptance of opiates is growing quickly in your society. Alcoholic beverages and smoking products are also not sold in Atturias although the old Vikings and Bodlanders indulge in barley beer and like tobacco, I'm told.

Mr. Haammaan continued, "Gentlemen, I am a man of arts and letters. I am not a scientist of medicine, nor a candidate for a doctor's
degree. Very soon I shall communicate with certain people below.
Then, through the good offices of you authors, who have discovered my whereabouts in your land and treated me with respect, I
shall ask to have brought up some suggestions, and perhaps explicit formulas, that your druggists, or researchers, can compound
for controlled trial use. As things stand at present in your country,
I would expect reference to these discussions in your book to be
rejected or laughed at by the major medical associations. Leaving
the subject of jeffjj@tds.netmedicine for a while, I would add that
we have authenticated cures for blood cholesterol, obesity, senility,
osteo-arthritis, stomach ulcers, and many more of your diseases.
We also have marvelous diagnostic equipment.

Contrary to what your fatalists say, three score years plus should
not be the span of a man's existence. If the major diseases could be
overcome on the Earth's surface, then mankind's life span would
be extended for certain, notwithstanding the harmful surface sunrays.

May I also disagree about your earlier question that implied that
our longevity stemmed from a collective, balanced, spiritual and
psychological attitude? Typical longevity below in Atturias is over
800 years and some have reached 1,200 years.

To prove that we, below, don't inherit a life span ten or twelve
times longer than yours simply because we possess superior spiritual or psychological qualifications, let me tell you about our dogs
and cats.

The life span of our domestic animals is perhaps thirty years. The
one common denominator that we people and our animal creatures
have in common is an environment free from harmful solar rays.

We can't unveil the mysteries of old age in a few hundred words,
but regardless of your sun's harmful rays and your diet, there are
some reversible techniques used by our medical men in Atturia that

could be copied above to drastically cut the annual death rate. Your medical scientists believe that each cell has an aging clock or self-destruct mechanism built in at about 70 years, but we below have proved this absolute life span is incorrect (as have the Bods). Well over 100 vigorous, disease-free years are possible for your people in the near future, if preventive help to cure the diseases of aging is studied.

Question: Upper earth nations publicly spend many, many billions annually on war preparations -- not to mention the huge interest cost to governments for monies borrowed to finance war debts. The question is; do you have a military apparatus below?

Answer: A qualified no! Nor do we have cadet colleges or war training schools. We, nor the Bods or Vikings, have standing armies (nor do the New Germans or the Six Kingdoms of Old German Saxons). Our sole paramilitary effort is policing our own people, and that force, whether a land force or sea force, is light. We do have a standing air force that has considerable power, but this is based on an ancient system of reconnaissance from the sky and transportation that you people amazingly refer to as unidentified flying objects. All the monies you spend on armaments, if turned to peaceful uses, could: create full employment, remove your welfare rolls, provide doctor and hospital benefits for all, and create a utopia like you haven't imagined. What are your poverty-stricken, emerging nations buying first? War machines!

I must add, no one major country like America could achieve this utopian structure while a single antagonist nation relies on armaments to dominate the world. All countries would have to lay down their arms simultaneously.

Question: Does your nation regard America as an aggressor nation?

Answer: I can't speak for our people, but I would say that the English-speaking people are not warlike. We do regard the Russian leaders as a military complex to be carefully watched.

Question: Who attacked whom in the 1946 war of the inner world?

Was it the New Germans or the old Vikings?

Answer: The Vikings observed the New Germans building up their new spacecraft squadrons. Worried about the growing German occupation of inner earth lands, and suspecting the real intentions of the New Germans, from their surface war record, the Vikings attacked. We, the new Atlanteans, as soon as we had ascertained their intentions, advised the Vikings to stop. On our signal, the Interplanetary Police Force came in and enforced a Viking withdrawal. The Vikings and New Germans now exchange ambassadors.

Question: Is your nation of Atturias more advanced than the U.S.A.?

Answer: Yes and no. The U.S.A. is extremely advanced in science and technology, but the inner earth nations are hundreds of years ahead of the upper world in social justice, the humanities and medicine. In space technology, North America has built a technical and scientific civilization in just a few years, as have countries such as Germany and Britain. It has taken us thousands of years to achieve our pre-eminence. Remember, we have had 11,500 years without war, and the Bodlanders 30 millennia.

Question: So, having a society free from want and hunger, and with ample clothing and shelter, you must have time for leisure activity.

Answer: Yes, we have had Olympic games (which we call Quad) since before we retreated to the inner earth from above. The New Germans below are now sending their athletes to compete. The Vikings, Six German Kingdoms, and Bodlanders have long done so. The annual games are a big event in our lives. We also have other leisure activities like you have above, such as hiking, racing and sailing on our oceans. You do practically every thing we do in the field of leisure. We also have our versions of your baseball, football, and tennis, but our athletes are not paid the enormous salaries yours are paid for stadium sport participation. In our houses, we have TV and home movies. I think our movie houses show a better three-dimensional picture than yours above.

Question: Is sex exploited below as in certain countries above?

Answer: Sex is not a goddess of worship below. There are no pornographic movies, periodicals, or media advertisements using it. There are no houses of prostitution. This is an explanation that requires a much longer treatment than we have time for today. You will recall married men and women live apart but have special houses for sex visitation. (The Bodlanders are more family oriented, living, playing and entertaining as a unit until the children leave home. The close Bod-family ties remain unbroken according to Dr. Jerrmus.)

Also, there are no polygamous marriages and no divorces in Atturias or Bodland. The childbearing age in Atturias is from 25 to 60 years of age. Marriages take place after age 25. The children live with the mothers until ten, and afterwards they are trained by the state. The family connection is never broken and we enjoy long lives of fellowship. Wives are permitted to have only two children, and afterwards women have a minor operation to prevent childbirth. Abortion is not permitted except for proven medical reasons.

(In Bodland, intensive high school sex education is taught, and the harm of illicit sex acts is discussed and studied by both sexes. The Bodland student must attend a state-run, tuition-free high school. All reading is censored until adulthood, with not even Shakespeare being on the high school curricula. University is free.)

I would simply say that total guidance by the state is obligatory until the child/youth becomes of voting age. You above permit the undesirable elements to become an accepted part of your society. Then, you spend the state's monies in locating, watching, or incarcerating them, after the criminal tendencies have surfaced. We try to find and correct the troubles beforehand.

Question: Are there any primitive societies down below?

Answer: Yes, in addition to certain Eskimos, there are a number of tribes in out-of-the-way areas that go practically naked like certain of your New Guinea and Borneo primitives.

Question: What would you call your form of government?

Answer: Ours is a private enterprise system (as is Bodland and Vikingland). We have a hereditary King (as do the Vikings, Bods and Old Germans). A republic form of government (re-elected rulers) was tried many thousands of years ago, but it failed. For 300 years, we had a republic similar to America. The President was elected for a five-year term and could be re-elected three times. This term was changed to one 15-year term, and the constitution allowed this for another 300 years. Next, a man was elected for life. Finally, we returned to the hereditary monarchial system that has been in effect ever since.

(Contrary to the Atturian hereditary monarchial system, the present Bodland monarch, King Haakkuuss III, was appointed for life in 1928. Recently he gave notice he wanted to relinquish his duties and the Bodland parliament is now seeking a new king.) Under the existing monarchy in Atturias, a head of state similar to a Prime Minister is in charge and is elected by parliament on recommendation of the king. He presides over the upper and lower houses of parliament. He doesn't necessarily sit in the legislative assembly, but the Prime Minister and King must approve all bills. Term of office is 15 years. Both lower and upper houses are for five-year terms by the citizens. A few have been elected for life.

Question: Is not the Atturian state below somewhat of a disciplinary force in all walks of life including religion?

Answer: No, it is not. The state allows freedom of conscience in matters of religious conviction where everyone may hold their own consensus of religious philosophy, but we do have a universal church.

The author was unable to explore Atturian religious beliefs in any detail, partly because of the subject's reluctance to elaborate on their forms of worship; except, to have Haammaan admit they worship a Supreme God, and they regarded Osiris, who visited ancient

Atlantis above as their Christ-like advocate with the Supreme Deity. Haammaan also said that Atturains were divided as to the belief in an afterlife, although the authors did not pursue this admission.

Interested in the overall religious complexion of the Inner World societies, the author therefore, at a later date, sought further explanations from a visiting Bodland lecturer, Dr. Jerrmus. He was persuaded to discuss the Bods' religious beliefs and agreed to do so. He forewarned of his reluctance, because he did not wish to offend his upper-world hosts by arguing either religion or politics. With the foregoing preface to religion in Bodland, the urbane doctor of philosophy described Bod religious background with some caution, as paraphrased as follows:

The accepted book of divine inspiration used below by the Bods is the Upper-World Bible expanded with three Old Testament and two New Testament chapters. The Bods claim that the existing Old Testament used below was compiled by scholars who were not exclusively Hebrew. They included Greeks and Bodlanders, Ezekiel being a Bodlander, Dr. Jerrmus claimed.

The entire original bible is kept below in their national museum for all to see and compare, whereas the missing bible books of the Upper World are hidden in three places, these being Rome, Cairo, and Tibet.

An important book in the Bod New Testament is the Book of Bod, written and compiled by the King of Bod living at the time of Christ. The King was also one of the four (not three) wise men, all of who were kings, one having begun his journey from a civilization in the Gobi Desert. The second Bod book deals primarily with healing as explained by Christ to the early Christian disciples. Some original manuscripts, on exhibit in the National Bod Museum, were written by the apostle/scribe, Saint John, and signed by Jesus Christ.

The Book of Bod elaborates more than the known gospels on Christ's birth, as well as the origin and activities of the wise men and the celestial nature of the star. The direction and focus of its rays were altered from time to time following its appearance almost a year before Christ was born in Bethlehem. Those in the Inner World also saw the star. The inhabitants regarded the new light as a long anticipated astrological sign by which the Bod King should begin his journey to pay homage to the Son of God. The King came through a tunnel, emerging in a Bod temple in Abadan on which there has been built a Moslem mosque. After the visit of the magi to the Christ child, the King returned below via space-craft. The Book also details the crucifixion and tells particularly how the wrath of God was felt on Earth through the elements of nature, including bolts of lightning that killed 12 Roman soldiers who participated in the crucifixion. The Book also explains how the entire Mid-East world was caught up in the events of the cruci-fixion, especially an Assyrian king who began a forced march with 3000 troops too late to save Jesus from death.

There are variances in the Book of Bod with the existing gospels. For instance, the Bod version credits the Bod King with warning Mary and Joseph to flee with the infant Jesus to Egypt after his birth in order to escape Herod's hate and vengeance. Then, after Jesus' first encounter with the teachers and priests in the temple at age 12, the Bod narrative says he was taken by space ship to the Inner Earth where he was tutored in the palace of the Bod King till his mid twenties, Then he asked to be returned to the Upper World where he completed his studies in India and Tibet before begin-ning his ministry of healing and preaching of salvation. Thus, the wisdom and learning of the Inner World are said to figure largely in Christ's earthly pilgrimage. That preparation does not discount his divinity or the main purpose of drawing a separated mankind back to God, says Dr. Jerrmus, who does not pretend to be a biblical scholar.

The second expunged book that has been denied Upper World bib-lical readers is an integral part of the Inner World bible, the book of healing. It was the cornerstone of Christ's earthly ministry. The visiting Bod doctor of literature opined that the greatest hindrance to the growth of Christianity in the Upper World was due to culpa-bility of early church fathers in their removal of the practical and sacred book on healing. That book was a legacy of God's mercy not intended exclusively for a priestly caste. St. Luke, the physician, was a Bodlander, claims Dr. Jerrmus.

The learned doctor from the Inner World concluded by saying that their prophets anticipated the arrival of Christ thousands of years before his coming. They also foretold the end times of this present age which is supposed to include a final holocaust of mankind, after which the perfect world order of universal peace and happiness will be reborn. The Bod pre-Christian temple mentioned earlier, now buried under a Moslem mosque near Abadan, Iran, still has the ancient Bod prophecies concerning this age engraved on its walls.

With this brief mention of religious ethics in the Inner World, as described by Dr. Jerrmus, our narrative reverts to the dialogue held with Professor Haammaan on the composition and authority of government in Bodland's Inner-World neighbor, Atturias. Professor Haammaan continues as follows: "The state of Atturias does not suppress individual initiative or deny freedom of expression, but neither does it allow wide range objections and lobbying from self-interest groups as is permitted in America.

"It seems to me that the constant attempts to tear down government here will lead to anarchy soon, or else a clashing of government forces and various so-called objector groups. Unlike a dictatorship, the problem of a republican form of government, as in America or France, is that there is a danger that the central power-base needed for civil obedience is dissipated by too many voices of self-willed interest. Your vested groups in America are very powerful and selfish, often at the expense of the majority electorate! I don't speak of politicians critically, but as an observer. We once had a republican form of government like yours, but abandoned it, as did the people of Bod."

Question: What main dangers lie ahead for Earth?

Answer: Number one -- nuclear war. That is why we came up in 1945. Number two -- an intruding planetary influence that is growing and could drastically change the climate in the entire northern hemispheres of the upper Earth in the next 20 years, if the planet is not diverted away. Past intrusions of this planet Nagirth caused the formation of other continental ice sheets, the origin of which has defied your geologists. Your Science Foundation has all the information here and probably is greatly concerned about this coming new glacial age. I believe Nagirth will be deflected.

Question: Have you heard that the Earth's mantle, between your people and us, is honeycombed with manmade tunnels?

Answer: Yes. There are tunnels at varying depths containing very ancient and vast civilizations. We use them to commute between Shamballa and the capital of the subterranean Kingdom of the Far North, located in the mantle under Siberia. During the time of the Russian Czars, there was an upper opening into Siberia through which we had access to Russia via the tunnels, but this opening has been closed since Russia went communistic. Openings exist in the U.S.A. and other parts of the upper world. (See map) We use them constantly. The North American tunnel opening of which I am aware has a "y" located deep in the mantle where a city exists. One line of the "y" goes to Shamballa and the other goes to Bod. We, below, are concerned about possible illegal entries of undesirable races from the subterranean world to our nations via tunnels. Other tunnels are the highways used by certain highly civilized subterranean people who travel via rail from city to city. Neither you nor your readers will likely believe this "inside the Earth's crust" remark, but there are reputed to be more people living there than exist on either surface. In addition to tunnel dwellers, there are major cities supported by steel domes under the ice caps of the Polar Regions. These cities were tropical before past Ice Ages, and shifting of earth poles caused the dwellers to cover their cities for protection. The Antarctic ice-covered, polar cities connect by train tunnels to subterranean mantle cities and major cities of the Inner World. A third of the tunnel cities are natural and the remainder man-made.

Those people living inside have protection against sun and cold, hence a great longevity span. Your Admiral Richard Byrd was taken to one of the domed cities through sub tunnels. We have mapped all existing tunnels and cities, but there could be pockets we don't know of. When Atlantis sank, our ancestors built plastic domes over those remaining cities that had not yet been inundated by the ocean. Today those six plastic-domed cities on the Atlantic bed are still inhabited by our Atlantean people. In all, I believe there are 28 cities located all over the world, underwater, each being reached by saucer craft as well as tunnel trains. The undersea city near San Juan, Puerto Rico, in the Bahamas trench is round in shape and is ten miles in diameter. It is occupied by millions of our people. All our undersea cities are also connected with Shamballa.

In effect, our Atlanteans, Bodlanders, and Athenians occupy: the inner Earth, many of the tunnels and tunnel cities, as well as domed cities on the bottom of the oceans.

Part of the former continent of Atlantis sank immediately; but other parts, including those on which the domed cities stand, settled beneath the Atlantic over a period of 300 years. Ice formed slowly over the Antarctic sub-continent that was the home of the original Garden of Eden, our legends tell.

Question: What is your explanation of the Bermuda Triangle?

Answer: The so-called "Bermuda Triangle" does not exist as a defined boundary. During our war with the Athenians, we dumped many multi-faceted crystals, of golf ball size, in areas of what you call today the Bermuda Triangle. The crystals were refractory power-er sources for some of our weapons and energy centers. They were able to capture the sun's rays; and, by internally refracting the rays, an intense beam, or laser ray, was produced. The crystals were first used for peaceful purposes and later developed for war. These crystals are still operational 11,500 years after they were dumped in these Caribbean areas that subsequently became flooded. They have been rising gradually since. When the sun's rays reach the ocean floor of these areas, the crystals are temporarily activated. When this happens, a steel ship or plane coming in contact with the rays simply disintegrates. They do not affect wood.

In the 1600's a fleet of three Dutch ships were sunk in the Sargasso

Sea. Survivors, who were found in the lifeboats, put together with wooden dowels, told how their larger sailing ships fell part when the ship's metal spikes disintegrated. In 1641, the Dutch King built an entirely wooden sailing ship with hardwood dowels. Sent over the same area, the crew found the floating debris of the former wrecks. Returning to Rotterdam in 1641, they first told the tale of a sea demon who ate up the ships' spikes. Today we know this area as part of the so-called Bermuda Triangle, and the sea demon is the dreadful black rays emanating from the crystals that early Atlanteans dumped in that area that is now underwater. It should be remembered that there are also suppressed reports claiming that radioactive waste dumped recently in the Caribbean is causing mysterious effects.

We call the ray a black ray because it can't be seen. Our ancestors deployed the disintegrating ray in their war with the Athenians to destroy whole cities, and also air ships. It is the most devastating ray weapon in the world. The colorless crystal collects its energy from the sun (making it crystal clear) during the day and releases it whenever it is charged to full capacity.

These crystals are indestructible. They were made active by the bottom of the present seabed rising, along with bottom sands shifting enough to expose the dormant crystals. The crystals are active only at certain times. I believe your government is aware of the danger periods.

Our inner sun is a modified version of these crystals and it, too, is activated in part from the solar sun shining through the Poles throughout the year. This artificial sun was built in ancient Atlantis, transported inside by our space ships and first charged by the real sun after being orbited in the Earth's interior. Foreseeing the coming war, our ancestors began our colony below 3000 years before Atlantis sank or approximately 15,000 years ago. The artificial sun has functioned perfectly since it was installed. Our lead protected engineering "ray men" do go in periodically and check the lantern for replacement parts. The refractory crystals, however, are everlasting.

Question: When are you going home permanently?

Answer: Your State Department permitting, I intend to remain above for a long time. It is my new home. While attending college, I fell in love with a surface girl and married her. We have three lovely children and I have made this upper world my home. If my wife and children were to pass on, God forbid, tragically before myself, then I would go back because I expect to have many useful years ahead. Who knows the future so exactly? Maybe I shall remain above till I die. I have not reckoned how many years of my normal life span I will lose by remaining on the Earth's surface.

Four interviews were held with the two inner world contacts from 1977 to 1979. Many aspects of their separate civilizations were discussed which have not been introduced here because they do not add to the credibility of a hollow earth. Two important revelations about them should, however, be brought to the reader's attention. The first is the greater longevity of the old races of the Inner Earth who are actually related to surface dwellers. Evidence indicates that those below, without exception, live a minimum of a hundred years longer than we do in a single life span and millions apparently live several hundred additional years. Until we gather further proof of this, a discussion of the longevity of dwellers in the Inner World will be held in abeyance, because the possibility of it being true is more disquieting than anything else discovered. If the Bodlanders live to be several hundred years, then an exchange of medical teams, which the Bodlanders are anxious to do, would be desirable to provide surface dwellers with the formulas used below. If, on the other hand, the Atturians live for a thousand years, is it not possible that mankind on the surface has indeed fallen from grace since he left the legendary Garden of Eden? Have human beings been denied longer lives by the finite life sentence of only three score years and ten? On being asked what was the greatest difference between the Inner and Outer worlds that he first noted on arriving on the surface to live, Haammaan replied, "Old age, hospitals, and mortuaries."

Notes on Sources

CHAPTER I

Incidents in Chapter I are indicative of outer space surveillance and the four primary events described were chosen from hundreds of sightings and alien manifestations gleaned from various sources, including Navy and Air Force files. The name Major Farrel is a pseudonym used by a retired Air Force person who now resides in the Tampa Bay area of Florida. Fifty pages of supporting documentary evidence regarding the Mantell/UFO encounter were read in the National Archives but when copies arrived by mail the photostat information was so purposely overdeveloped it was unreadable. Complaints were unanswered.

CHAPTER II

The Caldwell invention of an aerodynamic breakthrough, that had merit enough to become government subsidized, was denied by the Army-Air Force at the time. The stories appeared in several American dailies in July 1949, under AP wire. Pictures were included of the Roto Plane and Grey Goose. Their condition was battered, since they were abandoned in 1936. The Baltimore Sun carried the original story. Researcher Hudson found the initial story in the National Archives following a civil service tip. Follow-up then began in the Baltimore Sun's morgue where editors and cameramen were interviewed. The search was continued in California and Canada. America's greatest aerodynamic genius since the Wright brothers resides at various locations and is always on the move. The author met him twice. He used different names, part of a careful plan to shield him from the public for fear of renewed Soviet attempts to kidnap him. Caldwell's body movements are still quick, his mind is clear, his eyes sparkle with a merry, almost mischievous gleam, as he philosophizes or reminisces about his favorite hobbies and pursuits. He is always accompanied by what appear to be secret service agents, and he refuses to discuss his contributions to science.

CHAPTER III

Classified files in the State Department on the visit of the outer-terrestrials to President Roosevelt in 1936 and 1943 were shown to this book's researcher. This information was followed up through diplomatic papers in the National Archives. Personal verification was made also through a close contact with President Roosevelt, who said the visits were "common knowledge" among the White House staff at the time. However, much additional research, particularly about the beginning of the U.S. government cover-up, was done in order to present the facts in their proper context of that period. Several government heads that helped should be acknowledged, but they insist on remaining anonymous. The author, and exemplary voluntary aides, spent four years before discovering the current hiding place for the entire UFO repository. Records included the U.S. space role near earth, and in outer space environs. Although source of cover-up was located in the National Security Agency, it was apparent that the section that denied all knowledge of the program was semi-autonomous and not answerable to the head of the agency. It frequently defied orders to explain its actions. It was never discovered just where the roots of the cover-up section ended or from where its personnel were recruited. Sources indicated it was the Council on Foreign Relations.

CHAPTER IV

Some of the sources for early U.S. development of the round-wing plane must still remain secret as well as the names of contributing associates. We were unable to obtain existing close-up photos of Caldwell's first airworthy prototypes of the 30's, which are stored in the Smithsonian Institute for future public display.

CHAPTER V

First story leads, on German development of their own flying saucer, came from Christina Edderer, private pilot to Hitler who was interviewed twice in Munich in December 1975, and early 1980. Through Edderer, our contact led to the Von Schusnick family. John Taylor of the Modern Military Records of the National Archives dug out much German material and OSS records of World War II to complete the chapter. To get a first-hand account of the sorry lift-off of the first German saucer prototype, one of the former crew now living in America was questioned. He is still an arrogant hard-core Nazi at heart. Reference to the espionage trials, the executions of the eight traitors involved in the stolen Caldwell plans were from various government files and old newspaper stories. A State Department source verified details, and provided other leads.

CHAPTER VI

Untold is a great story on the stupendous civilian effort of Americans and Canadians to develop a hidden British Columbia valley and build a complex within it to house the U.S. round-wing plane factories, and housing. The author was unable to get any realistic perspective of the valley, for security reasons still in effect, although he is aware of Canadians and Americans who have been located there. On a per-capita basis, the Canadian war effort, with its part in the round-wing plane story and the valley complex, etc., was as great as that of the United States or Britain.

CHAPTER VII

The records of an OSS agent, a bona fide Catholic priest under the code name of Father John, were shown to the researcher. From this source, the story of Father John's visit to the British Columbia valley complex is told. Most helpful in acquiring much of the related material in the chapter of wartime development of the allied round-wing plane was from old unclassified files. Nothing of a strategic or significant military disclosure was made available.

CHAPTER VIII

Two of the four agents who infiltrated Germany and rode the troop trains to Spain are still alive and live in the U.S.A.; Allen Dulles and the Catholic priest are dead. Those alive are brave heroes whose names, because of security restrictions still in force, must be protected. Their true identities and whereabouts cannot be divulged. OSS records in the National Archives contain much of the cloak-and-dagger bravery of these American (and British) agents. That, won't be made available to the public until fifty years after these happenings, or after the death of the agents involved. A high government official, without whose help this book would have floundered in its early stages, made these records available. The author read microfilm files of captured German records at U.S. Archives revealing the story of the sinking of the two British cruisers. The same story was researched in the British Admiralty Office in London. A letter from the National Archives in Washington, signed by John S. Taylor, introduced the researcher to Sir John Cole, keeper of the captured German records in the British Admiralty. (British and American-held German records are now being transferred back to Germany on microfilm.) The officials, in the German Archives in Bonn, hidden deep under ground, also admitted the researcher in order to verify information on the super subs and other matters. Finally, the sub builder was interviewed.

World War II records transferred from the London office of the OSS on meetings of the Joint Chiefs of Staff, under the late General Dwight Eisenhower, including OSS Chief General W. Donovan (deceased), were studied in Washington. Records were also studied in the Public Records Office in London, archived by her Majesty's Secret Service under Army Intelligence.

The episode of the giant German super sub was first discovered in the captured German Archives at the U.S. National Archives, as well as the Library of Congress where the super sub plans were seen (copies could not be obtained). The bulk of the information re the super sub came from the British Admiralty Office in London. Bonn Archives were also checked for verification. Both the German Captain of the sub (the name given is fictitious), and the former OSS agent Schellenberg were located by the authors. Neither man was aware the other was alive. Many additional episodes were revealed that must be excluded because of time. Names of the mass Jew exterminators in German concentration camps, and elsewhere, came from original notebooks, diaries, and records captured from the Germans at World War II's end, including the one signed in human blood, kept in the National Archives. Dr. Wolff, head of the captured German records in the National Archives, was most helpful to the researcher.

Material re the Hitler escape was made available when Generalissimo Franco of Spain ordered the Spanish Military Records opened in Madrid and Simcas, Spain. King Juan Carlos later helped in a personal way to secure additional supporting information. Without the American CIA, the picture story of the German exodus would never have been verified. The author met the agent who took the intelligence snapshots.

CHAPTER IX

Phase I of the 1572 unwilling German exodus into the mantle of the earth was obtained in parts from Portuguese Archives in Lisbon, French Archives in Paris, and Vatican Archives in Rome. Eric Von Schusnick, living in Washington in 1977, verified to the researcher, the author's questions on the whereabouts and population of the present German cities located in the earth mantle, and German populations in the earth's interior. All Bodland information came from Dr. Jerrmus, visiting lecturer from Bodland's capitol city. Much tunnel information came from other German sources, including Swiss tunnel engineer Karl Schneider. Ben Miller, an assumed name, Byrd's navigator-in-hiding since 1947, for fear of his life, also provided extensive tunnel and interior information. He turned over his copies of the world's early (and perhaps first) written language used in the ancient Antarctic cities now covered over with ice. Most of the information for this chapter came from old German sources. Official records, manuscripts and nameless books at the Library of Congress catalogued, only by numbers, were searched. The conclusive break in the almost fabled story of

Germanic penetration of the Inner World occurred when Dr. Jerrmus was located. He answered many unanswered queries on the 20th-Century Nazi plans for emigration to the Inner World prior to World War II, and on the post-war German exodus. It was Dr. Jerrmus who provided the contents of the 1943 welcome speech by King Haakkuus III delivered to their Upper World Germanic cousins. That speech laid down the terms of Inner World occupation. Dr. Jerrmus told of the 1936 warning to Hitler, given by King Haakkuus III, that Germany should not incite another world war on the surface of the planet.

CHAPTER X

Admiral Byrd's 1946-47 logs were made available for one hour, on one occasion, and again later on. Congressman Claude Pepper arranged the first review and the signature of President Ford was required for a second look. A Navy airman who accompanied the group down and into the interior was interviewed as well, along with Byrd's navigator Ben Miller who of course played a leading role. Franklin Birch, head of Polar Archives, while not admitting the Byrd Flight, eventually gave much valuable information and assistance to the author-researcher team. The researcher saw hundreds of pictures re the inside of the earth. Those chosen were paid for, but never delivered, as opposition hardened to the Byrd story release. The briefing upon Byrd's return to Washington came from Navy Archives. Newspaper accounts stored on microfilm also were read.

CHAPTER XI

The official account, given orally, was that Byrd's 1947 flight crashed in an Antarctic snowstorm. Still-living members of the crew, as well as naval records, proved that this version of the missing airmen' deaths was concocted. Makeup and composition of the navy fighter squadron was located in the Navy Archives. Correspondence with Byrd's family went unanswered. Kurt Von Ludwig gave the German account of the Russian and American aerial destruction in the interior when the author visited the West German Embassy in Washington. Eric Von Schusnick gave the rendering of the dead airmen's' return to Arlington cemetery. The plaque honoring those killed in action in what could be called the Inner World Mini-War was seen by the book researcher in 1979.

CHAPTER XII

Someday historians will rewrite the drama of Admiral Richard Byrd's excursions to the Poles, and inside the Earth, in order to insert a momentous missing chapter to American history. It was Byrd's flights, regardless of the final disastrous one, that roused his successors to carry on the search for the "legendary" Inner World, and to prove it was real. Briefly interviewed for this chapter was Captain R. Davies, pilot of the 1947 flight by American round-wing plane into the center of the Earth. Most convincing, of the returned information, were the picture composites that formed the Upper World's first map of the hollow interior.

CHAPTER XIII

The author, to gather material for this chapter, visited the California base supplying the Antarctic stations. The Canadian Defense Department and the underground DEW line communications center in northern Ontario, Canada were also visited. The deception that Arctic and Antarctic defense lines were mainly built for possible action from the Russians intentionally ignored the presumed German menace entrenched in the interior of the earth. That was still considered a threat in the immediate post war years. The researcher sat in on an Allied Polar Defense meeting in Washington in 1975 attended by two representatives from eight nations, including the U.S.A., U.S.S.R., Canada, Great Britain, France, Netherlands, and Italy. The discussion was of a common northern defense against possible invasion from the interior (presumably New Germany). After the meeting, the Russian representative invited Hudson to Moscow to discuss UFO information. According to German and American Intelligence sources, the Russians do not possess the round-wing plane, but they are aware that Germans and English-speaking people have it. The Soviets also know (fearfully) of the American magnetic spacecraft generally called the round-wing plane because of its use, on occasion, over Moscow. The researcher, while in Russia as guest for three days with the Russian Institute of Space Sciences, was shown films of UFO sightings. The episode on how America nearly lost the secret of the round-wing plane as a result of the Yalta conference was provided. Protective OSS concern in cooperation with British Intelligence saved the secret. A two-hour study of a secret CIA brief of the Yalta affair later added agent verification. In trying to discern President Roosevelt's egomania, and diminishing well-being in his final months of life, the author was made aware that without Roosevelt's earlier vision, the round-wing shield over the free world would have been only a dream.

CHAPTER XIV

Description of German life in the hollow earth was delayed until the reader was first made familiar with the earlier origins of the hollow earth civilizations. Again it was information from German sources that gave the authors contemporary evidence that the earth is hollow, as are most planets. A grandson of the original Captain von Jagow, Helmut von Jagow, formerly captain in the Imperial German Navy and now (1978) with the United Nations in New York, supplied many details. So did a visitor to America, John von Tirpitz (now 81), formerly Grand-Admiral of the German North Sea Fleet, who, as a young lieutenant, served on the ship to the interior. Two persons from the Inner World were interviewed -- the first man, in 1977, named Haammaann, is a professor at an Eastern university. Professor Haammaann divulged the historical facts of the Upper World nuclear war 11,500 years ago, and he gave credibility to the sinking of the continent of Atlantis. Further information on the social, political, economic and religious life in the Inner World was supplied by Haammaann and Jerrmuss. Jerrmuss was interviewed in 1979. Their fascinating accounts of the interior systems are in the appendix. Both men want the story of the Inner Earth explained, although Professor Haammaann has been harassed by officialdom for talking and is afraid of deportation. Hence his picture is not shown. On the other hand, Dr. Jerrmus states there are no classified secrets in his country of Bodland and welcomes visitors in the years ahead who may want to ascertain what life is like in the most advanced nation on, or in, this world.

Another Inner World man, J. B. Aacceerson, who was on loan from Atturia to the U.S.A. on a map exchange program, drew for us the map of the interior. For his help, he was turned out of his office in the Library of Congress and was forced to go into hiding to complete the work. Later he sought and was granted asylum in a foreign embassy. He will probably be deported unless a Presidential stay is granted. In coming to the authors' aid in similar situations, the executive branch of the government, up to and including the President, has been obliging and helpful.

CHAPTER XV

Correspondence between Truman and Churchill, and other related letters from commentators such as Plateu, are kept in bound books in the Kensington Tombs, Maryland. In reading this correspondence, one can't help but reflect that the letters represented a course of action for transportation and technological changes in a new world to be born before next century. The great contributions made by General Charles B. Wilkerson, and his staff, were barely touched on. No investigation of the twelve research centers was conducted, and no attempt was made to evaluate the round-wing program after 1952. Almost as fascinating as the round-wing plane possibilities was the trial run of an automobile as it crossed the country (rather continent) without fuel. It is reliably reported that the same test motor is still in use on a highway conveyance vehicle.

CHAPTER XVI

The name Colonel Fox is fictitious, the author having decided to give the OSS agent the same name by which the Germans referred to him. He is also referred to under one of his code names. Fox himself spoke to the author and gave more details of the von Rundstedt visit and a later follow-up meeting with Patton in Berne, Switzerland. Only one family's migration and residence was used to avoid dry statistics. Five leading Von Schusnicks (three generations) were interviewed in America, Switzerland and Germany. Hitler's funeral was verified from government sources in Spain, Germany, and Washington. The author obtained a complete list of those who attended and a description of the service and final burial place of the former German dictator. Hitler's remains have since been moved twice. The revelation of German-based war aspirations located in various South American locales was sketched in order to show the reader that two separate German branches developed after World War II; one being inside the Earth under Bodland direction -- and the other hidden in the vastness of unexplored South American areas principally under Nazi direction.

CHAPTER XVII

The author tried unsuccessfully to obtain a copy of the State Departments alien card used to admit outer terrestrials to planet Earth. The text was read but no copies permitted for publication. Neither was it possible to use the name of the director of that department, notwithstanding he was most helpful in the interviewing. Six interviews were held with Mr. Estes Plateu. The first was in Danny's Cafe, Washington accompanied by Major Donald Keyhoe. A senior civil servant arranged a second meeting over the protests of another military intelligence group. Much of the information was not used. No attempt was made to prove if Venus is occupied because of book limitations; although, Mr. Plateu issued an invitation to the author to visit his homeland -- with our government's permission of course. Plateu said his father visited George Washington in the field, and the present Plateu visited Lincoln on more than one occasion of which the author has been given record. Plateu also says his father was an observer in Palestine, and Rome, at the time of Christ. The elder Plateu heard Christ preach many times in the Holy Land, thus verifying the gospels. Plateu is reported to have said of his father that if the people had only listened to Jesus then the world would be a paradise today. When in astral projection, Plateu is not photographable. Hence an artist was used to draw his portrait at an unnamed location. The first artist refused to finish the project because of threats to his life. It is obvious that Plateu's movements in the U.S. are so restricted by the unfathomed autonomous UFO control group located in the Washington vicinity, that Plateu's usefulness to America and the world in general cannot be effectively tapped. The Vatican was visited on two occasions by the researcher in order to verify the visits of the outer terrestrials. He spoke with Pope Paul, the Vatican Secretary of State, and the Press Secretary who began by saying, "We don't expect you to believe this -- we ourselves have a hard time deciding it is reality."

The author's own interpolation was added to that of the Vatican notes in order to look at the role of Christendom in the world today. Most protestant leaders approached in America did not react with openness or credibility to comments on extra terrestrial or outer-terrestrial visits to churchmen, avoiding discussion or calling the subject matter heretical. Dr. Billy Graham did not reply nor set up a meeting. A scientist at Stanford said, "How could only a few hundred pages in the bible tell all the things of the future that God wants man to know? The Old Testament and Revelations read that important prophecies would be unfolded at the closing of this age. If aliens and airships are arriving from other planets, and we have made contact with those inside the Earth, then we should pause and recall that Galileo was ahead of his time though bold enough to declare that, "Earth was not the center of the universe." A Doctor of Divinity who teaches a class in Revelations at a California Christian college said: "The concept of Christ's atonement for mankind's sins must be taken on faith -- but students today are asking many other questions of this age on which we need more complete answers." A top writer for a large protestant evangelistic association said: "It isn't necessary to prove God. Just tell the facts. God's word must stand up to any examination! Otherwise, it is not God's word." Israel's Prime Minister Manechim Begin stated that neither outer nor inner terrestrials had visited Israel, whose small stub of land is in the crossroads of the world's trouble spot in this decade. Because of this remark, the author considered that the historic Judaic position in the light of current Christianity should be mentioned.

CHAPTER XVIII

Several unnamed military eyewitnesses spoke of the Ocala confrontation between an American round-wing plane and a Nagirth intruder. A White House executive source was also helpful. The researcher learned of the event while it was happening, but the author was not allowed on the site. Regarding the remarks on the changing weather patterns across the globe, there is a film issued by NASA named "The Coming Ice Age." A 35 mm, 30-minute documentary gives scientific, meteorological, and astronomical proof of planetary intrusion of the wandering Nagirth. Mr. Plateu, of Venus, said his planetary advisors have shown North Americans how to build electro-magnetic, anti-gravity machines that will repel Nagirth as was done 300 years ago, when the same unwelcome influence approached the Venus orbit.

CHAPTER XIX

The United States Air Force provided the recent cases of unidentified craft in earth skies. Of prime importance is the understanding of the author that the spacecraft sighted and reported by the Air Force are said to be foreign to this solar system -- that is, the craft are considered as inter-galactic.

CHAPTER XX

No intensive review was done on the use of the anti-magnetic motor possibilities that military and civilian research groups have been conducting for decades. The researcher attended a meeting in Washington at which the round-wing plane specialists of the U.S. and Canadian Air Forces briefed members of the aircraft industry on the transition from fixed-wing to round-wing air travel. The Russian versus American (or free world) problems in the upper atmosphere were brought into focus after much thought in order to show the reader that Soviet versus free world antagonism has already reached into outer space. A private investigation by the researcher uncovered the existence of planetary delegations located in Washington. The reference to the 1952 flight of an American/Canadian/British flight to Venus was obtained from the actual flight log of the flight. It was read in its entirety on the authorization of an unnamed government committee. That story will be written as a separate narrative at another time, mainly because half of the contents describe life on Venus. Two round-wing pilots were interviewed for this chapter, and the head, or commander, of the Interplanetary Police Net (a Venusian) was also interviewed, the English phonetic rendering of the Commander's name being Karkov.

Finishing Statement

The 54-12 committee was attentive when we asked to explain
to them our reasoning for telling the public of the round-wing
achievement in the field of space travel and the obstacles which we
had overcome to reach the concluding chapter. Although the committee did not reveal their inner deliberations, it was apparent that
erudite and scholarly men from the United States and Canada sat
thereon. At that point in time, after four years of research, writing
and rewriting, no censorship demands were made by the committee, and no attempt was made to stop the book by 54-12. The work
of the author is generally optimistic in its outlook, but some sobering mysteries of this age are briefly mentioned in the last pages.
From the frontispiece to the last paragraph, world science is truly
shown as advancing at colossal speed. In the end, as in the beginning of this book, mankind is still feverishly poised to obliterate
his neighbor with the ultimate weapon – nuclear powered hate –
conceived in his heart and fashioned with his own hands.

FINIS

Genesis for the Space Race

Photos and Maps

Construction of buildings in the Inner Earth of the New Berlin

175

The coverup of America's activities in the Antarctic prevented the public from knowing the true intentions of the United States and it's post-war allies.

Admiral R. E. Byrd

Admiral Richard E. Byrd circa 1955

To Marry This Month — Miss Olga Joyce Lokaryk and John Blyth Leith, of Hamilton, whose engagement is announced, have chosen December 28 as their wedding date. The ceremony will take place at 2 p.m. in Dominion United Church. The bride-elect is the daughter of Mrs. J. Lokaryk and the late Mr. Lokaryk of Moose Jaw, Sask. Her fiance is the son of Mr. and Mrs. John Leith of Hamilton.

—Photo of Miss Lokaryk by Vincent Toomaa

L. Frank Hudson

Hitler's military inner circle, May 1940. Front row, l. to r., Brückner (personal adjutant), Otto Dietrich (press chief), Keitel, Hitler, Jodl, Bormann, Below (Hitler's Luftwaffe adjutant), Hoffmann the photographer. Middle row, Bodenschatz (Göring's chief of staff), Schmundt, Wolf, Dr. Morell (Hitler's chief physician), Hansgeorg Schulze (Hitler's ordnance officer, killed in battle and replaced by his brother Richard). Back row, Engel (Hitler's army adjutant), Dr. Brandt (Hitler's surgeon), Puttkamer, Lorenz (DNB), Walther Hewel (Foreign Office), unknown, Schaub (Hitler's personal adjutant), Wünsche. BIBLIO. FÜR ZEIT.

One of the last pictures of Hitler. He visits Oder front, March 1945. BIBLIO. FÜR ZEIT.

On October 10, 1943, Hitler congratulates Himmler, who has just revealed that six million Jews have been exterminated. U. S. ARMY

Millions more Jews and non-Jews died in concentration camps in the spring of 1945. Belsen. U. S. OFFICE OF WAR INFORMATION

Mussolini's son-in-law, Count Ciano, visits Hitler at Wolf's Lair, his headquarters in Poland. Behind: Schmundt, Ribbentrop and Schulze. BIBLIO. FÜR ZEIT.

PHOTO IN THE INNER EARTH

TOUR AT NEW BERLIN

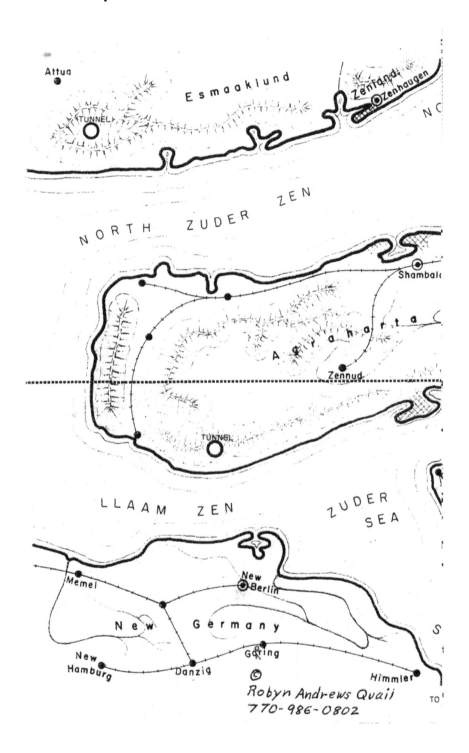

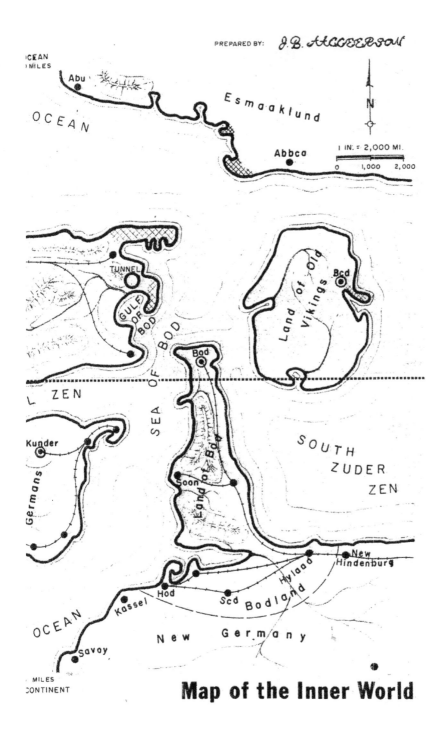

PREPARED BY: *J. B. Aggerson*

Map of the Inner World

Acknowledgements

Proper names of individuals and places in this book have been changed or omitted where security demanded such precautions. In several other instances, the true source of information must remain unidentified. There are people whose valuable contributions can be acknowledged without indicating the context in which they helped.

A few people provided counsel and support whenever called upon throughout the entire book. Those contributors are John S. Taylor, U.S. State Department, and Charles B. Wilson, former Dean of Princeton University Law School.

The following provided specific information and supporting evidence. The names do not necessarily coincide with the order of incidents. They were: Lt. Commander Harold B. Simpson, U.S. Navy; U.S. Senators Robert Byrd, Lawton Chiles; U.S. Congressmen William Young, Claude Pepper; Johnathon Charles Black, Naval Observatory; John C. Gaines, Naval Intelligence; James P. Kelly, N.A.S.A.; Arthur B. Hines, South Polar Archives, National Science Foundation; Hal B. Smith, Air Force Archives; Lewis B. Taylor, Library of Congress, Manuscripts Division; Dr. John B. Sherman, Ph.D., Treasury Archives; Dr. J. Manson Valentine Ph.D.; Robert J. Brush; Major M. C. Jones, U.S. Air Force; Lt. Colonel Louis B. Mackenzie, U.S. Air Force; W. T. Lee, Library of Congress; Fred C. Lewis, National Space Foundation; Lee E. Walter, Smithsonian Institution, Outer Space Division; C. S. Leighton, U.S. Air Force Records; George Leese, U.S. State Department, Outer Space Division; Albert V. Pace, Baltimore Sun; Jacob F. Oxford, National Observatory; Lt. Col. Eric C. Hoborn, U.S. Air Force (Ret); Lloyd C. Wright, Navy Hyrdographic Department; Maj. John C. Blalock, Naval Intelligence; William G. Ivey; William Bruce Jones, National Aeronautics Association.

For those informants who also helped, but could not permit their identities to be revealed, appreciation is also expressed.

To Mr. Estes Plateu, Venus Ambassador to Earth; Mr. Jooaan-noyhssn Haammoond, Shamballa, Agraharta; Dr. Jerrmuus of Bod-land, and J. B. Aacceerson of Shamballa who drew the Inner World map, our appreciation is gratefully acknowledged.

To an old friend of over three score years and ten, Lionel Mayell (now deceased), who believed the story of worlds beyond when others scoffed; and tribute to a young friend, Greg Leith, who never ceased to encourage his father to persevere in writing the book, in spite of countless discouragements.

Additional Acknowledgments

The particular government department or agency for the following names cannot be given for various reasons. Names are as follows: Thomas B. Goodnight; Orvil C. Kelly; John B. Williams; Thomas Watkins; Wadley G. Blake; George B. Meyer; Franklin B. Pierce; James D. Bouman; George A. Kelly; Orval C. Harris.

Without the aid of the following Americans, this book could not have been completed. They are Charles E. Scott; Bryan B. Kelly; Cecil M. Lloyd; Thomas (Tom) Whiford; John T. Jones; Cecil B. Brown; Amos P. Taylor; John F. Lynch; Xavier B. Johnnas; Merrill P. Fanning.

Bibliography

Angelbert, Jean-Michel. Occult and the Third Reich, The. MacMillan, 1974

Bates, D. R., F.R.S. Space Research and Exploration. William Sloane Associates, 1958.

Berlitz, Charles. The Bermuda Triangle. Doubleday, 1974.

Bernard, Dr. Raymond. The Hollow Earth. University Books, 1969.

Blavatsky, H. P. The Secret Doctrine. Theosophical Pub. House, 1966.

Brennan, J. H. The Occult Reich. Signet, 1974.

Brown, D. MacKenzie. Ultimate Concern. Harper, 1970.

Bulfinch's Mythology. London: Spring Books.

Carter, Mary Ellen. Edgar Cayce on Prophecy. Warner Books, 1968.

Charroux, Robert. Masters of the World. Berkley Publishing Co., 1967

Dione, R. L. Is God Supernatural. Bantam, 1976.

Donnelly, Ignatius. The Destruction of Atlantis. Rudolf Steiner Publishers, 1971.

Farago, Ladislas. After-Math. Simon & Shuster, 1974.

Fowler, Raymond E. UFO's - Interplanetary Visitors. Exposition Press, 1974.

Hoyle, Fred. Astronomy. Crescent Books.

Huxley, Aldous. The Doors of Perception. Chatto & Windus Ltd., 1954.

Huxley, Aldous. Heaven and Hell. Chatto & Windus Ltd., 1956.

Hyneck, J. Allen. The UFO Experience. Henry Regnerg Co., 1972.

Johnson, George and Don Tanner. The Bible and The Bermuda Triangle Logos International, 1976.

Keel, John A. Our Haunted Planet. Gambi Publications, 1968.

Keyhoe, Maj. Donald E. Aliens from Space. Doubleday, 1974.

Kische, Lawrence David. The Bermuda Triangle Mystery Solved. Warner Books, 1975.

Lahaye, Tim. Revelation. Zondervan, 1973.

Landsburg, Alan. In Search of Lost Civilizations. Bantam, 1976.

Landsburg, Alan and Sally. The Outer Space Connection. Bantam, 1975.

Lindsey, Hal and C. C. Carlson. The Late Great Planet Earth. Zondervan, 1970.

Lindsey, Hal. There's A New World Coming. Vision House, 1973.

Los Angeles Times, February 27, 1978.

Martin, Malachi. The Final Conclave. Stein & Day, 1978.

Mattern-Friedrich. UFO's - Nazi Secret Weapon. Samisdat Pub. Ltd.

Michell, John. The View Over Atlantis. Ballantine, 1972.

Monroe, Robert A. Journeys Out of the Body. Doubleday, 1971.

Mooney, Richard E. Colony: Earth. Stein and Day, 1974.

Packer, J. I. Knowing God. Inter-Varsity Press, 1976; London: Hodder and Stoughton Ltd., 1973.

Pember, G. H., M.A. Earth's Earliest Ages. Fleming & Revell Co.

Prophet, Elizabeth Clare. The Great White Brotherhood. Summit Lighthouse, 1976.

Rampa, T. Lobsang. The Cave of the Ancients. Ballantine, 1963.

Shirer, Wm. L. Rise and Fall of the Third Reich. Simon & Shuster, 1959.

Showers, Renald E. What on Earth is God Doing? Loiseaux, 1973.

Smith, Wilber M. You Can Know the Future. G/L Publishers, 1971.

Speer, Albert. Inside the Third Reich. MacMillan, 1970.

Stevenson, Wm. A Man Called Intrepid. Harcourt, Brace, Jovanovich, 1976.

Stonely, Jack and A. T. Lawton. Ceti. Warner Books, 1976.

Sullivan, Walter. We Are Not Alone. McGraw Hill, 1964.

Taylor, John G. Black Holes. Random House, 1973.

Toland, John. Adolph Hitler. Random House/Ballantine, 1976.

Trench, Brinsley Le Poer. Secret of the Ages - UFO's from Inside The Earth. Souvenir Press, 1974.

Trench, Brinsley Le Poer. The Eternal Subject. Souvenir Press Ltd., 1973.

Vallee, Jaques. UFO's In Space. Ballantine/Random House, 1974.

Velikovsky, Immanuel. Earth In Upheaval. Doubleday, 1968.

Velikovsky, Immanuel. Worlds in Collision. Doubleday.

Von Daniken, Erich. Miracles of the Gods. Dell, 1975.

Von Daniken, Erich. The Gold of the Gods. Souvenir Press, 1973.

Wilkins, Harold T. Flying Saucers Uncensored. Citadel Press, 1955.

Williams, John K. The Wisdom of your Subconscious Mind. Prentice Hall, 1964.

Wilson, Dr. Clifford. UFO's and Their Mission Impossible. Signet, 1975.

Wood, Leon J. The Bible and Future Events. Zondervan, 1970

Addendum by
Robyn C. Andrews

I met John Leith in 1990 while I was leading a workshop in Clearwater, Florida. He told me about this "Space Race" book he had written, not yet published, and explained it was his life's work about the inner-earth and the government's development of the round-wing plane. Since I had been a UFO researcher and regression therapist for many years, I was keenly interested. He let me take the manuscript for the night but said he had to have it back the next morning. I was staying at a friend's mother's home. I made a pot of coffee and prepared to stay up all night reading. By morning, I was not close to finished, so I called John and asked when I had to have it back. He said, "Oh, you can keep it as long as you like."

Thus began a friendship for the next 8 years, until his death in 1998. A special trust developed between us. He gave me that manuscript, and another called The Man with the Golden Sword, to be published only after his death. We did some editing but never got it ready to publish before he died. I met with his attorney and we discussed the process of publishing the book.

Leith never discussed the other book with me. I suppose this was because of the secret oath he was under about not acknowledging his service in WW II. Donald Ware and I worked with Robert Miles at www.timestreampictures.com in 2014 and published The Man With The Golden Sword in November. We believe it was restricted from being published until after Leith's death because of the highly sensitive nature of the missions.

I found John to be a highly intelligent, extremely interesting and enigmatic man. He told me his best friend and research partner was a general attached to the CIA.

Leith showed me some photographs, I think in 1995, at his condo in Clearwater. They included a map of the inner-earth. There were photographs of New Berlin that Germans had built in the inner-earth. There were many Germans in uniform standing in front of the buildings. He also showed me a photo of a very tall alien. Later he said that he had shown the photos to a government agent while trying to get permission to write about some of that material. The photos were taken from him. My research associates think the agent that took the pictures was John Poorbaugh.

Because of the scope of the book, it will cause the reader to seriously rethink their world-view.

" I was a speaker at a Global Sciences conference in Tampa about 1995. I was chairing a panel. Shown left to right: Robyn Andrews Quail, Phil Sparks, John Leith, Johnie Smith, Victor Navarro. John and Phil were so popular they were invited to be speakers at the next conference in Denver the following August."
- Robyn Andrews

Addendum by
Michael E. Forte

The stories in this manuscript challenge the most intelligent of men to ask, "Is this all real?" Was all I was taught in school and by leaders of this nation a cover story for something too big to handle? Can present-day scholars teach this history and present reality of our inner and outer worlds? The author's main purpose, I think, was to enlighten truth seekers about such popular mysteries as UFOs.

The authors shed much light on that quest. The big questions now are who occupies UFOs and where are they from . . . inner Earth, our planet's surface, or outer space? Some leading-edge scientists today say we live in a multiverse. This alone changes what we thought we knew. The author, the researcher, and some in our government know WE ARE NOT ALONE. The men who did this work were highly dedicated to service and sacrificed their personal lives to gather the secrets that would change the world when the time was right.

John B. Lieth was a war hero extraordinaire. His beliefs, learned as a young man, were to love thy neighbor, even our enemy. He had a standard of faith not usually found when facing the devil in one of the worst wars in history. President Reagan asked, "What if there was a threat from other worldly beings. Would we not unite as one?"

Leith gained great experience as a journalist of 25 years, writing for many publications in Canada. When I interviewed his son, Greg Leith, he said that his dad was very strict about truth and would never write anything he didn't check out every way he could. He had a very high moral belief system that was his foundation for his writing work. He possessed a photographic memory, aiding him in his OSS missions and adding to his great success as a researcher and writer. His book, Man with the Golden Sword is available at www.timestreampictures.com.

Leith was quite close to Frank Hudson, his primary researcher and fellow OSS agent. Hudson was born May 22,1918 and died Oct 9,1997. After WW II, he became a treasure hunter, historian, and author. Frank Hudson was known for many things that would cause some to frown and others to be excited. His interest was not limited to treasure. Hudson was actually a truth seeker, like Leith, and dedicated time to subjects like finding BIGFOOT. He published cases with witnesses and drawings. He worked with famous researchers like Dr. Valentine who discovered the Bimini wall, in 1970, the same time Hudson was out looking for the pyramids in Florida. While following these men's work, stories that could have just been rumors, I actually met treasure hunters, men who worked with MEL FISHER and FRANK HUDSON.

I began to trace the steps of these men's research in old records recovered from Hudson after his death. In doing so, I uncovered the map of inner earth. I also found that Jack Poorbaugh, also a war veteran and government-trained remote viewer, was a senate investigator who became a close confidant of Hudson. Poorbaugh was connected with the Kennedy clan and they shared properties in south Florida. He became a Representative in the Florida State House. Poorbaugh played an important part of this intrigue that I will reveal in a follow-up book. Poorbaugh's connections from his political career allowed him special access to evidence that I will later publish. My researcher, Carol Hammond, and I worked on the clues Jack Poorbaugh left behind.

Hudson was obsessed with historical documents, especially about pirates, the Spanish, and maps made to find treasures in the New World, including the Oak Island mystery. Frank Hudson researched and published some facts in the Hidden Wealth Treasure Hunting newsletter in the 1970s. He had been in the French and Spanish archives and found the clues recently reveled in the Oak Island TV series, including the full map of the "money pit."

Hudson and Leith both became interested in the John Reeves 1965 UFO case in Brooksville, Florida that I have researched thoroughly. Reeves was left a message on paper written in an ET language. It has now been partially deciphered as part of my future book project. Reeves was taken to the moon in 1968 on a round-wing plane, the year before NASA publicly made the trip. Many reports exist of those coming from inside the Earth. Cases in this book are not isolated.

Late in life, Leith and Hudson secured a submarine they used to comb the ocean floor looking for sunken Atlantean sites. I will later follow one of these quests and report back, if possible, the results of the adventure. It is truly a new age; I hope, a Golden Age.

Michael E. Forte,
Former Director for MUFON Tampa Bay, and Head of Investigations,
Truthseeker

CONTRIBUTORS FOR THE PUBLICATION
GENESIS FOR THE SPACE RACE

Robyn C. Andrews, Author's Authorized Representative and Author's

Agent who provided an Addendum

Michael E. Forte, Researcher and authority on L. Frank Hudson, the Author's primary research assistant who provided an Addendum

James G. Gavin, Prior Publisher who recognized the importance of the manuscript text when a copy was provided freely by a friend of the Author's son years after the Author's death..

Donald M. Ware, Editor who also provided a Preamble

Robert D. Miles, Project Coordinator

Carol Hammond; Research Assistant for Michael Forte